John Iona and Ralph Allen are long
The initial idea to pen this autobiog
their local hostelry, The Rising Sun,

Stan, the man of many words, said, 'Hey, do you know, no one's ever written about me,' as we all, lager in hand, rested our elbows unsteadily on the bar.

So that's how it started and we've all had a great time along the way; the memories are priceless.

Three friends together – one famous and the other two still hung over!

Stan Bowles
The Autobiography

Stan Bowles

with Ralph Allen and John Iona

ORION

An Orion paperback

First published in Great Britain in 2004
by Orion
This paperback edition published in 2005
by Orion Books Ltd,
Orion House, 5 Upper St Martin's Lane,
London WC2H 9EA

A CIP catalogue record for this book is available
from the British Library.

ISBN 0 75286 539 0

Printed and bound in Great Britain by
Clays Ltd, St Ives, plc

www.orionbooks.co.uk

To my father for pushing me along the way. I certainly would not have played football without his guidance and direction.

My mother for being there for me.

Ann for our beautiful children Carl, Alexandria and Tracy.

'It was like watching a player from another era.' Jimmy Greaves

'Bowles has 100 per cent skill. No one in English football can work a ball better at close quarters.' Denis Law

'He was easily the best player that I ever played with.'
Gerry Francis

'His tight control, balance, change of pace and cool, clinical finishing, stamp him as one of the most talented players I have seen.' Don Revie

'It would be difficult to name any player since Stanley Matthews who takes the ball so close to opponents before beating them.'
Dave Sexton

In terms of playing alongside other players, I think that he is one of the finest I have ever known, and I don't say that easily.'
Terry Venables

'I always felt that the skill which I possessed throughout my career was natural, and it never changed. I never knew why I had it, and I didn't know where it came from. It was just there. If I'd had to work hard to achieve that level of skill, I would not have been a footballer. I sometimes wondered what all the fuss was about.' Stan Bowles

Contents

Foreword

By Terry Venables

Stan Bowles was a special player. Those of us who played with him know that. He had the ability to know when to hold the ball, and know when to knock it off – so few have that skill.

He fell into the Dalglish and Beardsley category. Was he a midfield player going forward, or a forward coming back? I don't hesitate to put him in their company either, he was that good.

As well as a great footballer, he's a lovely guy. He has a very amusing, dry sense of humour, and he breeds a sense of affection from the people around him.

When Stan joined QPR I didn't know much about him, but he blended in straightaway. He was never an overly ambitious player, but was naturally gifted. He also had the ability to weigh up people and situations very quickly.

He had a wonderfully relaxed attitude and I'm sure that helped him to be the player he was. Some people were frustrated that he didn't make more of his talent, especially at international level. But that frustration lay with them, not him.

I know some managers had their problems with Stan, but I don't think he would have been difficult to manage. He just needed to feed his needs, and you had to appreciate that. He simply wanted to get through the day and enjoy it. In fact Stan Bowles hasn't changed one iota.

Chapter 1

What's Happening Today?

Yes, what is happening in the football world today? Gambling- and alcohol-related incidents seem to be ruling the front and back pages of the newspapers. It seems that the media are promoting these exclusives as if this sort of behaviour is new to the game. I can assure you that this is certainly not the case, it was even worse in the seventies.

I was amused to read Danny Baker's recent article in *The Times* where he talks about Michael Owen's reckless gambling antics, following in the fine tradition of *Stan the Man*. He wrote:

'Of course, none of this would have come about if only local councils had taken my advice and furnished every school library in Britain with a copy of *Stan the Man* [the original edition of this book]. Had this been made law then, the preposterous modern image of footballers, as responsible role models, would not now be lying in smoking ruins.'

It's no secret that the two main passions in my life have been football and gambling – probably not in that order.

It's fair to say I was a good deal better kicking a football around than I ever was at backing horses. My mother always used to tell me that if I ever bought a cemetery people would stop dying. The problem is – has been always – the fact that I don't half get some enjoyment out of gambling. Well ... sometimes.

One of my team-mates said I was either the most fearless gambler in the world, or the world's worst. My bank balance would suggest I'm down there among the also rans. My favourite ever gambling quote is, 'Hope makes for a good breakfast but a bad supper.' Gamblers all over the world will know exactly what those words mean.

It was Ernie Tagg, my boss at Crewe, who coined the now immortal phrase forever to be associated with me, 'If Stan Bowles could pass a bookmaker's like he could a football he'd have no problems at all.'

That phrase has followed me around for most of my adult life; dusted down and trotted out whenever I'm interviewed. I might as well have the words labelled and nailed to my back because they follow me

1

everywhere like a lost puppy. I'm not saying the words aren't appropriate, just a little repetitive. There are two mavericks in this world, according to the press – James Garner and me.

Gambling might not be a hobby exclusively confined to the working classes but if you take a peek in any of the betting shops I frequent, the best dressed man is usually decked out from head to toe in approximately £25 worth of clobber. The air is typically heavy with smoke and expletives, as the motley crew stare at the screens and bemoan their cursed luck. Each man an expert in his own right who never got the breaks. Usually, each and all are desperate to unload their heart-rending stories of cursed luck, that has conspired to deny them of a fortune.

A good many footballers gamble. In my days at Forest, players like Charlie George, Peter Shilton, Kenny Burns, Martin O'Neill and Peter Taylor all loved a punt. In the modern era John Hartson, Eidur Gudjohnsen, Paul Merson, Keith Gillespie, Steve Claridge, and – perhaps most surprisingly of all – Michael Owen, have all lost out to the bookies.

Michael went up in my estimation when it came to light that he liked a punt. He has this image of being squeaky-clean, a guy who looks like a young copper. He doesn't drink, doesn't smoke; but to me he isn't someone I'd class as a gambler in my league. I don't mean that as an insult but as a compliment, because the only time I don't bet is when I don't have any money. Footballers are getting the sort of money these days that they could only dream about in my day.

A great deal of fuss was made about Michael Owen losing between thirty and forty thousand quid during the World Cup campaign. That's chicken feed when you consider he's earning something in the region of £70,000 a week. To me it's no worse than a plumber spending three-quarters of the £400 he might earn in a week; probably more considering what they charge these days to stop a dripping tap.

It's all relative, you're just betting with bigger denominations as a high-earning footballer. To me, a proper bet has to hurt you, cost you something if you lose, or there is no point in placing it. If the outcome does not affect you in some way – positively or adversely – then it isn't worth having. You need that buzz, the adrenalin rush – a fix. Basically, that's why I bet. There is a school of thought I've never really understood, that says gamblers are only ever happy when they are skint. I've never seen anyone in a bookie's scream out, 'Yes, my horse has just been pipped in a photo finish depriving me of two hundred quid and no money to take back to the family, what a bleedin' result.'

I've never been one to dwell on the losses or analyse too deeply the psychological reasons why I bet. I think it would drive me quite mad. Nor do I want to be seen as an example of the stereotypical seventies' footballer. I'm unique – just like everybody else. I bet because I enjoy it, there's no point saving money, no point in being the richest guy in the cemetery. To me it is an extreme act of stupidity to die with £50,000 in the bank.

I think Paul Merson is overreacting when he claims that, 'The biggest danger faced by footballers these days is gambling. It wrecks more lives in football than any other vices.' And Arsenal legend Tony Adams believes that, 'Betting can be just as dangerous as any other addiction. They (gamblers) lose their self-respect and before they know where they are, they are nicking money out of their kids' savings to have a bet.'

Never mind gambling, how do we tackle the problem of therapy-cases who can't stop banging on about addiction? I do admire what Tony Adams has done in setting up a fund to financially help high-profile stars who have encountered trouble coping with their addictions; but that's usually when I'm filling out the application form!

In the near future, I can see gambling and football getting even closer together in an attempt to bring more revenue into the clubs. I don't think it will be long before casinos are integrated within football stadia, just as today you can bet on the first goalscorer and correct scores. I've been in a few casinos myself, but never played the tables – they just don't interest me. I've always preferred losing my money on the horses and the dogs.

In the 1970s there was a trivia question doing the rounds: 'Which footballer has appeared at Wembley the most times?' Answer: 'Stan Bowles. Three games for England, and 982 appearances at Wembley dog track.'

It's well known my regular haunts in London were White City, Walthamstow, Wembley, Hackney and Shepherd's Bush. I've owned several (slow moving) greyhounds over the years, and that's one of the reasons I've sometimes had trouble making ends meet. People often ask me: 'What's the most expensive part of owning a greyhound – the training or the veterinary fees?' Neither – it's betting on the buggers. One of the main drawbacks of being a gambler is that, more often than not, it leaves you without a placepot to piss in.

During my lifetime I've had a hell of a lot of wagers, most of them losing transactions. In fact you could probably paper Buckingham

Palace a couple of times over with all the losing betting slips I've thrown away. Ask any punter which bets tend to stick in the mind, and they'll all give you the same answer – the unlucky ones. As you can imagine, over the years I've had more than my fair share of mishaps.

One such bet that sticks in the mind was an unusual little wager we regarded as an absolute banker. After we'd finished training, my best mate, Don Shanks, and I, would often scratch around for a few bob and see if we could use it as stake money for a trip down the track. Whenever we could we'd pool all our funds and travel to White City to chance our respective arms. Typically, in the middle of the week, we often operated off a shallow pool. A few of the other players at the club liked a flutter from time to time, but it's fair to say no one was really in our league when it came to betting. Consequently, they had more money than us at any given time, but we wouldn't swap our lifestyles for theirs. When we had money we gambled; when we didn't we found something else less exciting to do.

We popped into our local café for two cups of tea, to read the papers and discuss what we would be able to bet on when we were liquid again. As we were reading the papers, Don suddenly spluttered on his tea and started jabbing wildly at the paper he was reading. His finger was pointing at a photograph of two players in a league match, challenging for the ball in the air. Don was one of the players going up for this header against an Arsenal player. Nothing unusual in that, you might think, but this particular photo was being used for a Spot the Ball competition.

The newspapers ran a popular weekly competition at that time, where the ball was airbrushed from a photo of a recent football match. To enter you had to mark with a cross where you thought the missing ball might be. Anyone putting a cross exactly where the ball should be would win a cash prize up to £10,000.

Well, Don and I had 'inside information' on this one and thought we were certainties to scoop the top prize. In fact, Don was so sure we'd win, he even suggested we should split the money on a 60:40 basis; after all it was him heading the ball, and him alone who knew precisely where it was. I agreed immediately thinking it would be better to renegotiate terms once we got our mitts on the £10,000 cheque.

Don had headed the ball, I was in the background yards away from the incident looking on, and all our team-mates also had a clear view. Where could we go wrong? We both remembered this particular header in any case, because Don, by his own admission, wasn't too clever in the air and didn't win too many duels. I used to tell him that he wasn't very impressive on the deck either. But to give him his due, Don always gave his all in a match and had won this header well.

According to Don's memory, he had headed the ball to the side, towards the centre half. Shanks was completely convinced as to the whereabouts of the missing ball. He even remembered Webby picking up the flick-on, and knocking it long to Dave Thomas. I agreed with his recollection of events, even though I wasn't quite as certain because the photo looked as though he was heading the ball forward. Don laughed and told me not to follow any of the other players' eyelines, because Don had entered these competitions in the past, and the ball never appeared where you thought it would be.

Don didn't leave anything to chance. He approached the manager and coaching staff, and counselled their opinions, the majority opinion tallied up with Don's own view, even if they were more concerned with discussing tactics for the following Saturday's game

We entered the maximum number of crosses allowed by the rules and smothered them across the area where we thought the ball was. We then entered the competition four times and virtually covered the entire photo in crosses. All we had to do now was wait a week, until we were announced the winners.

The original photo appeared the following week, revealing the location of the ball and the names of the competition winners. We weren't on the list. The ball had materialised somewhere behind Don's left ankle, nowhere near any of the crosses we had marked. Don cried foul play, and swore there was no way in the world the ball could possibly have been there. It was another losing bet.

Luckily, the law of averages dictates that anyone who bets as much as Don and I, had to back some winners sooner or later. We liked nothing better than backing our own team in a match. As you know – from press revelations about today's game – you aren't supposed to back your own team, or bet against them; but it goes on – at least it did with Don and I.

We played West Ham in the Cup after drawing 1–1 at Upton Park. The bookies had both teams priced at 6/4. We fancied ourselves strongly against the Hammers, whom we always believed had more show than steel. Sure, they had players like Billy Bonds, who could put it about, and skilled players who could turn it on when the going was good, but if the going got tough away from home they were capable of chucking it in.

5

Don and I raised £2,000 and stuck it on QPR via a private bookmaker in the Shepherd's Bush area, who took singles on football matches.

It rained all day and by the time kick-off came round the pitch was flooded. The playing surface at Loftus Road was always bad around the edges because the rain would drip off the terrace roof and drop on to the touchlines. On more than one occasion, I lost a boot as it was sucked off into the mire as I ran up and down the wing. About an hour before kick-off, the referee gave the green light for the game to go ahead.

During the team talk, we were reminded of the importance of a good Cup run, as there was a great deal of money at stake for the club. Don and I were more interested in the money *we* had at stake and were guaranteed to give the game our all.

In the first few minutes of the match, Trevor Brooking bursts through our defence, drops his shoulder and pulls the trigger back. Don Shanks sprints over at a pace I didn't know he possessed. Don's got a grand at 6/4 on us winning and he knows if we go one behind early on, it's going to be an uphill battle, so he's really busting a gut to get the block in. Don slides in brilliantly for the block challenge, but unfortunately for us, Brooking has dummied to shoot and Don is now sliding past Trevor and towards the corner flag at a pace the Icelandic bobsleigh team would be proud of. As Don is skidding away he has time enough to arc his neck back to watch Brooking slide the ball casually past Phil Parkes. One down and our continued participation in the FA Cup was in peril, as was our £2,000 stake. However, by half-time we are something like 5–1 up and the game and the bet were in the bag. What a result!

Don and I used to bet on football matches quite regularly; we didn't discriminate about what we gambled on. If there was a book on it, chances are we'd have a bet.

Shanks came round to my place to watch the England v Scotland match in 1978. We put £1,300 to win £800 at 8/13. We thought the price was very generous as we had a strong line-up and the match was at Wembley. We got some beers and some snacks in, and settled down to watch the expected rout.

As usual, things didn't turn out that way. England just couldn't seem to score. Eventually, when we'd all but given up on winning the bet, Steve Coppell popped up to notch the winner with about five minutes to go and then, as I recall, Scotland hit the post in the last minute to give us the jitters.

Another time QPR played Nottingham Forest in an FA Cup-tie and we were 3/1 to win at the Bush, a massive price. Don and I backed ourselves for a couple of hundred each. We went one up but they equalised in injury time. We got our money back on the replay because we were a massive price to get a draw at the City Ground. Forest were a top team at the time so we had another big bet and won our money back. We would always back our own side to win because we were confident in our ability.

Gambling to me is a hobby, a commodity of magnificence and I don't expect people who know nothing about gambling to understand that. I mean, a lot of people tell me how beautiful the sunset looks, and what a picture a full moon is by night. To me the moon is simply a big yellowy white circle in the sky, and sunset a big red one at half-mast. How can they be more enchanting than a winning betting slip? Yes, I do see them occasionally, and I will concede that rainbows look half decent; but you can hardly spend your life dedicated to a rainbow, unless your name is Geoffrey, Bungle or Zippy.

I do have a reoccurring nightmare that one day I'm found dead and my possessions are handed to my next of kin in one of those polythene bags. There's nothing in it except for one of those little blue bookie's pens, that don't even work in the first place. If you could symbolise my life with two objects then a ball and a bookie's pen would be as close as you could get.

When we were at training, Don and I would bet on absolutely anything we could imagine: the colour of the next car that came round the corner; two raindrops running down the window; or which team would win the training game match.

We even participated in a betting competition known as the 'Deadpool'. The Deadpool game is where everyone puts some money in the pot, and each and all predicts a celebrity to kick the bucket. You win points if your selection dies, the younger the victim the more points they are worth. The person with the most points (i.e. correctly forecast deaths) wins the pool.

I don't see anything wrong in it myself. I mean, we're all racing certainties to die at some point with the only uncertainty being when. I actually won the competition once when the 'double' of Benny Hill and Frankie Howerd, turned up their toes within a couple of days of each other.

I've had my ups and downs with the bookies over the years. I'd like

7

to say it's been something of a roller-coaster ride, but in all honesty it has just been one long continuous slide into poverty.

One of the unluckiest bets I ever struck (and there have been more than a few), was when Don and I bet £100 at 12/1 that there would be a white Christmas. That is to say, for us to win the wager it would have to snow on Christmas Day. Temperatures had been cold with forecasters predicting a big freeze on the way. This was a bet we reckoned we just could not lose.

All gamblers are skint at Christmas; it just works that way as a fact of life. You can't back a winner when you need to. It was about four days to Christmas and our bet was looking like banker material, meaning that the festive period might, after all, be bright and cheery. Whole streets were covered in snow, we had avalanches of the stuff everywhere. The bookies suspended the betting on a white Christmas, as it was now considered a formality that it was going to snow on Christmas Day. All we had to do was wait till the bookies opened on Boxing Day to collect our £1,300.

The rules and conditions of the bet stated that it had to snow between 9 a.m. and 5 p.m. on the GPO tower in London on Christmas Day. If it did, then we won the bet. The Christmas period is a busy time for a footballer, but the weather was so bad that year that all the games were called off five or six days in advance, because pitches across the country were frozen solid.

So we were out partying on Christmas Eve, cracking open bubbly at a pal's house in Hertfordshire. I rang up a mate in London as soon as I woke at around seven on Christmas morning, and he confirmed that it was snowing heavily. I went back to bed and kipped; safe in the knowledge our bet was a winner. I woke again at nine o'clock and rang up the same pal only to be told that it had stopped snowing at around half past eight, but that it was still freezing cold. I didn't worry too much because it still looked a nailed-on certainty that it would snow at some point during the day.

It got to about three o'clock and no white stuff falling from the sky. I was beginning to worry. Suddenly, to our disgust, the sun popped out and the day started to brighten up. I rang my pal in London and asked him what the weather was like there. He told me it was still cold but no more snow had fallen since my last call, and, yes, he had been looking out of the window every five minutes. By the time it got to ten minutes to five desperation had crept in. We just couldn't believe that we were going to miss out on what we thought was another sure-fire bet. Well, you can guess what happened next. At 5.15 it started to snow again, and I mean snow. Snowballs the size of cricket balls descended from the skies. Don just looked up forlornly at the heavens and said, 'I don't believe this, even the man upstairs is bleedin' crooked!'

Talking about crooked, I remember being in a casino in Manchester playing poker with a few friends, who had close ties with gangsters. One of my pals – Jimmy – a pretty bad-tempered type at the best of times, was about five grand down and getting increasingly annoyed that Lady Luck wasn't with him that night. During a break in the play, Jimmy decided to disappear to make 'an urgent phone call' before retaking his seat at the table. Nobody thought anything of it at the time.

About fifteen minutes later a masked gunman appeared suddenly from nowhere and ordered everyone to empty their pockets and place the pool of money in the middle of the table, to be put into the carrier bag he was holding. It was a pretty scary moment, because in this sort of situation you never know if the gun is going to go off, intentionally or otherwise. I wasn't as scared as I might have been, because I knew the gunman well – it was Jimmy's brother, Len, who was also a pal of mine. I knew it and so did everyone else in the room because Jimmy's brother was six foot five and spoke with a lisp, 'Plathe all the catsh in the bag or elth thumone geth it,' spits Lenny. The mask wasn't fooling anyone, but nobody was going to call Lenny's bluff.

Len was well known in the area as an out-and-out fruitcake and no one was willing to second-guess his moves and end up with a big hole in their chest. He could quite easily have pulled the trigger at any moment if you gave him any backchat. I was a little bit worried, because I didn't have any money to hand over to him, as I had lost it all earlier in the evening.

Lenny took off with his loot, and Jimmy did his best to act really annoyed. Calling the police wasn't an option in these circumstances, but Lenny had to leave the area as he was a marked man in Manchester from then on. Nobody would dare accuse Jimmy of staging the raid for fear of reprisals; you see, Jimmy was well-connected.

Growing up in a deprived area of Manchester gave me a good grounding in life. I've rubbed shoulders with the rich and famous, but deep down I've always preferred keeping company with the type of people

I grew up with – ordinary working-class folks, who sometimes have to sail pretty close to the law to make a living.

I have been friendly with George Best over the years and still keep in touch to this day. I read recently that he was selling his football medals at auction to raise money to buy a house. I didn't receive many medals during my football career; however, I did collect a few England caps.

Of the five caps I won against Portugal, Northern Ireland, Wales, Italy and Holland I have only two left and they are hidden away in my daughter's attic, to which I am not allowed access. One was given to Jim Gregory's wife, one I lost in a game of cards and the other I sold for a couple of hundred quid. The first cap I won – against Portugal – was a special moment for my parents, so I gave it to my mother as a memento, expecting her to keep it as a proud souvenir. My mum still lives in Manchester to this day, and I would occasionally pop back to see her when I was playing for QPR. She didn't really like football, or know anything about the game. In those days, the caps were specially handmade and embroidered and you had to wait three months before you received it, via your football club. Nowadays, you get them off a conveyor belt.

I remember having a cup of tea with my mum, when I went to visit her after playing a game in Manchester. I noticed her dog, a little shih-tzu, coiled up in a moth-eaten rag covered in hairs. I thought the material looked a little familiar and so I asked mum what it was. She said it was, 'That England cap you gave me, it's no good to me but the dog finds it quite snug in there.' My England cap – probably worth a couple of grand – was being used as a home for a dog! I was never too keen on those tiny oriental animals. They don't look like a proper dog anyway.

The cap was absolutely rotten, and after the dog died my mother gave it back to me. My chairman at QPR, Jim Gregory, kindly paid to have it restored. I gave Jim the cap to thank him for everything he had done for me. Years later when I attended Jim's funeral, his wife Fluff asked me if I wanted the cap back, but I thought it would be in bad taste to have said yes at such a sad time and so I tentatively refused. Now things aren't so good I wouldn't mind having it back. I know I could cash in the two caps at my daughter's house for about four grand. Unfortunately, she won't leave me in the house unattended, and whenever I visit her the ladder to the loft cannot be found.

Reflecting on my relationship with George Best, I am very sad to hear of his recent problems with booze and the women in his life.

In my playing days I struck up a good friendship with George, despite my best pal Don hating him, with a passion, for nicking his girlfriend. I like a drink now and again, but I never went over the top and certainly never drank before matchdays. George would drink until he couldn't drink any more. I saw him a while back and he was drinking out of a glass the size of a fishbowl.

Alex, his wife, could drink a fair amount herself, as far as I could tell, but they seemed to be happy together. George is without a doubt the best player I ever saw and great company off the field. He often used to say that he drank only to make other people more interesting. Bestie is one of the most charismatic people you'll ever meet, even if he is more unreliable than me! George loved to tell people he liked to go missing quite often ... Miss America, Miss England, Miss Canada ... but, Don's girlfriend happened to be Miss World and George is lucky to be alive today.

One Friday, the night before a QPR game up at Newcastle, me and Don went off to the local dog track at Gosforth. As it happens, Mary Stavin – the reigning Miss World at the time – was there doing a presentation of some sort. At the time, the Swedish beauty was going out with Mr Medallion Man himself – Graeme Souness – although he wasn't with her in Newcastle that night.

Now, our Don was a right womaniser who could charm the girders off any girl. He had all the patter and would invent stories about having a high-flying business, buckets of cash, and a penthouse flat up west. This night he was determined to chance his arm with Mary. She'd gone into the restaurant, which, on this occasion, had been reserved for special guests. Even so, Don somehow blagged his way in there and made a beeline for the beauty queen.

I chuckled to myself. No chance, Mr Donald, I thought. This Miss World was the most stunning bird I'd ever seen in my life. I shrugged, left him to it and just carried on betting. In those days, the two of us used to pool our money, so I was betting for both of us. I ended the night winning a few bob, and was pretty happy, especially when Shanks returned Miss World-less.

However, Don had found out that she was flying back to London on the same flight as us. He was pretty chuffed and reckoned he was well in. So I bet him a hundred notes that he couldn't get off with her. Don was up for it; he couldn't care less whether she was seeing Souness or not, because he hated the bloke. And I have to admit, I wound him up a little bit about it, because I didn't like the twat either.

To my surprise, by the time we arrived back on Saturday, Don had pulled her and they'd arranged a date for the following week. So the slippery bastard had copped a ton and Miss World, all in the same night. I can't remember the result of the Newcastle game, but the way his luck was in, Shanksy probably scored with a volley from the halfway line.

Of course, Mary had no idea that Don was living with his mum in a council flat on the White City estate, but this was never going to present a problem for old silver tongue. Shanksy could always lay his hands on some readies, so, after only a few dates, they rented a smart place in St John's Wood.

I thought that Souness would know what was going on, but, just in case he didn't, I decided to tell him, when we played Liverpool a few weeks later. In the dressing room, before the game, I said to Don, 'I'm gonna tell him on the pitch.'

'No, leave it out!' said Don, horrified.

'No, I'm gonna tell him. I don't like the fucker anyway!'

The rest of the lads were geeing me up, because they'd travelled back on the plane, and had sussed out the situation. As soon as the game started, I ran up to Graeme.

'Did you know that Don's giving Mary one?' I said, grinning all over my face.

For some reason, Souness didn't take too kindly to this. Next time the ball came anywhere near me, he went in and I got a few studs down the back of my legs. David Webb, my minder, came up to see if I was all right.

'You've seen what he's done to me, Webby?' I said to him, all hurt pride.

'Leave him to me mate,' growls Webby, 'I'll sort out the bastard.'

Sure enough, later in the match, Dave got a chance to go in hard on Souness, and nearly took off his legs. Souness didn't come near me after that. I caught up with him after the game, though. I said: 'If you want to see me, I'll be in the players' bar.' But he never came in, wise man, because the Notting Hill boys – notorious villains and hard men, whom you don't mess around with – surrounded me.

So, now the affair between Mary and Don was out in the open. It lasted for about three years, and Don managed to keep her in the lifestyle that she had become accustomed to. He always had the knack of getting money from somewhere, even if he was down on his luck.

Mary was incredibly beautiful and Don used to keep her under wraps as much as he possibly could, which I could understand.

Towards the end of their relationship, I heard that Mary had been seen at Morton's, in Berkeley Square, with George Best. I didn't tell Don, but eventually he found out, and was furious. As far as he was concerned the relationship was still a goer. Don found out which hotel George was staying in and he met me in a pub in Shepherd's Bush. I could see that he had totally flipped. 'I'm going to stab him,' he said, wildly.

Next thing, Don pulls a bloody great knife out of his pocket, and starts waving it around. Few things shock me, but I was gobsmacked when Don produced the blade. I was saying to him, 'Oh yeah, Don. I understand, yeah.' But all the time I was thinking, Jesus Christ, how can I get the blade off him?

He'd definitely lost it; he had a mad look in his eyes, and if he'd seen George that would have been it: no more comebacks for Bestie! I didn't want to see Don ruin his life by doing something stupid in the heat of the moment. On top of that, me and George got on well, so that was another reason I wanted to avoid a disaster. 'Give me the knife, Don,' I pleaded. 'You're not taking that with you. If you want to sort it out, do it man to man.'

After a while, I calmed him down and managed to get the knife off him. Don went off to the hotel that night, squared up to George and punched him out. So Bestie got a right-hander, instead of something more serious. On the way home, I threw the knife in a dustbin. Don and George had several further confrontations, because it took Don a long time to get over the shock of Mary leaving him. Even to this day, Don avoids talking about her. Eventually, she moved in with George. Later on, I used to go to George's wine bar in the West End, but Don would never come with me. I suppose he couldn't trust himself.

Everyone knows that George was a right lad; in and out of trouble over birds and booze. But I wonder how often he came that close to having GBH perpetrated on his talented frame. More than once, would be my guess!

After I finished playing for Brentford, I took a call from George and he asked if I would like to play a few charity matches with him in coastal resorts, for a team he had put together. He offered me £200 a game and 'the opportunity for a few beers after the match'.

I popped round to George's house in Cheney Walk to meet up with him before travelling down to the first game in Bournemouth. It was

13

only nine in the morning and he was absolutely smashed. He invited me in and offered me some breakfast – a can of lager. I realised George was heavily intoxicated when he started trying to balance a grapefruit on his head, something he found hysterically funny. Somewhere in the region of 10,000 people turned up in Bournemouth to watch us play, and when Georgie didn't take the field they were all screaming for their money back.

I had to laugh when I read in George's book that after the charity matches, 'Stan was always first in the bar and the last to leave.' I used to have a good few beers, but I wasn't quite in George's league when it came to drinking. George used to tell me that his grandfather swore by liver salts. Apparently he drank a pint of the stuff every day and lived to be ninety-four. When he died his liver was still functioning and had to be beaten with a stick for an hour until it finally packed in. However, George hated the taste of liver salts. He was a great storyteller when he had a drink, and that was pretty often. George could drink and drink and drink. He didn't ever seem to get drunk until at least seven hours on the sauce. The women adored Georgie, and George knew he could pick up any woman he wanted and that often happened, but usually well after closing time.

I first met George in the Brown Bull pub in Manchester when I was starting out for City and he was playing for United. I made my league debut in the Manchester derby when George was playing for the reds and we struck up a friendship. We were pretty much the same age and had similar interests; although George was more into clubbing, whereas I was fixated with gambling.

A few years back I desperately needed to get hold of George because I had promised some United fans a signed Bestie shirt. They had travelled all the way from Ireland to pick up the shirt and meet Bestie at a time when he decided to go on the missing persons list again. In trying to track down George I shrewdly decided to begin the search by ringing round the pubs he frequented. George drank in a pub called the Phene Arms in Cheney Walk. I rang up about nine times asking for George but the bar staff kept telling me he wasn't there. I said, 'If I call at eleven o'clock will he be in?' She replied deadpan, 'Try nine o'clock.' And he was there!

His missus, Alex, had as much chance of changing George as getting a council house in Belgravia. In fact, when I saw him, eventually, he had a shiner – administered by Alex. According to George, he had bought Alex a Pashmina scarf from Marks and Spencer and she wasn't happy with the gift. Apparently, she went mad and hit him in the eye with a stiletto shoe, when he was asleep. It did make me wonder what kind of scarf a Pashmena was. I made a mental note never to buy one as a gift, an unlikely possibility in any case.

George ended up sleeping on his favourite bench by the walkway in Cheney Walk. Anyone passing the unshaven, unkempt figure curled up with a bottle of wine, would be forgiven for thinking that George was just another homeless tramp and not the finest player in the British Isles ever to lace up a pair of boots.

Back then George was on to his third wife, first liver and countless blonde. It was obvious to everyone that he couldn't maintain that lifestyle. George was writing cheques that his body couldn't cash, eventually something had to give.

As I have said my main vice has always been gambling, whereas George liked a beer and a blonde – in that order. I like a drink now and again but I know when to stop; Georgie could go on and on and on – he often did.

Yes: football and gambling. The two main passions in my life but why don't we start from the beginning.

Chapter 2 •

Streetwise Stanley

As I understand it, some time in the late 1930s the Germans switched from playing football to town planning. That must have been the case because they certainly spent a few years trying to rearrange the houses round our way! Thanks to their passionate interest in English architecture, there was a massive shortage of housing after the war. So thousands of one-storey houses, made from prefabricated concrete, were put up all over the country as a temporary solution to the problem.

The walls in these prefabs were so thin that if you punched the bedroom wall, your fist would end up in the living room. If you farted in the kitchen, you'd blow off the front door! These little boxes were meant to stay up for only a short while, until proper houses were built, but some people are still living in them now – sixty years on.

It was into one of these prefabs in Collyhurst, Manchester, that the infant Stanley Bowles made his England debut on Christmas Eve, 1948. I was actually born at three minutes to midnight; my dad often used to say to me, 'If you'd hung on another few minutes you'd have been Jesus'.

Collyhurst was one of the roughest areas of Manchester and very few people there had any hope of experiencing a normal existence. But those were the cards we were dealt and you just had to play the best hand you could. As much as our parents loved us it was a constant struggle, and our daily lives certainly made us streetwise very early on. There were only three ways out of this slum environment: become a professional footballer, a boxer, or a criminal.

When I was little, my dad was a window cleaner, employing eight or nine local people. By the time I was five years of age, there were already three children in the family: Anita, Steve and myself. But I was always the governor. I think I developed a certain individuality at a very early age. There is a photograph of us, taken a little later, on holiday in

Blackpool, in which I was wearing a white mackintosh – the style of mac which later became my trademark.

I began my education at a Church of England school. In those days you were either a John Bull or a Mickey Finn: a Protestant or a Catholic. Religion was an important factor in our area, and the Catholic priest came round to our house every week and tried to persuade us to change our religion. Eventually, I think I was converted into the Catholic faith, because all of a sudden I found myself at St Mary's Junior School.

The rule there was that if you didn't go to church, you couldn't play for the football team. The teachers used to ask you what colour robes the priest was wearing – green or gold – and what the sermon had been. You were in trouble if you guessed, or told lies. Whether you were picked or not depended solely on the church you went to, or if you even went to church at all.

I think I either went to church a lot or was a bloody good liar because I got in to the school team. Straightaway it became obvious that I was streets ahead of the other kids; something I remember being aware of almost immediately. In the end, the headmaster used to make me play in goal, to make matches more evenly balanced.

When I was about eight years old the funfair came to town and set up in a field facing the air-raid shelters, next to Broadhurst Fields. One of the fairground attractions was taking penalties, where you tried to knock down a line of skittles; if you were successful, you won a couple of bob. So every night after school I went to the fair. For three nights, I never missed a skittle. The stallholder was pulling his hair out, he couldn't believe it. My friends were giving me a penny each to knock down skittles for them. They were pulling in a fortune!

On the fourth night, I was banned from the fair and went home crying, so my dad went down to have it out with the stallholder. The poor man was virtually in tears; he said I was putting him out of business. But he still wouldn't let me have another go; I stayed banned. I felt sorry for the bloke, there weren't many people who lost out on a gamble with me, as you will see. It was the first – but not the last – time in my career that I got on the wrong side of the management.

At the age of eleven, I went to New Moston Secondary Modern School, where I started playing football more frequently. At this school you were judged only on how good you were at football, not on your knowledge of a priest's fashions. I was picked to play for Manchester

North Area team alongside Brian Kidd, and eventually we went on to play for Manchester Boys. Our early careers in football followed parallel lines, and we were both in the team that beat Middleton Boys in the final of the *Manchester Evening News* Cup.

We were also very successful in the English Schools Trophy, winning our divisional rounds and playing teams with a long history of breeding top-class footballers. In the fifth round we played East Northumberland Boys, who were one of England's outstanding school teams. They had produced international players like Jackie Milburn and Bobby Charlton, who had played against Manchester many years before. When the teams had last met in 1953, Manchester Boys had won 3–0 and we continued the trend. We were also involved in the final of the Lancashire Schools Cup and the North Manchester Schools Trophy. But, being me, I just took it all in my stride.

One day, though, in late 1962, during the Cuban missile crisis, the headmaster, Jim Davy, was explaining to the class the seriousness of the confrontation between the USA and the Soviet Union. He frightened the life out of us kids, by talking in detail about an international crisis and the possibility of nuclear war.

Afterwards, he pulled me to one side and said: 'Look Stanley, if nothing happens, I think that you'll make it in football.' It was the only time any teacher had given me any encouragement; but I thought it was a joke, because playing football was so easy for me. I believed that to be successful in any career you had to work hard; and I had already been made vividly aware, by my upbringing, that nothing comes easily. I also played for a Sunday morning team called Broadhurst Lads, and it was during one of these Sunday games that I came into contact with Manchester City scout, Harry Goodwin. Being a local man, Harry used to regularly watch all of the Sunday games on Broadhurst Fields, which was a massive expanse of football pitches. He liked the look of me and persuaded the club to take me on.

He swore that when he went to sign me at my house, we were sitting at the table while my little brother was underneath it, with his hand in Harry's pocket! He started going through the signing-on paper with me, and he was a bit nervous because it was the first time he had ever actually signed a lad. He'd had a letter from the headmaster of my school, thanking him for taking me away for the day, so I think that made him even more nervous. The forms took ages to complete and when it came to the part where it asks about religious denomination, he says, 'What denomination are you, Stan?'

'What's that mean?' I asks, then shouts upstairs to my mum, 'Ma! What denomination am I?'

'I don't know, son. You'd better ask your dad when he gets in!'

We didn't use long words like that in our house, but I signed school-boy forms for Manchester City, anyway. I was fifteen, and just received my bus fare as expenses for going training twice a week.

Money didn't really bother me; we were, as they say, poor but happy. I had enough, and I had my mates. One of the great strengths of kids growing up in rough and deprived areas is that you develop a bond that can never be broken. Your friendship lasts a lifetime through the ups and downs. Also, you can be flat broke or a millionaire and it doesn't matter. You continue to have that inner strength that carries you through life.

I was a part of the clan, if you like. When we were young we helped each other to survive as best we could, and we all stuck together. It wasn't like today, where you have guns and knives. We would just have a fight, then shake hands afterwards. We would try to protect each other if trouble came our way.

It wasn't easy to find an apprenticeship, trade or anything like that, so your first job would be on the market. If some of the lads didn't earn enough to pay their keep, they'd have to thieve the rest. Your mother was always first to be paid. Now and again, some of the lads would be sent away on a day trip, with a long shopping list and only sixpence to buy the lot.

They'd ask, 'Mam, how am I going to get all them with only a tanner?' And the answer would be, 'Go in Woolworth's – you know what to bloody well do!' These were the days when you left your back door open and everyone knew each other's business, like a big family. You'd just walk in and out of people's houses. Despite the hardships, I think it was a great time to grow up.

At school either we played football all day, or spent our time fighting in the gymnasium. We didn't used to bother much with lessons, so most kids found it very difficult to pass the 11-plus exam. We used to laugh when the teacher slapped our hands for doing something wrong, or for playing truant, because it was nothing to what your dad would do with a belt. I suppose that punishment did teach you respect for your superiors.

I managed to get out of the district, whereas others are still caught up in it. The same would have happened to Nobby Stiles, who lived locally. If Nobby hadn't been a footballer, he would have been an undertaker like his dad. Many of the people from those times are like brothers to me to this day and I see them whenever I can.

My father would come and watch me play football on the local parks when I was very young, but he would never stay too long. He would stand on the touchline, saying, 'That's my boy playing over there.' This gave me great encouragement; but then I would look round and he would be gone. He couldn't stay for some reason, but I never found out why.

None of my parents' family played football, although my dad, a Manchester City fan, used to enjoy watching the game. Dad was proud of me but couldn't legislate for the way I was. Even in those days I was what you might call temperamental. I certainly had my own way of doing things.

When I left school I started work in a raincoat factory in Cheetham Hill, on ten quid a week. I worked on the press. Every time I see the laundry room in *Prisoner Cell Block H* on television today it reminds me of the press in that factory. Every time the laundry came in, that big press would come down. It was always the same – all day every day. If you wanted to experience heat, all you had to do was sit in that room for a few minutes – it was unbearable. It made the stories they'd told us in primary school about Hell come to life.

In Cheetham Hill in those days, most of the rag trade was run by Jews as it was in the East End of London; especially in areas like Petticoat Lane.

My having to find a job was a result of earache from my dad, who kept on at me to go out and earn some money, so that I could give my mum a fiver a week for my board and lodgings.

'All right,' I said, 'don't get so excited.' And off I went with a swagger into the big, bad world of business, pressing raincoats. I lasted three weeks – it was bloody murder.

After I quit the factory, my dad gave me a job working on his window-cleaning round. He used to clean shops and restaurants in the city centre and had the same round for over thirty years. He employed a friend of his, Brian, and took me on as a sort of apprentice.

From day one, Dad had always said that when he died he would pass the round over to Brian; which eventually happened. You couldn't fault their loyalty towards each other. Although Brian was a heavy drinker, he would, without fail, be at work bang on six in the morning; no matter how pissed he'd got the night before. He was a lovely man and used to cover for me, because normally it would be half-ten before I turned up. Whether I'd had a drink or not!

Dad used to wake me up at 5.30 in the morning.

'I'll see you in an hour,' he would say.

'Yes, Dad!' I would reply.

Then, I would turn over and go back to sleep. Hours later, I would tumble out of bed and drag myself off to work.

Brian would just say: 'Get working on that fucking shop!'

One of our customers was Dorothy Perkins – a big department store with huge windows. I liked that job because all the birds used to be in the window. Brian used to say, 'Do that, and I won't tell your Dad!' And, God bless him, he never did. Eventually, I became quite handy with the chamois leather and the scrim – this was years before the squeegee was invented.

My old man used to give me a wage packet every week. After he had deducted the fiver for my week's keep, I still had a couple of quid left over to spend on myself. Needless to say, I always spent it, I never put anything away. I suppose I was practising for the future!

Later on, when me and my first wife, Ann, were on the verge of splitting up, Dad and me fell out. He wasn't happy about what was going on and always believed that you and your missus should stick together, no matter what. Sadly, we didn't speak for a long time and only made it up years later when he was very ill.

When I was seventeen years old I signed as an apprentice professional with Manchester City, who were managed at the time by Joe Mercer, the former Everton and Arsenal half-back. I was put under the guidance of Dave Ewing, the reserve team manager; a big Scotsman with a loud voice. He decided what tasks had to be done every day, and gave instructions to the top apprentice, who handed them down to us new recruits. Joe Corrigan, a giant of a goalkeeper, and Tommy Booth, a centre half, were there with me, and altogether there were about ten apprentices on City's books.

I used to arrive at Maine Road about 9.30 every morning, which, for me, was an early start. My duties were easy enough: sweep out the dressing rooms, hang the first-team kit up on pegs, and get all the boots ready for training at eleven o'clock. When everybody was changed, we travelled by coach to Cheadle – about fifteen minutes from Maine Road – for training sessions.

The City stars at the time were: Colin Bell, a very good inside right, but a quiet lad; right-back Tony Book, a nice fellow signed for Plymouth Argyle; Johnny Crossan, an Irish international who was a bit of a wild lad with the women; Mike Summerbee, a right-winger, had been bought from Swindon; and Francis Lee, a stocky goal-poacher who joined us from Bolton Wanderers in the summer of 1967.

However, we apprentices had no real contact with the first-team players. We only spoke if spoken to – those were the rules. If Dave Ewing saw you talking to the pros, he would send you to clean the toilets, or some other dirty job. He was like a sergeant major: a big, frightening man. If you didn't come up to scratch, you were quickly replaced. It was quite a tricky situation, so you had to prove yourself sharpish, because no one would be carried, and apprentices were coming and going all the time.

We were given fitness and skill training, and had to collect up the kit and the balls at the end of the session, and take them back to the ground. Then we would start cleaning the boots, ready for the next day. We were there until 3.30 every afternoon.

I quite enjoyed this part of my life. When we all got to know each other we had a lot of laughs, and got up to some daft pranks. I soon became chief apprentice, and it was my turn to dish out the duties. I had never liked Joe Corrigan, who was a bit of a bully, so in the winter I sent him out in the freezing cold to paint the terraces, while the rest of us were mopping the floors in the warm dressing rooms. By the time I started my second year as an apprentice, I was in charge of all the recruits.

The teams within the club were made up of first, reserve, A and B teams. I progressed to the A team at the start of my second year. We played against Manchester United, Burnley, Oldham, Blackburn and other teams within a forty-mile radius.

Obviously, we all wanted to sign for City as full-time professionals, and although we knew we were being assessed all the time, nobody knew when they would be called in for the chop, or the offer of a full professional contract. The decision would just come out of the blue. One day you would be called upstairs to Joe Mercer's office, and you knew what was coming: either you were signed up, or it was 'see you later'.

When it was my turn, Joe told me that they were signing me at twenty pounds a week. The contract was for the minimum period of eighteen months; obviously this was a sound contract for them on such a small wage, because anything could have happened during that time.

But the main thing was – I was in.

Chapter 3 •

Moss Side Blues

When I was eighteen, I was playing in front of about 200 fans in the A team. Then I was promoted to the reserves, whose games were played on the Friday night prior to the first-team game on the Saturday.

Once in the reserves, we started to broaden our horizons from playing local teams to the likes of Newcastle United. We progressed from the local pitches, used as the clubs' training grounds, to the main stadiums. I remember one pitch was right next to the local mental hospital and all the patients used to come out and watch us. This progression was obviously preparing us for the big stage, if we were good enough to take that next step in to the first team.

Sometimes, say for a local derby with Manchester United, the reserves drew crowds of over 20,000. I played in the second string for about six months, and thought I was doing reasonably well. Then, one Wednesday evening, I arrived at the ground – intending to join the reserve squad – and was called in to first-team coach Malcolm Allison's office.

'I'm a bit concerned about Tony Coleman's injury,' said Malcolm, without looking at me. 'So I'm going to put you on the bench.' He looked up. 'I might give you half a game.' So there it was. I trotted off, a teenage sensation in the making, if I didn't fall flat on my arse.

I made my debut for Manchester City in the League Cup, against Leicester City on 13 September 1967. Leicester had a long history of introducing young players into the side, almost slipping them in unnoticed, as did Manchester United. Both clubs had a gold mine of talent in their youth teams. The United manager, Matt Busby, was renowned for pitching unknown youngsters into the cauldron of the First Division, much to the dismay of the Manchester City faithful.

This time, the tables were turned and it was me who was thrown into the lions' den; in front of more than 30,000 supporters. I had no time to feel nervous. One minute I was just someone sitting on the subs' bench, the next, I was pitched into battle. Our inside left, Neil

Young, couldn't continue, because of a heavy cold, and on I went – in a complete daze. The players around me were helping by saying, 'Don't worry, take it easy, we'll look after you.' They did and we thrashed Leicester 4–0.

Incredibly, at the end of the game, my team-mates, as well as the fans, gave me a standing ovation. It was the supreme accolade, a dream come true. I had produced the kind of fairy-tale performance that all youngsters fantasise about, but I couldn't take it all in – everything was a blur.

Next day, one newspaper reported that: 'In 45 minutes, Bowles scored twice; nearly scored again with a superb header; and strutted off with the confident stride of a youngster who knew he could do it all the time.'

Some people said it was the most stunning Maine Road debut in years, but the management were very careful not to get too carried away with the euphoria. Joe and Malcolm told everyone that I was still very much in the grooming process, still standing on the bottom rung of the ladder, but looking very much a player to watch out for in the future. Harry Goodwin, the club scout, was suddenly in the spotlight for signing me as a schoolboy. He told people that all he did to coax me to join City, was give me a packet of mints!

Some of the papers were also careful to keep everything in perspective. One said: 'These are very early days in his career, and he must be given time to develop, time to grasp the essentials of the game, which cannot be accumulated overnight. Don't look for miracles from young Stan. He is nothing more than a youngster who possesses fine ability.'

Joe Mercer then told me there was every chance that I would make my league debut against Sheffield United the following Saturday. Tony Coleman was out with an ankle injury, and suddenly I was being considered as a first-team player.

Ironically, I was picked as a left-winger, the position that I filled for Manchester Boys. Until now, City had felt that I was too small for this position and were planning to turn me into a wing-half. The team was going well, we were attempting to win our sixth successive game and I was going to be part of it. Again, the impossible happened: I scored two goals; making it four goals in 135 minutes of first-team football. It seemed I had already won the hearts of the City fans.

It was a dramatic and unexpected rise to fame. It didn't happen overnight though; it was a long, hard struggle. Early on, I had been so physically frail and unsuited to the world of professional football that City had put me out to grass with Broadhurst Lads in the Manchester Junior Sunday League. We won the league and cup twice in two seasons, and, over that time, I started to get stronger, taller and broader. When I made my first-team debut my weight had gone up to about 10 st 5 lbs, thanks partly to a course of weight training in the Maine Road gymnasium.

As a treat for being picked for the first team, I bought myself a new suit. I felt on top of the world, with a little bit of money in my pocket. At this time I was going out now and again with some of the pals I had known since childhood. Peter Pandolfo, a good friend who worked in his family's ice-cream business, had a minivan and sometimes, about ten of us used to pile into the back and head off into town.

Just after the Second World War, Peter's dad used to walk around the local estates with a pushcart delivering ice cream. In those days ice cream was made by hand in bowls, placed in tubs of crushed ice and sold round the streets from handcarts. Mr Pandolfo later moved up to a pony and cart and then, in the late fifties, to a van. I used to hear the van's jingle as it cruised the streets, and when I was occasionally allowed to have an ice-cream cone it was one of the highlights of my summer.

Round our way, the ice-cream van used to cause many household rows, and there were many disappointed young faces looking through the curtains. Now, I could afford as many ice creams as I wanted – twenty quid a week seemed like a fortune.

Peter always seemed to have money in his pocket and we used to go to the Portland Lodge in Manchester for a drink or maybe to pull pranks. Like putting fireworks in the letter boxes of people who had rubbed us up the wrong way. We used the local miners' club as a watering hole, and would often end up in a nearby Indian restaurant. Somebody would decide not to pay, and all ten of us would leg it out the door. The police chased us one night, and caught Peter and a few others, but not me – I was too fit to get caught.

Mind you, one night our little ruse totally backfired on us. Me, Peter, Joey Leach, Ricky Gore (who became an MBE, as it happens) and a few others, were getting it down us in the local Chinese restaurant. Pleased as we were with the food and the service, we decided to do a runner. Unfortunately, they must have been used to this sort of caper because, unknown to us, they had installed a central locking system on the door. The second we made our move, the shutters came down.

We were completely trapped – it was like *Indiana Jones and the Temple of Doom*! They beat the absolute crap out of us with these huge great sticks; poor old Ricky took a right hiding. I was as slippery as an eel who'd been bathed in oil, so I avoided the worst of it. Even after the thrashing, we still didn't have enough money to pay the bill, so it was left at that. The bruises healed pretty quickly and it was soon laughed off. Mind you, the funny thing is that I can't eat Chinese food to this day!

We went out most nights, just messing about, and getting up to no good. It seemed a normal thing to do in those days. We were happy and life seemed uncomplicated and easy. I suppose it's pretty much the same for young lads today.

As it happens, Peter Pandolfo owned a multi-million pound business supplying ice cream to major supermarket chains, so we can't have been all bad. I suppose we have both been lucky in our different ways, but, I admit, in those days we were a bit rebellious. While Peter was starting on the road to ice-cream riches, I was selected to play for City against Manchester United, on 30 September 1967. This was, of course, the main event in Manchester football. At the time, the government had set up a committee to investigate the causes of football hooliganism, and look for possible solutions. There was a great deal of publicity when it was discovered that a member of the committee, who was a psychiatrist, was attending the derby match among the capacity crowd of almost 63,000 rabid fans. I fancy he picked up enough material for a bloody big book on the subject.

There was the usual steady trickle of pissed-up louts, being dragged out of the ground by the police. The packed stadium echoed to the constant chanting of obscenities. There was such a fanatical desire for victory that you could cut the atmosphere with a Stanley knife. Even the most mild-mannered supporters in the 'grandad seats' were on their feet, savagely screaming hate when their favourite players copped it.

Out on the pitch there was plenty of petty, vicious fouling. Once again, I hit the headlines, but this time for the wrong reasons. I exchanged a flurry of punches with Brian Kidd, who had been drafted into the United side. It was ironic that the two new boys who had grown up together, were now scrapping on the big stage. The bust-up happened near the end of the game when someone grabbed me round the neck from behind, and I just lashed out, not knowing who the offender was. Tony Book and Pat Crerand successfully pleaded clemency on our behalf and referee, Kevin Howley, booked us and issued a stern warning.

This didn't go down too well with the boss. Joe Mercer always emphasised the importance of sportsmanship in the game. He felt that if you lost a match, you had to lose it with dignity. Joe thought that it would be a good idea to make up with Brian the following day, and shake hands publicly in front of the press. Brian didn't want to do this kind of thing, thinking that it would only make matters worse. I didn't mind at all. Not because I was a chastened young man, but because I was being paid by the newspapers. We met in a public park in Moston and then went to Brian's house where they somehow got the picture of the flare-up on the TV screen, so that it looked as if it was on the telly. Then they took pictures of the pair of us with our arms around each other in front of the TV screen, so that it looked as if it was on the telly. We were saying our lines: 'That has taught us a lesson, we won't be doing it again.'

The referee, Kevin Howley, said, 'It was a serious situation and one which called for clear judgement. But I not only booked the boys, I gave them a wigging that I'm quite convinced they wouldn't forget for a long time. I was left in no doubt that they got the message.' It was obviously designed to appease the public, but I didn't learn my lesson.

Going back to the game itself, the result ended up 1–0 to United. One situation that I will always remember was going into the dressing room at half-time, already down 1–0 and Malcolm Allison immediately having a go at one of the players – Dave Connor. Before the game started, Malcolm had told Dave not to worry about the ball at all, during the game. His job was to follow George Best about wherever he went; of course, as usual, Bestie had played a blinder.

So Malcolm fired into Dave. 'I thought I fucking told you to forget about the ball and just fucking follow Georgie Best around.' Dave took off his shirt and threw it at Malcolm shouting: 'You try it, it's fucking impossible.'

Malcolm immediately substituted him, and Dave just sat there with his head in his hands. I must admit I had to agree with Dave and I am sure that many since have endured the same fate, trying to do a marking job on the great man.

I was still earning twenty pounds a week, with a small bonus if the crowd was over 35,000. In those days the size of your wage packet was dictated by the amount of punters coming through the turnstiles. Also, to bump up the wages, if you were one of the top six clubs in the division, you would be given extra bonuses.

In May 1969, when I was almost nineteen, I married Ann, my girlfriend, who was pregnant. I had to borrow the money off my dad to pay the registrar for the marriage licence, because I had gambled my wages away. In the sixties, families still stood by old-fashioned principles: if you made your bed, you had to lie in it. In those days marriages were meant to last for ever – whether you loved each other or not. Not getting on was no reason to break up, especially when children were involved.

We had met on my sixteenth birthday, and, once married, ended up living with her mum. We both had a lot of learning to do in those early days. Ann, who came from a fairly stable and sheltered background, was only fifteen when we first went out together. Thankfully, she didn't seem too concerned that I went out with the lads regularly, and used to gamble a little. She was dark-haired, slim and pretty. Quiet and a bit shy, I'm not sure if Ann knew what she was letting herself in for. But we were happy together, and that seemed to be all that mattered. In many ways it was a relationship that was made to last, despite a backdrop of ignorance and naivety. We couldn't see any further than the bond between us; and that bond grew in strength. I was hoping that she would come to understand and accept my occasional irresponsible behaviour. It was some hope!

A few months after our wedding, I was again in trouble after a misunderstanding at Manchester City. A two-day training trip had been organised by Malcolm Allison; I didn't attend. We used to go on occasional trips to Southport for training, but Joe Mercer had told me that, with the birth imminent, I needn't go this time. When the team returned from Southport, I was training with the reserves at Maine Road when Malcolm saw me. 'Why the bloody hell weren't you at Southport?' he roared. I explained that Joe Mercer had given me permission to stay in Manchester, but he flew into a rage. 'I'm in charge of this team,' he bellowed, 'and I decide who stays at home.'

Malcolm was a big, forceful bloke – certainly not the sort you start a fight with – but I don't like anyone taking liberties with me. When they do I tend to lose my rag a bit, which makes me far too brave for my own good. Malcolm started to push me around, and that was it. I saw red.

He threw the first punch but I ducked and lashed out, catching him

29

with a right-hander to the side of the head. I knew that I was in trouble as soon as the punch landed because Malcolm was twice my size. Luckily, Johnny Hart, the reserve team coach, dived in to pull him off me, just as he was about to tear me apart. Johnny dragged me away, and told Allison, 'Leave him alone, this is my training session.'

Malcolm hardly ever spoke to me again after the fracas. That punch-up was the beginning of the end for me at Manchester City.

In July 1969, I was picked to play in a pre-season friendly against Ajax in Amsterdam. This was a prestigious game and we were instructed to be at Manchester Airport at ten o'clock in the morning; but unfortunately, I overslept. In a panic, I rushed off to get advice from my mate, Andy Slattery, who lived in New Moston. We realised that the plane was due to take off in forty-five minutes and it would have taken an hour to drive to the airport. Andy suggested that I still go to the airport, even though I would miss the plane, but I decided not to go at all. It turned out that, due to engine trouble, the plane had been delayed by four hours, so I would have had plenty of time to make the flight.

This would have been my first game against a foreign club, and a chance to establish myself as the team's regular outside left. Joe and Malcolm were making frantic phone calls all over Manchester trying to trace me, to no avail. Eventually, I was posted as a missing person, and the police were out searching for me. I knew there was something wrong when the coppers turned up at Andy's house while I was still inside. Again, I panicked and hid in a wardrobe, begging Andy not to tell them I was there.

The following day, the national newspapers had a field day. Said one: 'The mystery of nine missing hours in the life of Manchester City footballer Stan Bowles was still unsolved last night. His career must now be in jeopardy.' Another had it that: 'Stan must be the only person to miss a plane that was four hours late taking off.'

Not surprisingly, I was very wary about the reception that I would receive from Joe and Malcolm when they got back. The press were building up the event saying: 'Manchester City's missing footballer will turn up in manager Joe Mercer's office this morning and try to explain why he missed his chance to play in Amsterdam. He is trying to blame an alarm clock with a softly, softly ring for a mistake which may have ruined his career.'

Luckily, I think they came to the conclusion that I had panicked, being so young, so they decided to overlook the incident. I received a warning and was told never to let it happen again.

I only played one full game in the 1968–69 season, but made twelve appearances in 1969–70. This was a successful time for City – League Champions in 67–68, FA Cup winners in 68–69 and League Cup winners 69–70. But I wouldn't say that they couldn't have done it without me!

Although I had scored four goals in my first two appearances, I knew that the policy of Manchester City was that once established, more experienced players came back from injury and regained their fitness they would immediately get back into the team. I knew that I would have to wait until someone was injured before I could step in. Those twelve appearances in 1969–70 were scattered over the season when the top players were injured. Young players were brought along slowly at Manchester City.

Ann and I had lived at first with her mother, and then moved out to a corporation flat in Ancoats, paying three shillings and sixpence (approx. 17p!) a week in rent. We were struggling every step of the way, especially with a one-year-old daughter, Andrea, to look after.

In the 60s, the selection process for the first team was very different to the way it is now. Even though I had excelled on my debut – and in subsequent games – as soon as the established player came back from injury he automatically got his place back in the team. At nineteen you were thought of as a baby, and clubs were prepared to wait and develop their players slowly.

Malcolm thought I was hanging around with the wrong type of people, and resented the company that I was keeping. He was hearing reports from all quarters that I had been seen in seedy parts of town, and there was an ongoing argument between us. Malcolm frequented nightclubs such as the Cabaret Club, and he was known as Champagne Charlie. He had a bee in his bonnet about me, and wherever he went the conversation would, at some point, come round to me. People would always say to me, 'Oh, Malcolm's just been in, slagging you off.' Wherever I went, it seemed that Malcolm had already been there.

He was an excellent coach; very creative and passionate and not afraid to take chances in a game, or use innovative tactics. But, at the same time, he was very flamboyant, bold and abrasive, and found it difficult to handle people – unlike Joe Mercer, who everyone regarded as a sort of uncle. You certainly wouldn't go to Malcolm with any personal problems, because he might fly into a temper at the slightest provocation. Despite this, he thought of himself as the manager of the club, and didn't like it when anyone questioned that view. When I broke into the first team in 1969–70, our outside left, Tony Coleman, used to say, 'Do you want to come out for the night?' So off we would go and soon we became good friends. In the end, I was staying at his place a couple of nights a week. We used to go round everywhere together. Tony was a great one for the birds, but not me – I was already heavily into horse racing and anyway, I was a happily married man. Everybody went to discos at the weekends, this being the heyday of soul music; but I would just be at the bar, not dancing.

One night I was drinking in the Cabaret Club with Tony, when Malcolm came to our table. A row started between the two of them. Tony was a lot older than me, and Malcolm was trying to accuse Tony of leading me astray, saying, 'What are you doing bringing a young player into this club?' Tony kept quiet, but I couldn't. 'Why don't you shut up?' I said. There was a huge silence, then Malcolm threw a punch at me. So I threw one back, and it all started again. Tony jumped up and smashed a pint glass on the table.

It could have become really nasty, because Tony was a right handful in those days, but the brawl was broken up by the owner of the club. That was to be my last battle with the Manchester City establishment.

I went into training one day soon afterwards and Dave Ewing said, 'Malcolm wants to see you – he's going to get rid of you.' So I picked up my boots and left. I knew I was walking away from one of the biggest clubs in England, but I wasn't bothered either way. At the time I was too reckless to care. I'd half expected it anyway, so I just got on with life – as usual. The official version was that City had decided to release me.

Joe Mercer even gave me a two-week suspension, as well as my cards, but City held on to my registration to ensure that any club wanting me would have to do business with them. The club press release blamed the walkout on the fact that I had refused to sign a new contract, because terms could not be agreed. Malcolm said in the press: 'He can come back in two weeks, but if he still feels the same way he will be suspended again.'

I knew it was all over, and there was no turning back. Immediately I fell back in with my old pals in the Manchester underworld, where the wages were far better than the pittance I was earning at City. I decided that I was finished with football and the trappings of being a 'starlet' as they called me. I stopped training, except for running to the bookmakers for the two o'clock race, and lost interest in football.

The club placed a £30,000–£40,000 price tag on me, designed to frighten off smaller clubs looking for a bargain buy. The news that I had left City sparked a surge of interest among lower division clubs, particularly Oldham Athletic, Crystal Palace and Sheffield Wednesday; but nothing materialised.

Once again I was back on the streets. I seemed to be able to move between the football world and the underworld as easily as if I was stepping from one room to another. I accepted both with a kind of nonchalance that would bewilder most people. My early background contributed to my acceptance of fate, without questioning it too much, or reflecting on what could have been.

So, I teamed up with one of my best pals, Joey Leach, who thought nothing of spending £300 a night, which made my twenty pounds a week wages at City look a bit pathetic. There was money to be earned in Manchester far in excess of what I had been used to in football, which helped smooth the changeover. We were at the end of the swinging sixties; a time of hippies, drugs, and a sense that you could do what you wanted. Mind you, I was that kind of person anyway, I didn't need the current fads to tell me how to behave.

I had many friends who were connected to the Quality Street Gang, a firm who were the inventors of what became known as the 'slow count'. This was an effective little trick used in betting shops. A slip would be written out for, say, £500 to win on a horse in a sprint race. The bet was handed over the counter at the off, and the money would be counted out slowly. If the horse was obviously not going to win coming into the final furlong, the punter would just pocket the cash and do a runner out of the shop. If the horse was in front and looked like it was going to win, the cash would be pushed across the counter for the cashier to check. Either way, the only loser would be the bookmaker. The QSG invented many a fiddle and eventually they became notorious in underworld circles. Most of the time, I walked round in amazement at what was going on. Although I was never actually involved in any crimes, some of my friends and acquaintances were criminals; and I was looking in from the outside. There was always something going on, and I found it difficult to keep pace with it all. It was certainly a far cry from cleaning boots in the Manchester City dressing room.

Some people I knew, were involved in a scam trying to acquire Cup Final tickets. In those days you collected vouchers out of the club programmes, and after you had saved the required amount you could apply for a Cup Final ticket. It was a way of not only rewarding loyal supporters, but also increasing the size of the gate every week. Of course these mates had contacts on the inside, and amassed enough vouchers to send away for 200 Cup Final tickets. After painstaking preparation, they were set to earn loads of money by selling them on to the highest bidder. Unfortunately, after weeks of waiting, the tickets never arrived. They didn't receive a single ticket, and, of course, they couldn't complain in case they were investigated. I think what happened was that someone in the ticket office had creamed off our tickets and sold them on himself, knowing full well no one could do anything about it at all. Criminal, isn't it?

One particular friend, actually bought a betting shop off his first wife's uncle and turned out to be the biggest gambler in the shop. It became so bad that he couldn't pay out the punters on winning bets. In the end, they glued his locks up so that he couldn't get into the building. He just walked away from it and never returned. Everything in those days seemed open to exploitation. If something didn't come off, they would just move on to the next opportunity. There was big money flying around.

These characters had a lot of tenacity, and a strong drive to earn a living; but some escapades were a mixture of hard-nosed gangster work and the Keystone Kops. Plans succeeded and failed to the same degree, but they always saw the funny side of things. They lived from day to day, and nothing seemed to bother them too much – which was a mirror image of my own personality. There were a lot of laughs, and that's what made my links with them more exciting.

They would often do silly jobs, which didn't reap much reward. A typical example was when one of my pals, a very heavy gambler, had lost £3,000 on the horses. He used to frequent a little bookie's in Manchester by a canal, and he knew that the bookmaker walked home along the street next to the canal. My mate smashed every lamp-post in the street so that when the bookie came out of the shop it was pitch black. He ambushed the poor bloke, hit him over the head, and snatched his briefcase.

He was delighted with a nice little job well done. But when he opened the case, there was just the bookie's sandwiches inside; and you can't put a bacon sarnie on a nag. Another thing that made us smile was the fact that my mate was only a very small guy whereas the bookmaker was over six foot. To save himself further embarrassment, the bookie told the police that the person who attacked him was a massive tall guy. Obviously, when this description appeared in the press it took the heat off my mate.

The QSG were building a reputation in Manchester as the under-world gang 'who had things sewn up in the city' when it came to any villainous activity. Occasionally, they were threatened by rival gangs trying to muscle in on the action. One particular bit of aggravation came when they had to tackle a gang who were being a bit cheeky. This other firm started pushing people around, and belting one or two of our acquaintances. So the QSG confronted them, and they all left town with their tails between their legs.

One time, on the way back from a successful night's work, the gang members were unloading the tools of their trade. As one of them passed his shotgun to a mate, his hands were sweaty and the hair-trigger was somehow depressed. The poor fellow was shot straight in the bollocks. He had to have 180 stitches in his groin. Maybe crime really doesn't pay, after all.

The Quality Street Gang are mentioned in a book called *Gangland: Volume Two* by James Morton, and a couple of people I know quite well are singled out. The police always denied that any such gang existed, but I grew up with these people and still keep in touch with them. I was never involved in any of their activities; but I used to hear all about what went on. My policy was to turn a blind eye and keep my mouth shut. We used to meet socially and have a laugh about this and that. I was, I suppose, in the company of these lads almost every day and I don't regret a moment of it.

The QSG were hugely respected in Manchester, and in some ways, they were greater celebrities than the rock stars and footballers they knew and partied with. But they never hurt anyone too badly, and were never arrested for anything major; so I could never understand why they ended up with such a big reputation. However, they were legendary characters, and remain so even to this day. Maybe they did something that nobody else knew about ...

The gang aren't operating any more – they're all fine, upstanding citizens these days. But, so famous are they, that, since their retire-ment, other gangs have taken to using the name. I suppose it's a bit like an unknown football team from the back of beyond calling themselves Manchester United or Liverpool – they hope a little bit of the old magic might rub off on them.

When you are constantly involved in this whirlpool of action and hilarity, it's very difficult to keep track of time because one day is very much like another. My life just rolled along and became one long adventure. But, I eventually started to sense that it was getting out of hand, and I began to feel that I should somehow try to get back into football. This realisation came to mind more and more as each day passed. The time was probably right to walk back through the other door. And, as luck would have it, the football door was about to open once again.

Chapter 4

Bury ... Me at Sea

Bury Football Club had contacted Manchester City about the possibility of taking me on loan at the start of 1970–71. Colin McDonald, the former Burnley and England goalkeeper, was general manager of the Third Division outfit and Les Hart was the manager. Hart was on his way by the time I arrived, so all my dealings were with McDonald. At the time, Division Three contained some good teams, such as Preston North End, Fulham and Aston Villa, all of them pulled in far bigger crowds than the Burys and Rochdales, who lived in the shadows of their illustrious neighbours United, City and the Merseyside giants.

Bury is only about eight miles from Manchester, so I wouldn't have to move house. Although it would be a substantial drop in class, I decided to give it my best shot. I signed for Bury on a three-month trial basis. Peter Leigh, the club captain, was a long-serving full-back and he used to get on the train at Altrincham on training days. Then, on match days, he would drive me to the ground and home again. So, I had someone to keep an eye on me.

Unfortunately, I found myself in deep trouble almost immediately. As far as I was concerned, I had agreed to go to Bury on a basic wage of forty pounds a week, but when I collected my first pay packet I received only thirty-five. Hold on, I thought, someone's taking liberties again. I stormed into the manager's office without even knocking and started having a go at him.

McDonald looked at me, then brought out my contract. 'Don't you read things before you sign them?' he asked. Of course, I've never read a contract in my life, I used to rely on verbal agreements and handshakes; so although it stated thirty-five quid in the contract, I wasn't satisfied.

'We agreed on forty and that's what I want,' I yelled, sticking out my chest. He started shouting back, papers were flying everywhere and suddenly he lunged at me. I thought, Here we go again! I was just about to get stuck in when I heard someone crying. It was McDonald's secretary, who'd been sitting taking notes when I had charged into his office. I'd not even noticed her until then, but we must have scared the poor woman half to death. The tears were pouring down her face, and we were both so concerned about her that we forgot the fight. From that day on I decided that I didn't like Colin McDonald, and I'm sure the feeling was mutual!

In those days, you had to sign a register when you came into the ground on training mornings. Sessions started at ten o'clock, and if you hadn't signed the register by the stated time, McDonald would snatch it away and disciplinary action would follow. It was like being back at school. I was late a few times, so I got into more trouble. The final straw came when I arrived, in a taxi, half an hour late for an away game and asked the club to pay the fare, but they refused. I'd done my money gambling the night before, and I had to explain to the cab driver that he would not be receiving reimbursement for the journey. 'What can I do mate? Sorry!'

The bloke hung round for an hour or so, hoping that someone would come up with the cash. Eventually he gave up and drove off, vowing to run me over the next time he set eyes on me.

Eventually, I had another big row with McDonald and was sacked for constant breaches of club discipline. Bury reckoned I was more trouble than I was worth. McDonald issued a statement to the press which said: 'He [Bowles] just didn't seem interested from the moment he arrived here. We were never sure when he would turn up for training, and during the matches he seemed to resent being played at outside left. I had a big regard for his ability, but it was obvious we couldn't keep a player who carried on like this. We had no choice but to give him his cards.'

I had played in the first five league games of the season for them, and our only win was 3–1 at home to Gillingham in front of a crowd of 3,700. I didn't score in any of the five games. So I started playing for Bury on 15 August 1970 when we lost 3–2 at Wrexham, and my last game was at home against Brighton on 5 September, when we lost 2–0.

The truth of the matter was that I didn't like McDonald treating me like a kid. I thought he was petty and vindictive. Also, I didn't think he was all that clever when it came to football – he insisted that I played as an orthodox left-winger, which never suited my style. I needed to cut in from the right. I explained this to McDonald, as I had to Malcolm Allison, but neither of them took a blind bit of notice. All right, my timekeeping wasn't up to scratch, but you can't have everything can you?

My three-month trial had lasted only seven weeks, and I was out on my ear. Once again, my football career lay in ruins; and I had a free transfer back to the Manchester underworld. I didn't expect to kick another ball for a professional football club – ever again. The game's grapevine was, of course, buzzing with stories of me as a bad boy; a rebel; a liability; someone no manager in the country would be crazy enough to touch. I could always go back and run bets or pick up money for the Quality Street Gang. I used to get paid £150 a week, which was a lot of money in those days, much more than I was earning at football. That's why I wasn't really bothered if I succeeded at the game, or not, because I could always earn good money running bets.

I remember placing my first ever bet, which turned out to be a winner. Sadly, I never kept up that sort of success rate. I thought, This beats working every day of the week. I got a tip from one of the gang that a 100/8 shot (about 12/1) was well worth sticking on a couple of quid. I put a fiver on it and the horse romped home netting me sixty quid. I remember thinking to myself, that to make that sort of money, I'd have to iron raincoats for two months solid.

All of the Quality Street Gang went on to do prison sentences, eventually turned straight and made a lot of money. Joey Leach went into managing pop bands. He turned down the chance to manage a band called the Electric Light Orchestra (ELO), turning them down to look after a group called The Drones, an ensemble of four lads who together produced the worst noise I've ever heard. In contrast ELO went on to sell millions of records.

Chapter 5 •

All Change at Crewe

From being one of the best prospects in the country, I was now virtually untouchable. After being sacked by two clubs in a short space of time, I'd developed a reputation for being a rebel, and the whole of football was keeping me at arm's length. I was the football version of a leper.

Luckily, there was one manager in the Football League who was prepared to take a chance on me – Ernie Tagg, publican, and manager of Crewe Alexandra. Ernie had seen me play, and had liked the look of me.

At the time, my mate Paul Hince was playing part-time at Crewe, while trying to build an alternative career in journalism. Paul had warned me not to join Bury because he knew that Colin McDonald was a strict disciplinarian, and with my temperament it would be like showing a red rag to a bull. He had played me as an orthodox outside left which Paul knew never suited my style of play. He knew that it wouldn't last long, and he was proved right.

Paul played his first game for Crewe away at Workington and took the train to the match. He was late arriving and could actually see the football stadium from the railway station. Paul was in a panic; it was quarter past seven, and the game was due to kick-off in fifteen minutes, and there he was, running down the road, football boots in hand.

The first person he met at the ground was Tom, the odd-job man. Out of breath, Paul said, 'I'm very sorry I'm late, where's the boss? I'll go and apologise to him.'

'Don't worry lad,' said Tom, cool as you like, 'the manager's not here tonight. He's got a darts match at the pub.'

When Paul told me this story, I knew Crewe was the place for me. Paul phoned Ernie Tagg and told him that he had Stan Bowles with him, and said that, despite my reputation in the game, if I could get my head right, and start playing again, I would be a tremendous asset to the club.

All Ernie said was, 'Put him on the train to Crewe station, and I'll meet him there.'

'How much is the fare?' I asked. Paul rang British Rail and found out that it was about three bob.

'I haven't got any money,' I said. He lent me the fare for a single ticket to Crewe.

'What if I fall asleep on the train and miss my stop?' I said, 'I won't be able to get back again.' Paul gave me enough for the return fare – I was three bob up!

Anyway, when I arrived at Crewe station, the first thing Ernie did was give me some money because he knew I was on my uppers. That meant a lot to me and sealed the relationship from day one. I was at an all-time low at that particular point of my life, and, looking back, that three bob was probably the best investment anyone has ever made in me. I thank Paul for that lifeline. It may have been tiny in financial terms but in every other way, it was gigantic.

'This is your last chance in league soccer,' Ernie told me, bluntly. 'If you don't settle down at Gresty Road there'll not be another club in the country who will touch you again.'

I tell you what. I knew he was dead right.

Ernie gave me a trial for a month, but within two weeks I was given a two-year contract and a rented house in Crewe, literally five minutes from the ground – no more cabs for me. Soon, Anne and the children moved in, and everything, at last, looked rosy.

One of Ernie's skills was that he could spot talent. He had been watching me for a while, even in my early days in Man City's reserves, and had been impressed. He had even tried to get the club to sell me, but it wasn't on. He and Fred Chandler had actually gone to the ground to watch a more seasoned player and, quite by chance, noticed me. Both Ernie and Fred had an eye for up-and-coming players. He was always prepared to take on what he called 'the rum buggers' – players like me with a chequered past, ones who had run into trouble with the 'establishment'. His view was that they got into trouble because they played to win, and he believed he could channel their energies. Ernie tried to instil trust into players, and used to tell them to come in through the front door and go out the same way; not to sneak round the back. He was honest with you and expected the same in return.

The problem he had, was that he couldn't go to the board of directors and ask for money to buy players. Signing-on fees were never forthcoming, and he could only get involved in free transfers. In November 1964, Crewe Alexandra Football Club were on their knees; effectively down and out. The chairman, manager and secretary had all left the club.

A bloke called Alan Rowlinson took over the club when there was practically nothing left to salvage. A successful businessman, who basically wanted to balance the books, he didn't give two hoots about the spectators, the fans or the players. He did save the club, but they couldn't bring in any new players unless it was for free. I remember Ernie telling me that he could have once signed Jim Holton, who eventually became very successful with Manchester United. At the time he was playing for a club's reserves, and his manager told Ernie that he was free at the end of the season, but for a bung of £1,000 he'd make sure that Holton went to Crewe. Ernie told the chairman about it, saying that if we left it to the end of the season there would be a queue of clubs after Holton, but he wouldn't pay up and Crewe lost him. Arthur Rowley signed Holton for nothing, to play at Shrewsbury Town, and before the following season finished, they sold him on to United – for £90,000! Still, Ernie had his successes, sifting through the scrap heaps, and he is kind enough to say that I was his greatest success of all.

I remember him telling me that when he took over at Crewe, they were bottom of the league, staring at oblivion; but by the end of his first season they had scored over 100 league and cup goals and finished halfway up the table. He was a man with great vision, had the ability to bring a good team together, and still make money for the club in the transfer market. He used to say to me that he always had last pick, but he always found good players. His strategy with me was simple: get me away from the big city and my friends, so that I concentrated more on my game without all those distractions.

It must have been sickening for Ernie that he recognised talent, signed good players, and then had to sell them to the highest bidder and start all over again. Every time he had an offer for a player he had to tell the board of directors, and they were constantly pulling the rug from under his feet. Rowlinson had told him that he had to make £15,000 a season by selling players, and if he didn't make it one year he wanted £30,000 the next. Over a seven-year period Ernie sold eighteen players for pure profit. So I suppose Rowlinson at least kept the club in the black, and allowed them to continue in the league.

Ernie was a gem, but in some ways he wasn't the most imaginative person on the planet. He ran three pubs over the years, and they were all called The Vine! But he was a father figure to me, and before long, his faith in me was producing results. Ernie reminded me a bit of Joe Mercer, and would always put his arm around my shoulder. He was trying to smooth a way for me to rejoin top-flight football, and is on the record saying: 'I know Stan has been in trouble before, but since he has been at Crewe he has been a model of professionalism. He has played brilliantly for us, and I feel it is time that someone gave him one more chance to do what he is best at – playing football.'

I rediscovered my touch and appetite for the game, and was being widely acclaimed as the finest midfield player outside the First Division. I scored thirteen goals in thirty-seven league games in my first season at Crewe, and, best of all, I was enjoying my football again, after those traumatic exits from Manchester City and Bury.

I'm told that a cousin of mine, Paul Bowles, played almost 200 games for Crewe a few years later. People often ask me if I had put in a word for him, or if I'd suggested he went to Gresty Road. But the truth of the matter is that – as far as I know – I'd never even met him. The thing is, if he'd ever met me, I don't think he'd have wanted to follow me anywhere!

Before I arrived, the club had already been knocked out of the League Cup by Tranmere Rovers. When the FA Cup first round arrived in November, we were drawn at home to Doncaster Rovers, so my first appearance in the world famous tournament was in a 0–0 draw, but I did score in the reply as we produced a handsome 3–1 victory in front of over 6,000 fans. In the next round in December we faced a derby at Chester, where we lost 1–0.

I scored against Lincoln City in January, and again in February, and on both occasions their left-back was Graham Taylor, who went on, so I'm told, to keep a vegetable garden. In March 1971, we travelled to Scunthorpe, another small club which drew slightly bigger crowds than ourselves, and got a 1–1 draw. I remember that the Scunthorpe goalscorer was a young striker called Kevin Keegan.

We were cruising along fairly comfortably in mid-table, and I was doing my damnedest to live down my bad boy reputation. At Maine Road, the Collyhurst kid had the world at his feet, but he had thrown it all away. Now, I was playing well, and scoring regularly, but the bigger clubs were still refusing to reach for their chequebooks.

I'd like to say that there were a few good footballing sides in the Fourth Division, but to be quite honest the standard of football was desperate. Manchester City's youth side would have beaten most of them.

I just couldn't believe that people were getting paid to play. For me it was a platform to progress my career. The highlight of the season playing for Crewe, was when we visited Grimsby. We would each be presented with a box of fish to come home with; it was like a tradition. The box would be packed with ice and fucking freezing to carry, just what I'd always wanted.

After thirteen successful months, during which I made fifty-one league appearances and scored eighteen goals, Crewe decided to sell me on to swell the coffers. The speculation began almost immediately about which clubs might come in for me. Ernie was quite annoyed that potential buyers who were contacting Manchester City had been given bad character reports about me. He claimed that transfer enquiries were being blocked by the Maine Road club. At the end of January 1971, Ernie went public with his anger by issuing a press release which read: 'It is unfair if a player is made to suffer for previous misconduct. As far as we are concerned, Stan has behaved admirably and has helped to lift the side into a position of potential promotion runners. He has reformed and should not be punished again for his past troubles.' Manchester City immediately issued a statement refuting all charges made against them, and Malcolm Allison said, 'I have personally not dealt with any enquiries about Stan. We want him to get on, he has a lot of ability. Let's hope his past is now behind him.'

In the press, I was being linked with Newcastle and Sheffield United. In March 1971, Fulham were showing interest although they knew that I wouldn't be able to play in their remaining promotion games, but I would figure in their plans for the following season. Northampton, Luton and Brentford had failed to sign me, although they had put in bids – some of which included player exchanges – before the transfer deadline. It seemed nothing was going to happen. But, at last, something did.

Chapter 6

Ice Cold in Cumbria

In October 1971, Second Division Carlisle United, who were looking for a replacement for Bob Hatton, came in with a £10,000 offer, which the board considered seriously. As it happened, the offer was well short of Crewe's valuation of me, but everyone expected a compromise figure to be negotiated quickly. A wall of silence surrounded the deal, with neither manager prepared to admit that the signing was going ahead.

Ernie Tagg told the press: 'All I can say is that we seem to be in stalemate at the moment, and are waiting for another telephone call from Carlisle.' Meanwhile, Ian MacFarlane, the Carlisle manager, was giving a different version of events. He said: 'I am waiting for more information from the Crewe end. It is true that I have made a firm cash offer for Bowles, but it is too early to say what the outcome will be.'

The Crewe management were also suffering from a backlash from the fans, who didn't want to see me go. But the club claimed that I was too good a player to stay in the Fourth Division, and that they couldn't stand in my way. Eventually, a compromise was reached at £12,000, and I signed for Carlisle United. Behind this figure lay a story, though. Originally, Crewe had wanted £25,000 for me, but Carlisle had pleaded poverty. After much toing and froing the deal went through. I was signed at eleven o'clock in the morning and, that afternoon, Carlisle sold Bob Hatton to Birmingham City for about eighty grand. Not surprisingly, everyone at Crewe was incensed. The Hatton deal must've been done and dusted, so Carlisle knew what they were getting – they were pulling a stroke. Ernie Tagg was outraged and swore that they'd never do business with Carlisle again. I have to admit it did seem like they were taking the piss a bit!

After the deal had been done, Ernie called me into his office and told me, 'You don't have to go, but you're too good for this club. Go there, and if you crack it, I'm quite sure you will end up where you belong, right back at the top.'

He was only confirming what I already knew: that, in time, I would re-establish myself at the pinnacle of the game, but it was good to hear someone like Ernie saying it. I had a great deal of respect for him; he always placed other people's careers before his own success. He was a very special person, a great manager, and, I like to think, a good friend.

So I moved to Carlisle under Ian MacFarlane, a giant Scot who, at any opportunity, would whack me in the ribs, particularly at 9.45 a.m. before training started. That was Ian's way of saying hello and, perhaps, his way of showing who was the boss.

MacFarlane was a friend of Malcolm Allison's from his days of coaching at Manchester City. Allison recommended me to MacFarlane. He thought, I suppose, that MacFarlane could tame me a bit. Ian obviously thought he could, or he would have never taken me on. The nice thing is that Allison must have rated my game, otherwise he wouldn't have suggested me in the first place.

On the pitch, I continued where I had left off at Crewe – playing well. After eight goals in only thirteen appearances, I had rocketed into the £70,000 class. All of a sudden, everybody wanted to know me again. I heard rumours that two First Division clubs had pencilled the name of Stan Bowles in their notebooks. I was rapidly turning into hot property.

Spurs manager, Bill Nicholson, admitted that I'd looked a great player when I hammered Carlisle's equaliser in the third round of the FA Cup against them. Joe Harvey, Newcastle United's boss, had seen me at Brunton Park in the replay with Spurs, and was looking for a striker to team up with Malcolm Macdonald. They were the clear favourites to make an offer for my services.

Joe Mercer was even saying, 'It's ironic that while Stan had to drop right down to the Fourth Division to really learn what his priorities were, we have never been able to fill the gap he left.'

Carlisle were a very good footballing side and that suited me, so I was happy to continue playing at the club for the foreseeable future. Basically, I used to listen and agree with whatever Ian MacFarlane would say to me. I trusted him. If he had wanted me to go to any club, no matter how obscure, I would have gone. On the other hand, if he had preferred I stay at Brunton Park I would have been more than happy to oblige. He seemed to have the knack of knowing what was right for me, so I left my career in his hands and concentrated on my football.

I would travel back to Manchester after Carlisle's game on a Saturday and, usually on a Sunday night, I would ring Ian and make some excuse why I couldn't return to Carlisle. After receiving verbal abuse from Ian, I would snap and we would argue; but the end result was always that I would get a very expensive cab back to Carlisle that night. This happened many times, and I never figured out why I would do this for Ian and nobody else. I suppose I needed that kind of stern handling at the time.

In my first season at the club, I played twenty-eight league games and scored eleven goals, becoming top scorer. The following season, after only five games I got a call from Ian at my house; he explained that Queens Park Rangers had made a firm offer for me, and that I should consider it carefully. They were also in the Second Division, but that is basically all I knew about them. I didn't even know what the club was like; I was only aware that they played attractive football.

The next day, I went down to London by train and met Ron Phillips, the QPR secretary, who took me to watch one of their home games and put me up at the Kensington Hilton overnight. I was alone and didn't know a soul in London. After the game on the Saturday, I went back to Carlisle the following day. QPR offered me a two-year contract and five per cent of the transfer fee. I was told that I would be placed in lodgings in Shepherd's Bush.

MacFarlane had, by this time, been sacked from Carlisle; probably because he was having constant rows with the directors, and was very outspoken. There were also rumours doing the rounds that he was moving to another club and I think the chairman had come to the end of his tether. The board were from the old school and I don't think that they could handle his aggressive approach at times. His successor was a much safer bet and a lot calmer in the way he managed the club.

So Alan Ashman was back there as manager, and all he said to me when I left, was, 'Good luck!' He could have said a bit more, seeing as I was a fortunate buy for the club; Carlisle were making a thousand times more than what they paid for me.

I have a lot of memories of Carlisle – some good, some not so good. It was certainly no place to be skint in the winter. The snow piled up to six feet high in places, for two or three weeks at a time. The only way we could train was by playing five-a-side in the local gymnasium. It was pointless trying to clear the snow because as soon as you did, it all came down again. Eventually I realised why my neighbours used to come home with vanloads of groceries: they knew that they wouldn't be able to get out of their front doors for weeks on end. I couldn't find anyone to talk to after ten o'clock in the evening. In the winter, it was as if the entire population had gone into hibernation. The cold was unbelievable; there were sheep in my back garden, and I couldn't find anyone to lend me two bob. The people were great – when they could get out of their houses – but the weather was bloody awful. That's how I remember Carlisle in the winter.

I did make a lot of good friends there, however. A few years later some of them came to see QPR play at St James's Park in an FA Cup replay. We lost 1–0 and I missed a penalty. Because all these friends were there for the game, a big night had been planned and the Rangers players were invited. Unfortunately, after the game none of my team-mates fancied it – they were too gutted by going out of the Cup – but I couldn't let the Carlisle mob down. So there was me, as miserable as sin, out on the town. I think it took me about fourteen pints of lager to forget that penalty miss!

My best friend from up there is a lad I call Carlisle Peter. We're still the best of mates to this day. Peter loved a bet, too – and a drink and a laugh – and we usually managed to combine all three. I remember one time when we'd got a bit of inside information about the favourite in a three-horse race. For one reason or another, the jockey was going to jump off the horse – probably to keep its handicap weight down for a bigger race. Me and Pete think, Hello, we'll have a bit of this! So, we have £400 between the two of us on the second favourite at 5/2. The third horse in the race is an old knacker at 10/1 – a horse so crap that it should have been 100/1 even if it was the only nag running!

As predicted, when the horses are going down the far side, the favourite unships its jockey, leaving the outsider a couple of lengths clear. Three fences from home our horse hits the front. Into the last, up and over as sweet as anything, four lengths in front. Me and Pete – a couple of smart boys in the know – are already spending our winnings. Only trouble is, the 10/1 knacker catches our horse on the line and wins by a nose. Of course, with my luck, if I hadn't backed the second favourite, it would have romped home. I put the old Stan Bowles betting curse on the poor thing. In fact, in all my time in Carlisle, I can only remember picking one winner and even that wasn't what it seemed.

Me and Pete were sitting round at my house, watching the Cheltenham Festival on the telly. It's coming up to the last race and I've still got a tenner left. I pick a horse and Pete picks another. He goes off in the van to the bookie's to put our bets on. One thing that neither of us noticed, when we were checking the card, was that there were two horses with very similar names – say, Irish Jig and Irish Wig or something like that. When he gets back from the bookies, he says, 'It was 8/1.' 'No, 14/1,' says I. Pete looks at me gone out and we settle down to watch the race. It dawned on Pete, as we were watching them go to the start, that he'd put my tenner on the wrong Irish-Whatsit. He's mortified, but doesn't dare say a word.

Naturally, the horse I think I've backed walks away with the race. I'm jumping round the room, roaring my head off with delight. Peter's just sitting there, looking miserable. I think this is because I've had it off and he hasn't. Naturally, I want my money: one hundred and fifty notes. Pete knows that I haven't had a winner in months, so he doesn't have the heart to tell me the truth. Next day, he gives me the cash and tells me he's delighted for me. I didn't find out, until years later, that the poor lad had gone out that night and sold his stereo just to raise the cash. I'd have done the same for him, though – honest, I would.

Another time the two of us are in a pub one afternoon, desperate for a bet, but we haven't got a penny. So, Pete blags a cheque for fifty quid off this bird who's got a bit of a soft spot for him. We leg it off to the bank to cash it before she gets the chance to change her mind; unfortunately, while we're queuing up to collect the readies, she strolls in and does exactly that.

She says to Pete, 'Listen, if you want the cheque, come down to my flat at four o'clock and I'll give it to you then.' We're thinking, 'She wants to give him more than a cheque – and we were right. So, down we go to her flat at four that afternoon, but she won't let me in. I'm outside, pacing up and down, worrying about what's going on in there and thinking about who to back with my half of the money.

Inside, according to Pete, she said, 'Don't I get anything for this cheque, then?'

'What do you mean, like?' asks Pete.

'You know what I mean.' And he did.

She writes the date on the top of the cheque and then they go to bed. After that she writes the amount. Then she says, 'If you want me to sign it, you'll have to do it again.' And Pete lay back and thought of gee-gees. Of course, next day we lost it all.

My time living in Carlisle – and my subsequent visits – weren't all about sex and horses. Every Sunday lunchtime we used to go to the King's Head for a game of dominoes. It was never for big money, just for the sheer pleasure of it. The locals were a great bunch of lads and the landlord, Davie Spiers, was an absolute diamond. I could often be seen running across Eden Bridge, just to get to the King's Head in time for 12 noon opening. I think people thought I was putting in a bit of extra training.

One morning I was early, so I was strolling along with my nose in the racing pages, oblivious to everything. Next thing, I walk smack bang into a bloody great lamp-post, nearly knocking myself spark out. Quick look round and no one was about, so I thought I'd got away with it. But someone passing on a bus, spotted what happened and by the time I got to the pub everyone knew. They spent weeks taking the piss, wandering round, pretending to walk into lamp-posts. Oh, the joys of friendship.

Sometimes, I used to go and watch park matches in Carlisle. Pete wasn't a bad player, but I only went to see him play once. It had been pissing it down all night and the pitch was a mudbath. Early on, Pete was clean through, beat the keeper and shot, but the ball stuck on the muddy goal line. I left straight after that. Later on, in the pub, Pete comes up, all offended, and asks, 'Why did you bugger off, Stan?'

'Because of what you did, Pete.' He looks a bit puzzled. I drew myself up to my full height and said, 'Peter, my boy, always remember that there's no mud in the air.' Even now I don't think he's worked out what I meant.

Some of my nicest memories of Carlisle revolve around the park, opposite my house. Every Friday evening before a home game, the local kids would come knocking on my door, saying, 'D'you fancy a kick about, Stan?' I always did for an hour or so, even though Pete thought I was mad. It was just great fun and some of those kids were bloody good and all.

Some of the habits that I was to become well-known for, were developing well at Carlisle. The summer before I got transferred to QPR, I was on a £45-a-week retainer. This was paid every fortnight, so every second Thursday Pete would drive me down to Brunton Park to pick up my wages. And every second Thursday the ninety quid was spent by teatime and I'd have thirteen days to survive without a penny. We'd be running around looking for money to give to Ann to buy groceries. By the time I left Carlisle, I owed eighteen weeks' wages to the club. Start as you mean to go on, I always say. QPR should have been warned.

I think that perhaps the most memorable aspect of my stay at Carlisle or, at least, the fact the fans remember with affection and pride is our amazing run in the Anglo-Italian Cup. Believe it or not, in the not so dim and distant past, Carlisle United had a damn good go at conquering

Europe. The Anglo-Italian Inter-League Clubs' competition of 1972, was scheduled to take place in the early weeks of June, and the Mighty Blues had applied to take part.

The Anglo-Italian Cup was initiated in 1969 as a competition for English and Italian league teams, its primary objective to reward Swindon Town, who had won the English League Cup in 1969 but, as a Third Division club, were not allowed to enter the Fairs' Cup.

In the time-honoured tradition of smaller tournaments the organisers weren't happy until they'd tinkered with the rule book a bit. The competition was to be played with the teams divided into three groups. Each group would consist of two English teams and two Italian teams. The first two group games were to be played in Italy and the remaining two games back in England. Two points were to be awarded for a win with an extra point gained for every goal scored. The most bizarre rule applied to the competition, was that offside only came into force in the penalty area.

Carlisle were drawn with Stoke City, Catanzaro and Roma. It could not have been better. Roma were one of the best clubs in Europe, if not the world, at the time. Our first game was against Roma at the Olympic Stadium in front of 20,000. You could have counted on one hand the number of Carlisle fans who made the trip. They were the pasty-faced members in the crowd wearing scarves and woolly hats wondering where the snow had gone.

We had some good players in our team: Bobby Owen; Chris Balderstone – who went on to play Test cricket for England against the all-conquering West Indies team; John Gorman – now Glen Hoddle's right-hand man; my old mate Stan Ternent, now Burnley manager; Ray Train, who had a great name, I always felt; and a fellow named Tot Winstanley. I never did find out why he was called Tot; I think it was because he liked a drop of whisky.

We put in a great performance beating Roma 3–2 on their own turf. Three days later we beat Catanzaro 1–0 at their place with me notching the only goal.

In the return leg 12,000 turned up to welcome the mighty Roma to Brunton Park. Carlisle had played well – really well – in Italy, but needed to win convincingly at home if they had any real hope of reaching the final. United fan Hughie Boyes had this to say about that summer, when Roma came to Cumbria: 'Can't remember much about the match – too long ago. It was a warm summer night – an unreal atmosphere – something new; as was the reaction from the Italian players as their bus entered the car par to see eight Carlisle fans, myself included, sitting backs to the wall outside the south paddock turnstiles, eating fish and chips out of newspaper. The Roma players all had film-star looks, their wives and girlfriends looked like glamour models. Massive kitbags, and a manager who looked like a middle-aged playboy. The Carlisle players arrive, good cars, smart casual clothes, then ... a Transit van pulls up, out jumps Stan Bowles, scruffy T-shirt, dirty jeans and his kit in a carrier bag – never to be forgotten!'

The match ended in a 3–3 draw, meaning the only chance of making it through to the final now rested on inflicting a heavy defeat on Catanzaro in the remaining group game. We beat them 4–1 with me scoring two, but unfortunately it wasn't enough to see us into the final.

The competition did see Carlisle make many new friends and impress even more, with their flowing brand of football. Carlisle United's first venture into Europe was nothing short of a glowing success. They outplayed the Italian giants on their own turf, and showed the watching world that this little, unknown club played with pride and passion. Maybe we didn't conquer Europe after all, but we didn't half make them sit up and watch. For the record, Blackpool went on to lose 3–1 to Roma in the final.

Chapter 7

If the Shirt Fits

I was twenty-three when I joined Queens Park Rangers in September 1972, for a then, club record fee of £112,000. Rodney Marsh, the hero of the fans, had just been sold to Manchester City for £200,000. Rodney had made the number 10 shirt his own and, since he moved, no one wanted to touch the thing – it was taboo, nobody wanted to wear it. The shirt thing didn't seem a big deal to me. I hadn't really heard of Rodney Marsh, so I just shrugged and said, 'If no one wants it, I'll wear it.' They couldn't give it to me quickly enough – it was my fault that I hadn't heard of the great Rodney Marsh.

However, as luck would have it, I scored one and made another for Don Givens in my first game against Nottingham Forest on 16 September 1972. We won 3–0, and the fans seemed to take to my style of play; which, to them, was a bit like Rodney's. The fans had seen me previously at Loftus Road when I was playing for Carlisle so that might have helped a bit, maybe they knew what to expect. As far as I know, the QPR chairman had tried to buy me then. I'm certain of one thing though: volunteering to wear the number 10 shirt was the best thing I ever did. The fans desperately want to have a hero wearing a particular shirt – think of Newcastle fans and that number 9 shirt – and if you do a good job while you're wearing it they'll love you forever. Mess up, though, and they'll never let you forget it. I was lucky, getting off to a flying start and eventually I became the crowd's favourite.

When I joined the club, the manager, Gordon Jago, had already said that, although QPR were expecting to win promotion, he was phasing out some of the older players, so he had bought me, Dave Thomas and Don Givens to strengthen the team for the following season, when he expected to be challenging in the top flight against all of England's biggest clubs. Gordon wanted to take us up, and make sure we stayed in the First Division. He was building the side around Gerry Francis and myself, with the likes of Terry Venables in there as well, adding both class and experience.

Terry Venables was coming to the end of his time as a QPR player, and only lasted one more season. We had a mutual respect for each other. Terry recalls:

It was a big responsibility wearing the number 10 shirt. Rodney was the idol of the crowd, and you always felt that no one could replace him, because he was such a big name. From the lower divisions, QPR had made themselves a force to be reckoned with by winning the League Cup Final against West Bromwich Albion in 1967. We had the Morgan twins, Lazarus and Les Allen but, above all, Rodney was the king, so his number 10 shirt was going to be difficult to fill.

Then, of course, they bought Stan, who, for me, was an exceptional player. I don't think that he really got the credit for his ability. He was not only a skilful player, beating people, but he had that knack of knocking it off early. He had all the things that were necessary to be a top player. Although I am a big admirer of Rodney's, I must say that Stanley's all-round game was sensational, and I would rate his overall skill as better than that of Rodney Marsh.

Funnily enough, the first day he came training with us, we were having a small-sided game, and normally when new players arrive it takes them a while to settle in. Stan was in the same side as Gerry Francis, and they were playing one-twos off each other, as if they had been playing together for a hundred years. It turned out to be a combination that was very special. For a small club there were some outstanding individuals, and Gerry, Stan and myself played so well together. Then Dave Thomas came to the club and he actually increased the depth and width of the side, then McLintock and so on.

Stan's first touch was the key. He had a left foot like a hand, and could put the ball anywhere he wanted it to be. It wasn't a case of controlling the ball first, because he knew he could do that, it was what he was going to do after that. He was like one of those highly technical foreign players, he just had that type of ability. Stan was also a cheeky player, enough to sort of annoy you, but not enough to make you too angry, just a thorn in everyone's side.

He was also a bit slipshod when it came to observing the rules of the club, particularly when it came to turning up on time for matches. I think now, if he was one of my players we would have fallen out a bit, but everyone loved him. There was no nastiness in him and, where other people would be angry that someone had got away with something that *they* couldn't get away with, it was OK with Stan because he had such a lovely way with him. He had a great personality and sense of humour, and he's never changed. Nothing seems to get to him too much, and he just gets on with his life. In my capacity as a former England manager, I would say that Stan would suit today's game very well.

The first time I met Jim Gregory, the QPR chairman, was after my first, or maybe second game. I had taken over this shirt of Rodney's, and Jim used to like Rodney, so it was a good job I had a particularly good game. Jim was a bit spivvish, but I had been around a lot of spivs in Manchester, and I knew the type. The QPR boardroom was different to other boardrooms because, unlike at other clubs, a few players were allowed in.

The directors of the visiting club would take a very dim view of that, and ask, 'What are you doing in here?' as if we were scum. But it was different at Loftus Road. We would be larking around with Jim, who would pour us champagne in front of the opposing chairman and say to us, 'Don't worry about that lot!'

So I went in, that first time, and Jim said, 'I thought you had a good game today, have a drink.' And then he bunged me £200, which was quite a bit of money in those days. I thought, Hello, I could get used to this!

Jim was not your average chairman; very unlike those who wouldn't talk to the players. He liked rogues and I think he saw a lot of himself in me. A Jack the Lad character, he always used to come into the dressing room before the game and have a laugh with us.

I was one of the 'chosen few' players allowed up to the boardroom. Gerry Francis was another who could go up because he was captain for club and country. I put a word in for Don so he could be included in the fold, and as Don was a local lad, Jim sanctioned the invitation. Once I got Shanks in we would try our damnedest to relieve Jim of some readies; we planned it like a military operation. We'd shower after the match, have a drink in the players' bar and then go up and see Jim and start buttering him up. If I'd had a good game I'd get bunged some money, by and large around the £100 or £200 mark, which we'd then take down to White City. If I hadn't played well Jim would refuse point blank to pay me out and we'd have to go to the dogs with our own cash. When Jim said no, he meant it, and nothing would change his mind; even though we'd try every trick in the book. We'd say we needed the money to visit a sick relative; pay off some urgent debts; or spend on pacifying the wife. Jim knew the latter was the least likely scenario.

More often than not, after I played well, Jim would oblige with a cash drop. His customary method of handing over the money was by folding a wad of notes in half, before slipping them into my top pocket. He'd say something along the lines of 'Have a bet on me, Stan,' generally patting my top pocket as a signal that I could now depart. That would be my cue to say goodbye, pop outside, discreetly remove the money from my pocket and count what I'd been given. Once, for a laugh, I wore a double-breasted shirt with two top pockets, one on either side. So when Jim popped the money in one pocket and gave it a pat I drew his attention to the other pocket. He silently removed half the money from one pocket and put it in the other. Another time, Jim refused to hand over the cash so Don and I worked frantically on him for a good half hour to the point where we thought we had talked him round. Eventually, Jim appeared to wilt, held up his hands in mock surrender and said, 'Okay, okay boys I give in, go on have a drink on me,' with that Jim stuck his hand in my top pocket, shoved in the fold giving it a pat. Then he turned round, breathed an exasperated sigh of sub-mission and said, 'Now, just leave me alone.' When I got outside I put my hand in my top pocket wondering how much Jim's bunged me, only to pull out a Tetley tea bag. He was cute was Jim. I miss him.

Jim was partial to a gamble himself. On Saturdays, he would chal-lenge anyone in the boardroom to ask him a full-time score in any First Division game and up to four scores in the Second Division. If he couldn't name all the correct scores he would hand over £50 and if he could, you'd have to pay him forty. If you backed against him you'd lose your money every single time. He'd say, 'Mr Memory Man does it again.' He'd win money off different chairmen every week, pretending to be absent-minded when clocking the scores at full-time. 'Villa won didn't they?', 'No, it was a draw, Jim.' Suddenly, come wager time, Jim's memory was flawless.

Don Shanks met Jim by chance in a health club in Aldershot once, and Jim challenged Don to a length race in the swimming pool for £100. Well, Don loves a gamble but even he thought if Jim's betting a ton against a professional footballer at his age, he must be Mark bleedin' Spitz. Even though Jim was a short plump man, Don warily accepted the bet and after a furious amount of thrashing and splashing Don just beat Jim by a short head.

Many years before, so his cousin told me, Jim Gregory had started off in the family business, as a barrow boy in North End market, which was between West Kensington and Fulham Broadway. One Monday,

when his mum and dad didn't put out the fishmonger's barrows, Jim
went and bought three GPO vans. In those days you had to buy them
in lots of three. So Jim put the three vans where the barrows usually
stood – he sold all three the same day. Jim did that every Monday, and
eventually became a very big used-car dealer and made a lot of money.
He became a director at QPR in 1964 and bought the club in March
1965. He had taken over a small, obscure Third Division outfit, hidden
away among the housing estates of Shepherd's Bush, and planned to
turn it into something very special. A man who could make a fortune
out of clapped-out GPO vans, wouldn't have much trouble turning
round an ailing football club.

Funnily enough, Jim Gregory looked exactly like a car dealer. He
wore a short Crombie overcoat, had a little bald head, and a wicked
grin that said it all. He drove a navy-blue Rolls-Royce all the time I was
at QPR, buying a new one every year. Terry Venables thought he was
sharper than Jim, but he wasn't. There wasn't a lot in it, but Jim
definitely had the edge.

When I first arrived at Rangers, I was staying in digs with a Scots
couple in Acton. The trouble was that I wasn't much of a one for early
nights and was keeping quite late hours and, since I had no key, I kept
getting locked out. So Jim, generous as ever, decided to put me up in
the Kensington Hilton. This arrangement lasted for three months. I
was drinking champagne all night, having friends round to dinner and
just signing the bill. It was like I'd died and gone to heaven. Of course,
when Jim got the final bill he went mental, the whole thing cost him a
bloody fortune.

I settled into the club pretty quickly and soon began to enjoy living
in London, even though my only previous stay in the capital had been
with Carlisle, for a match at Brentford. I had imagined that London
and Manchester would be similar in many respects and I could only
compare the size, hustle and bustle to my recollections and knowledge
of the streets of Manchester. I had also been told by many friends that
Londoners didn't get on with Northerners, so I was a bit worried about
the kind of reception I would receive.

As it happens, this concern turned out to be totally unwarranted. I
almost immediately made connections and friends; some of whom
were doing business with friends of mine back in Manchester. So I
didn't find the transition too difficult. Even so, despite my connections
with some shady characters, I was still a little bit naïve. Although there
was a lot of publicity surrounding my move to QPR, I was still a

relatively poor Manchester boy; walking the streets of London for the first time.

One morning, as I was strolling down Shepherd's Bush Road, looking for a betting shop, I was approached by a likely looking bloke in the street.

'You don't know where there's a betting shop, mate, do yer?' I asked.

He looked me up and down. 'You don't come from around here, do you, mate?' he said, with a little smile.

I shook my head, 'No I'm a bit lost, as it goes.'

As luck would have it, this fine upstanding gentleman, decided to take me under his wing. He showed me where the local betting shop was and, just by chance, there was an illegal gambling club – where you didn't pay any betting tax – in the basement. I didn't realise it at the time that this person was an underworld character by the name of Slates. He was well known at the races, as a clerk who worked for different firms in London. Slates looked just like a spiv; a scruffier version of Arthur Daley, in a crumpled suit. Although he was wearing a shirt and tie, you could imagine that he had been dealt a few dud hands and was down on his luck.

I had stumbled across a man who knew the underworld activities of the area and there he was, luring me into a smoke-filled basement. When I look back, that episode reminds me of Oliver Twist meeting the Artful Dodger in the busy streets of London, and immediately becoming involved in the seedy world of the petty criminal. Within three days of moving south in a big money transfer, I had been introduced to the illegal gambling dens of West London.

So, anyway, there I was standing outside this betting shop with this dodgy character. 'You can come down here if you want,' said Gentleman Slates. 'Because the tannoy for the racing commentary is there, and you can place a bet without having to go upstairs.'

That's considerate, I thought, as I descended into the dark and gloomy world of London 'Society'. Talk about home from home.

Slates and I became firm friends; he was always a laugh and had a very quick wit. I remember one time we went to Toppers club in London, after we'd won a few quid down at the White City dogs. Toppers was a topless bar – one of those expensive clubs with 'hostesses' who would come and sit with you. This was the first time Slates had ever been there and he didn't know the form. This bird came and sat down at our table; I think Slates thought he'd pulled. She saw the look on his face and put him right straightaway: 'You know it'll cost you twenty-five quid to talk to me, don't you?' Slates's face dropped, then, quick as a flash: 'Well, talk to him and I'll listen!'

So, that was my introduction to London life – meeting the thieves and villains of Shepherd's Bush. Obviously, they paid a bit of attention to me as soon as they realised I was a high-profile footballer, but they didn't really treat me any differently just because of that. I had fallen into the same type of company that I had grown up with in Manchester, and I felt entirely comfortable in this new environment.

However, the rules of the card schools were different to those I was used to. As a result I was losing heavily, while desperately trying to come up to speed with the different gambling activities.

In the vast expanse of London there were endless opportunities to quench the thirst of whatever your addiction was. And one basement is much the same as another. These gambling dens were called 'spielers', and they were quite numerous around London. There would be one room for poker, and another for thirteen-card rummy; gamblers would spend all day and night playing for very high stakes, in these serious card schools. There was no drinking, because alcohol wasn't allowed on the premises. Thieves would come in throughout the day with the bits and pieces – jewellery, clothing, electrical goods – that they had stolen down the West End, hoping that whoever was holding the winnings would buy the booty. Later, when we had a spieler in Ladbroke Grove you could make a shopping list for the thieves, and they would go out and steal to order.

The police knew all about the spielers, but left them open simply because they knew where most of the villains were at any one time – gamblers being creatures of habit. If the police were looking for anyone in particular, they usually knew where to find them. I suppose these dens were a bit like open prisons.

I honestly believed that moving south would have given me the ideal opportunity to start afresh, and try to bury the darker side of me, once and for all. Could I win the battle? I had faltered at the first hurdle but, in my stronger moments, I was willing to give up gambling.

Unfortunately, Ann was finding it difficult to adapt to this new environment. I was out all day, and would just come home, have my tea, then go out again at night. So it was a tremendous strain for her – a young mother with two small kids.

I felt immediately that London was the place for me, because I knew that there was big money to be earned. I was enjoying my football, and slowly coming to terms with the pressures of the social side. But I knew I had to cut down on the gambling as it wasn't doing me, or my marriage, any favours.

Quite early on in my career at QPR, I had the fortune, or misfortune, to meet Don Shanks, at that time a Luton player, who became my friend and constant companion. I used to refer to him as Mr Donald.

The club sorted me some new digs out. I would be staying with Don's parents who lived a stone's throw from Loftus Road. I remember settling down in the living room with a cup of tea taking in my new surroundings, browsing the horse-racing section of the newspaper, when in walks Don with a copy of the *Sporting Life* tucked under one arm, and six pairs of tracksuits he was flogging in the other. Within minutes we were both wearing identical tracksuits, huddled round the paper trying to pick out potential winners. Thirty years later we're still looking for them.

Don became my constant companion from that point onwards even though he was playing for Luton at the time. Don has always been one of life's duckers and divers; great company, a natural talker with an eye for a bet, the ladies and making a few quid, should the opportunity arise. Don was a local lad from the Bush. He had been a schoolboy at QPR and was one of the first youngsters from the Shepherd's Bush area to make it into the professional ranks. Players like Les Ferdinand and Dennis Wise would follow in his footsteps.

Don got to the age of fifteen and, like a lot of kids around that age, was devastated to find the club he loved, supported and played for, wasn't going to offer him an apprenticeship. He played one of his last games for QPR in a schoolboys' final. Rangers were losing 4–0 at half-time and then Don goes and scores four in the second half but still ended up losing the match 5–4. If I've heard Don tell this story once, I've heard it a thousand times and I had to have it checked and double-checked, because I don't think Don scored four in his whole career.

After that impressive performance, QPR quickly changed their minds and offered Don an apprenticeship but by this time it was too late. Fulham had already shown a strong interest and so it was off to Craven Cottage for Don. At this time Johnny Haynes was the top dog – the first £100-a-week footballer – and it was Don's task to clean his boots. Don used to tell me that Johnny was an unbelievable player, left foot, right foot, no one could pass a ball like him.

Bobby Robson became the new manager of Fulham, and he decided to let Don go aged seventeen. This was a real blow, because he began to wonder if he was ever going to make the grade. But Don had faith in his ability and was handed a temporary contract at Luton, where he was selected to play for the England youth team, and played in a competition in Prague, which they ended up winning. Don had a good tournament and Luton manager Harry Haslam, known as 'Happy Harry' because of his permanent smile, offered Don a full-time contract. Some time later Don would join up with me at QPR but we'll get to that later.

According to Don, he had just read in the paper earlier that week about the reformed Stanley Bowles. There was a photograph of me with my long coat on, with the pockets pulled out to signify that I had no money left. The caption read: 'I'm finished with gambling. I've come to London now, and I'm a changed man.'

He asked me, 'So you're never having another bet, Stan? I've read the papers, is that it – finished?'

'Oh, yeah,' I said. 'Definitely finished – for good.'

We talked for a bit, then he asked me what I was doing the following night.

'Nothing much,' I said, 'I've got the game on Saturday, but otherwise I've nothing planned.'

So, we decided that we would go to the pictures. We went to see a film called *A Clockwork Orange*. It was an absolutely mental film, and we were both sitting there, fidgeting away until about 9.30 in the evening. We turned to each other and said, 'That was good, I really enjoyed this evening!' We never went to the cinema again. Next night it was the dog track, and for the next seven years we went down the dogs almost every night. We would go anywhere to gamble. We'd be at the dog tracks at White City, Hackney and Wembley; at the betting shop; or we would play cards. We just liked to be in that environment. I wasn't a very heavy punter that would gamble all of his money in one go. I would spread it out over the course of the afternoon or week. Unfortunately, the end result would be the same, but it just took a little bit longer to go. Mr Donald was different, he loved nothing more than a heavy punt.

He did me a big favour one day. He owned a very fast dog called Super Supreme, which he used to run at the White City track. He had an argument with the trainer, so he took the dog away and put it with a local publican, who was a friend of ours. The dog had won a race the week before. I hadn't had anything on it, so he was quite pleased, because if I have a bet, something very unlucky, or out-of-this-world would happen, and the dog would usually finish second or spontaneously combust, or something. So, Mr Donald started to race this dog privately.

He came to see me training at QPR on the Monday morning.

'How did you go over the weekend?' he asked.

'No good, no good,' I replied, shaking my head. 'They done me. I didn't have a winner. How did the dog get on?'

'Oh, it bolted in,' said he.

'Bolted in!' I croaked, as if in agony. 'What price was it?'

'Three-to-one,' whispered Shanks.

'Three-to-one? Did you have it off?'

'Yes,' beamed Shanks.

'Oh lovely, terrific,' I replied.

This happened for five consecutive weeks. The dog won every single time, and still I hadn't put a bet on it. He would go to the track, put it in the traps, and pick up the winnings. As far as Mr Donald was concerned, this was better than going to the bank – this was like owning the bank. Eventually, I cracked. 'Come on Don,' I begged, 'put me into the action, give me a chance! Come on, Don. What's the matter with you, leaving your old mate out like this?'

'All right, Stan, don't panic,' he said. 'You're in.'

The relief was enormous – I was about to start getting free money. 'Why don't you enter it in a race up near Manchester or Bolton, somewhere like that?' I suggested – because all my mates were up there.

So, Don entered Super Supreme for a race at Doncaster, and took the dog all the way up there himself. I arrived with my entourage – three mates from Manchester. I was never on my own and this particular night I was with my lifelong friend Joey Leach, whom I was treating to a night out. So anyway the dog, which has won its last five races, gets the perfect position, Trap 6. Don's having a grand on it at 3/1. The price is right, everything looks good.

Me and my mates go in heavy and suddenly the price is obliterated. It goes from 3/1 to 6/4 on favourite. The race starts, they leave the traps, they go towards the first bend, just about to turn left, and another dog runs straight into ours, breaks both his front legs, and Mr Donald has to have him put down. That was my big night out in Doncaster. My lifelong pal Joey Leach has done five hundred quid, and Shanks's dog is dead. I don't know why, but they both seem to think it was all my fault.

My main ambition at QPR was to establish myself in the side that Gordon Jago was putting together for the future. QPR had only ever been promoted to the First Division once before, and that was in 1968. The following year they had a disastrous season and went straight back down again with the lowest points on record. They only managed to pick up eighteen all season and finished twelve points behind the second from bottom team, Leicester City. Gordon wasn't about to let that happen again.

The team was playing quite well, and five wins in a row in October lifted us up to second in the table, behind Burnley. I was lucky enough to score eight goals in my first thirteen games. Everything seemed to be going smoothly, at last.

At the training ground in the mornings, Terry Venables organised all our little sessions, and Gordon Jago would arrive about an hour after we had started. At the end of the session, when Gordon went off to work in the office, Terry would take three or four of us – Don Givens, Gerry, probably Dave Thomas and me – and show us some little tricks of the trade.

Terry always said, 'Do what you've got to do, but this might help you along the way.' He was very good at that. You have to make your own decisions on the field, but little things did crop up where I thought, Yeah, Terry did mention that in training. He was good at putting things in to your mind, that's why he's made a brilliant manager. Previously, I would listen to my coaches, but I wouldn't take any notice of them. I would just go and do whatever I fancied. If they told me something that turned out to be right, I'd think to myself, Oh, yeah, he was right. But I'd never say, Thanks very much! I don't really know why, I expect it's my easy come-easy go attitude, although some people might say it's because I'm an ungrateful bastard!

Before we started training, Terry liked us to do a bit of ball practice, keeping it up, just to get the feel of the ball, especially when we had just come back from our summer holidays.

In those days, the summer break was a lot longer than it is today, and your touch definitely went. On the first day back in training, we wouldn't use the ball at all. Then, after a couple of days, somebody would chip a ball to me, expecting my close control to be exceptional, and the ball would be bouncing everywhere, which was unusual. I had lost that touch during the two-month summer holiday. But it didn't take long to come back. And when it did, it was like it had never been away.

Off the field, however, things weren't always going smoothly. In November 1972 I was involved in what could have been a very serious incident after Don Shanks and I had borrowed a Transit van from one of my friends – Carlisle Peter – who was in London at the time, but on his way to Jersey for a few weeks. At that time, Transit vans were regularly involved in robberies.

We used to go to Hackney dog track after training. Hackney was convenient – although it was the other side of town – because there were afternoon meetings, and I could always get back home to my wife and kids by early evening. This day, we'd had a few bets and just about broke even, and on the way back we decided to stop at a hamburger bar for a bite to eat. We pulled up in Holborn, at a Wimpy Bar near the West End. It was about 4.30 p.m. and workers were leaving their offices for the day, so it was getting busier, with crowds of people milling around an area where a lot of banks and places like that are situated. Into the Wimpy we go: cheeseburger, chips and a milkshake. Then we went home, well satisfied.

The following week it was the same thing again, but this time we actually had a good day and won a few quid. I was the banker, and used to keep the money in my pocket, even though half of it was Don's. I was in charge of the finances on that particular day. We've come back feeling happy; on a high, having won about £1,600. But we still went to the same Wimpy to spend a tenner, because it was the kind of people we were, it was all the same to us – whether it was the Hilton or a burger-bar, we didn't give a toss.

We pulled in at the same time, parked in the same place as the week before, and went in and ordered our cheeseburgers. As we were coming out of the Wimpy, I decided to nip off and get an evening paper, to study the next day's runners. Don says, 'All right, I'll just open up the van and wait for you.'

According to Mr Donald, as he walked back to the van, he looked into a shop window, noticing that it was very busy inside. There were about twenty people inside, and a woman outside wearing a big mac and he's thinking, I wonder what they're selling in there? Everyone seemed to be browsing, but no one's buying anything.

He wasn't worried about this and just walked to the passenger side of the Ford Transit, and put the key in the door. As he did this, he heard a sort of tapping noise on the glass of the shop window fifteen yards away. Suddenly, about twenty people come legging it out of the shop, grab him, throw him to the ground and thrust guns against his head. So he's lying flat out on the floor, surrounded by enough fire-power to take out a small country. A voice shouts, 'Move and you're a dead man,' to which Don whimpers, 'I'm not moving. I'm not moving.' Foolishly, I walk slowly up to Don and the group of people surrounding him with weaponry and ask, 'Don, did you forget to pay the Wimpy bill?'

The whole thing looked so bloody comical, I just had to laugh. Next thing, the police grab me as well, and we're off to Snow Hill police station; arrested, and about to be charged with attempted armed robbery. As it happens, the police had spotted the van the week before, taken its reg, put it through the computer and found that it had been stolen three years earlier, and used in an armed robbery in Manchester.

So they had put two and two together and thought: same time, same place, something's going off. Hence the heavy mob waiting there. They've rushed us, opened the back of the van, searched it and taken us away. Now we are trying to explain to the chief copper at the station that this is Stan Bowles, just signed for Queens Park Rangers for £112,000 and that Don plays for Luton Town.

The guy was laughing his head off. 'You're two comedians, aren't you?' he said.

'Look, we're telling you – we are footballers,' we said.

'Yes, sure you are; bang 'em away. You two are going down for five years.' I know it was serious, but I couldn't stop laughing, because I'm finding the whole thing hilarious.

'What are the charges?' asks Don. 'What have we done? I should be charging you for putting me under intense pressure, throwing me on the floor and putting guns to my head – for what?'

'Well, whose is the van?' they said.

We told them that we had borrowed it off a friend of mine who was in Jersey, and who would be back in a week. We then told them the whole truth about everything that happened. They still didn't believe us, so we ended up just sitting there, and Gordon Jago was called to bail me out.

When you are arrested they take off your jewellery, and all the money out of your pockets. I had £1,600 in cash, and Don had 50p. So, the police were saying as they were checking this, 'When arrested, Stan Bowles had £1,624 in his possession, Don Shanks 50p.' Don was thinking, Half of that's mine! Which, being Don, was the only thing he could think about.

Then, poor Gordon Jago came rushing in, white-faced and horrified.

'Stan, what's happened?' he cried. 'What have you done?'

'I've done nothing,' I replied. 'It was Don, he was driving this van ...'

I forgot to mention to Gordon that it was my friend who had lent *me* the van, and Don was driving me home and that he knew nothing about this. Gordon Jago blamed Don for about the next ten years.

The end result was absolutely ridiculous. They actually charged us and we had to appear in court. Of course, it was a field day for the papers, with headlines like: Football stars arrested with stolen van; committing an armed robbery, etc. And we were taking lots of stick from the other players at our clubs; digs like, Been back to the bank lately?

They took us to court and, to be honest, we couldn't stop laughing. Gordon Jago was there with his wife, who was a policewoman, and he's staring blankly at us, while were fooling around in the aisles outside the courtroom, before our case was called. I couldn't believe that they were going to go through with this case. It was like Victorian England – transportation to the colonies for nicking a loaf of bread. Eventually, we get into the courtroom, and it's full of Queens Park Rangers' supporters chanting: 'Rangers – Stanley – Rangers – Stanley!'

We started laughing, so the judge had to clear the court. He looked at us sternly and said, 'If the accused find this amusing I will put them somewhere for a few weeks, where they'll find it less amusing.'

Gordon Jago's face dropped to the floor. He turned around to me and whispered, 'Please Stan, tell Don to stop laughing. Please!'

The hearing proceeded for another ten minutes, and then the judge jumped up and said, 'Would the two officers who brought this case to court, please come forward to the bench.'

After a few moments of consultation, the judge announced: 'This case has been dismissed through lack of evidence.'

We received a public apology, and later a report was given to the press that the court had been misled, and we were totally exonerated. But by that time the damage had already been done and our names had been dragged through the mud. Carlisle Peter later got twelve months' jail for driving this van, knowing it to be stolen. This incident happened in the first couple of months of me joining QPR – a nice introduction for Gordon Jago. I suppose it's typical of me though, walking up to the van asking what was happening. I should have walked past and got the nearest taxi and buggered off home; which is probably what anyone else would've done.

My friend Peter had been in and out of prison a few times. He used to follow Carlisle United football club everywhere, and I bumped into him at one of our home games. He had been involved in small-time robberies, and knew my brother in Manchester very well. At this particular time he was on the run from the police, which was why he was going to Jersey – to keep his head down for a while.

I suppose, thinking back, that we were very lucky to get away with that incident; and the whole thing was a major embarrassment to Gordon Jago. But it didn't affect my game. During the time that the case was coming to trial, I continued to play out of my skin. We weren't exonerated until March 1973, during which time we had only lost one of our previous seventeen games, and were well on the way to promotion. I should have realised, there and then, that my friendship with Mr Donald was going to be incident-packed. We were like two cartoon characters stumbling through life, having plenty of laughs, but leaving a trail of destruction behind us.

At least on the football side, things were going well. Unfortunately, Burnley had built up a big lead at the top of the Second Division, and we just couldn't peg them back in the end. We won our expected promotion, finishing one point behind Burnley, and eleven points clear of Aston Villa. I was on the way to realising my dream of playing again in the First Division; which it looked like I had thrown away at Manchester City, four years earlier.

Even so, I still couldn't resist a little bit of controversy. The last game of the 1972–73 season was also the first time I got myself on *News at Ten*. That was the year Sunderland upset the odds by winning the FA Cup against a star-studded Leeds United team who were the previous year's winners. I had backed Leeds earlier on in the season to win the Cup and had watched, amazed, as Sunderland survived everything Leeds threw at them. I thought Sunderland a very ordinary side, and was mightily peeved that they had deprived me of a big pay-out. As it turned out, for our last game of the season we had to play Sunderland at Roker Park.

Ordinarily the season finishes before the FA Cup Final but Sunderland had a backlog of fixtures and were forced to play their last match (against us) after the final. The Sunderland management decided to treat the match as a victory parade by displaying the Cup on a trestle table beside the pitch.

A couple of friends of mine, including Carlisle Pete, had made the journey across Cumbria to watch the game. I met them before the match and the talk turned to the FA Cup. As we had already tied-up promotion I decided to have some end-of-term fun. I bet Pete ten quid I could knock the Cup off its stand. 'Don't be fucking daft,' says Pete. 'There's forty-five thousand Mackems in there – they'd string you up.' But he took the bet anyway.

So, we kick-off and I make a run down the left. The ball squirts loose, plops down in front of me, halfway inside the Sunderland half on the left side. My plan had been to knock the Cup off its stand at the earliest opportunity, and then concentrate my efforts on winning the game. The trouble was, I now found myself on the opposite side of the pitch and running forward, approaching the penalty box with a defender in close attendance, jockeying me down the wing.

As there was a tenner involved I'm not about to let this geographical inconvenience interfere with my mission. To the bemused amazement of the Sunderland defence, I suddenly turn back and start running towards my own goal. Now the defenders weren't sure whether to follow me in case I'm drawing them out of position.

To confuse everyone – my own team-mates, the Sunderland players and the crowd – I then start running across the pitch, feigning a couple of times as if I'm going to launch a ball into the box. Everyone is just staring at me – then, when I feel I'm close enough, I blast a fierce left-footed shot directly into the Cup. I knock it off the table. The whole ground knew that I'd done it deliberately. Everything goes deadly silent for a few seconds, then the Sunderland fans go apeshit! They want my balls in their sandwiches!

The game goes on and I score, which doesn't seem to please them at all. To make matters worse, one of their players – Micky Horswill – is giving me hassle all through the game. In the end I get pissed off with this and go down, pretending that he's head-butted me – as you do – and the ref sends him off. This is too much for the Mackems, they come swarming on to the pitch – with most of the ingredients for a sandwich at the ready. The ref, sensibly in my view, decides that the best course of action is to take the players off. It took twenty minutes to clear the pitch and, I'm glad to say, gonads on Hovis was off the menu.

At least I got my tenner, and my picture on *News at Ten*. And all because I was just having a bit of a laugh.

At the time, Ann was having Tracy, our third child, and she'd gone back to Manchester to be close to her family. There was a lot of talk in the press about Rodney Marsh being homesick, and wanting to come back to London, and that I was homesick for the North. In actual fact that was just paper talk, because my only intention was that I would be there when Ann had the baby, and after that I would go back to London. Gordon kindly gave me an open rail pass to visit Manchester, but people were saying that, like George Best, I was a runaway and that trouble followed me around. This wasn't how I saw the situation. As I said, on the football front everything was going fine and I was determined not to mess up everything again.

Also, although George and I were friends, we didn't really have much in common. As you know, he was more interested in girls, whereas I was a gambling man, so we were quite different personalities. Nowadays, people rate me as only slightly behind George as the best British footballer ever to put on a pair of boots but in those days all the press were interested in was trying to compare us as troublemakers who were bad for the game.

Not surprisingly, I suppose, Ann wasn't willing to come back down to London to the same sort of life that she had endured before. She had been on her own a lot, getting homesick for Manchester, and would now have three children to look after without much help from me. Also, she was finding it very difficult to cope, being married to a footballer in the public eye.

But, as it turned out, I persuaded her to come back, eventually. We moved out of our house in Ruislip, but we both knew that she would have been happier living back up in Manchester. But I wanted, if possible, to save our marriage.

These days, there is a lot of talk about drugs in the game: cocaine, cannabis and the like. I suppose there was a bit going on when I played. With me though, it wasn't performance-enhancing drugs that I was interested in. Back in 1971, a bloke called Johnny Hammond, who had just come out of prison, could get hold of 200 Valium for a tenner. He used to take them, and he suggested I try one, so I did. After that, I took Valium for about seven years. So that I did not have to go to John's house, another bloke started bringing them over to me. That guy ended up in St Bernard's – the psychiatric wing of Ealing Hospital – and was there for over a year. He used to swallow them like Smarties. He lived on his own in Hanwell for years and it got to him in the end, and he tried to slash his wrists. He went into hospital initially with a pain in his back, and they moved him into the psychiatric wing.

I used to take one Valium in the morning, and two later in the day. They range in strength from two to ten milligrams, and of course the longer you take them, the more likely it is that you will need the strong ones. A lot of people took them, even Mr Cool – Don Shanks – would take one occasionally when he couldn't sleep.

I told the QPR club doctor, Stuart Khan, eventually, and he prescribed them for me for a while. It was Dr Khan who got me off them. He asked me if I would see a psychiatrist, but I refused. If I'd said yeah, I think they'd have banged me up and chucked away the key. I also took Temazepam, which affected me slightly differently. They made me feel more outgoing – a bit aggressive, as well. Valium, on the other hand, calmed me down totally. One night I gave a Temazepam to one of my mates, Jimmy Fearon, while we were down the pub. Obviously the drink and the pill didn't mix too well, and Jimmy lost it. He was crawling under the tables in the packed boozer, biting the legs of total strangers.

We knew something was up because someone checked Jim's cards and he had three jacks. There's no way you start acting like a dog with a hand like that. I left him there. Next day, Jimmy and his wife came round and she had a right go at me. Apparently, he had been spotted running, stark bollock naked, through the churchyard at two in the morning. He turned up at his house, still naked, covered in bruises from head to foot. Naturally, Jimmy put the blame on me for leading him astray. His missus wouldn't speak to me for weeks. Suffice to say, I never gave him any more tablets.

All the time I was still gambling regularly, and among my many acquaintances was a heavy gambler, racehorse expert and con man, affectionately known as The Colonel, but whose real name was Jimmy Rogers. He used to socialise with the team and his opening words were always, 'My dear fellow,' which used to make me smile.

We've known each other for over thirty years and have always had a laugh together. Me and Don used to meet him at the dog track. The Colonel and I had a good thing one day from trainer Pat Taylor, a horse called Debenture. So, as it was running at Stratford, we thought we'd be clever; we wouldn't go by car in case we broke down, we'd take the train. Lo and behold, when we got to the station the train to Stratford had been cancelled.

We finished up going to Madame Tussauds, because there was a betting shop close by. We backed Debenture, which won by ten lengths at 7/1. We followed this with a trip to Wimbledon greyhounds and ended up in the Rheingold Club. So it turned out a good day, after all.

The Colonel reckons he owes his life to me – literally. Every Saturday, when Rangers were at home, he used to come to White's Hotel to have lunch with the players. He'd have a bit of a laugh and joke with us; and the Colonel, Donald and myself would always sneak off to the betting shop. One day at Sandown, he fancied five horses and like mugs we all backed them individually. A bloke we know once had a shilling Super Yankee and got sixteen hundred quid back!

At the time, the Colonel was looking very ill. He had some sort of weird skin complaint – that made it look like leather. He was in a terrible state. One day, he happened to ring up his brother because he'd heard that he was ill, and asked, 'What's wrong with you?'

The brother said, 'It took six specialists and professors to find out what was wrong with me. I've got a very rare complaint called porphyria which King George III had.' So he asked him what the symptoms were and, after the brother told him, said, 'That's what I've got!'

Anyhow, the Colonel went to the doctor at St Stephen's, in the Fulham Road, and told him about the conversation. 'You can't have that,' said the Doc, 'it's a Royal complaint.'

All the doctor did was keep giving him Betnovate to put on his head, but of course, it made no difference. It got so bad that he had to buy himself a ginger wig. One lunchtime he was up at the Rangers with me, and Frank McLintock had an itchy bottom and was going to see the club doctor, so I said, 'Why don't you go and see our doctor, tell him about your problem – he'll sort you out.'

So the Colonel dutifully troops off and tells Stuart Khan – and thankfully he advised him. From then, he went to Hammersmith hospital for treatment and got back to normal, after a lot of suffering. He said that he really owed it all to me, because if he hadn't had quick treatment, he said that his condition would have worsened rapidly. He'd been having treatment earlier but no one knew what was wrong with him. Even a well-known skin specialist, Beth O'Solomons, couldn't diagnose what was up. Unfortunately, the Colonel is now frequenting that big 'spieler' in the sky, impressing everyone with his flowery phrases.

We used to play cards together – 79-up – anything to pass the time away. I wasn't a big gambler, I just used to fiddle about for enjoyment. It was the way I liked to relax. I'm an easygoing fellow; pretty harmless really. I didn't say a lot but was always happy. I would see the funny side of things, so people like me and the Colonel got on really well together.

I should explain that 79-up is seven card rummy, where you try to get three of one and four of the other. Say, three jacks and four queens.

But in 79, you would only need three jacks and three queens, and if you had any card under a seven, you could call for another card. If I had three jacks, three queens and an ace, I would call for one card and my 79 would become 78. Whatever you have in your hand, if you have not got a set, you have to count up all the points. If you had 40 points, your 79 becomes 39. It is a very quick game, and we used to play for big money.

When we played 79 with the Colonel, me and Don Shanks had a little scheme going. Don would be scoring, so he could see the hand that Jimmy Rogers was holding. He'd say, 'I thought Gillie had a good game today, Stan.' I'd say, 'Yeah, he did, as it happens.' Ian Gillard was, of course, our number three, so I'd know that the Colonel was after a three. Same if he was after a seven, 'Dave Thomas was a bit quiet today.' The Colonel never worked out what was going on.

According to the Colonel:

> Stan never used to act like a superstar, and was always good company when we were out and about. All of this talk about Stan's gambling was in my opinion, overstated. He was only a small beer player, he wasn't a gambler in the true sense of the word. I used to laugh when people said that I was taking advantage of Stanley because I can assure you no one really could, he was too sharp and streetwise for that.
>
> We were going to have him managed by Peter Skelton of Lynx Travel, just for TV, general appearances and the like. Well, the papers kicked up such a fuss about us taking advantage of dear old Stanley and that kind of thing. Jim Gregory even, interfered and we had to call it off even though Peter Skelton had already given Stan £1,000 as a retainer to manage him, of which Stan gave me £500, and £500 worth of credit which Don Shanks knocked out in one day.
>
> On the field Stanley was a genius, he could win a game with one move. He would be worth £20 million today, he was a marvellous player. He was different class to the likes of Gazza, and all of those other pre-tenders. Rodney Marsh was only a juggler and a loudmouth, whereas Stan was a very skilful player.
>
> He should have been a millionaire because he had more talent than anyone I have ever seen. I don't think that there is one English footballer playing today who could match his skill. In my opinion, he was as good as George Best. The trouble was that he was on small wages, he should have been earning five times what Gregory was paying him. He had the

smallest wage bill in the First Division, and that's why he used to slip them a few quid because he owed it to them.

The Colonel used to say that his real name was Geoff Parts and he claimed to have joined the army aged eighteen, going straight in as a corporal because the top brass didn't want anyone addressing him as Private Parts.

If anyone came in asking him to repay a loan they usually ended up lending him more after 'a brief review of the facts'.

Quite often he didn't say much and when he did, he still didn't say much. The Colonel's favourite expression was, 'A fool and his money are some party.' Another favoured expression of his was, 'At this point you are thus far – and no farther.' I never really understood what he meant by that, however he did say it with great conviction.

Mr Donald used to get me opening butchers' shops and things like that to earn money for gambling, but he was a man who could turn £50 into £50,000, unlike me – I was strictly small-time. I'd play fruit machines, and was just happy playing cards or having a bet. I didn't really care whether I won or lost, I just did it for the excitement. The Colonel always said that you have to bet to win, but I wasn't bothered, I enjoyed it either way. Sometimes I would have big bets, and sometimes I would have small bets, so he couldn't work it out.

I'd bet on anything though. I remember Jim Gregory wanted to have a race with me one day over a hundred yards. So I said, 'Why does he want to race me? I'll slaughter him.' It was Frank Sibley who marked my card because you had to race over Jim's course. 'Don't you take that bet, Stanley,' said Frank. It turned out that Jim had already done Rodney Marsh previously for a hundred quid because what he used to do was manage a false start and race down a back alley between two sets of houses near the ground. Of course, once the race had started, because the alley was so narrow, and Jim was in front, no one could get past him. Like I say, Jim was a slippery customer.

Around about that time there was a lot of speculation about Bill Nicholson wanting to take me to Spurs. This involved swapping me for Martin Chivers, plus cash. However, the fact that Gordon Jago didn't mention Spurs to me was a sure indication that I wouldn't be going anywhere. Even at this early stage, I had made my name at QPR. If Gordon had sold me so soon after selling Rodney, he wouldn't have been able to show his face in Shepherd's Bush ever again.

Obviously, we were hoping for an excellent season when the

1973–74 campaign kicked off, but we started off very badly with four draws and a defeat, although our performances were better than those results would suggest. Gordon was still spending and had bought Frank McLintock from Arsenal, in the close season, and Frank proved to be a big asset to the club.

In November we went to Manchester City, my old stamping ground, and there was a big press preview about this being a duel between me and Rodney, who was playing well for City at the time. It was a little bit sentimental for me because my family and friends all come from Manchester. It turned out to be a nondescript affair, and it took a Franny Lee penalty to win the game for them. It just goes to show that when the press build things up, they often fall flatter than a pancake on Ash Wednesday.

We then played Stoke at the Victoria Ground and suffered a heavy 4–1 defeat. Mike Pejic, their tough left-back, was booked for a tackle on me. As it happens I lost my temper a bit over that. Afterwards, the Stoke manager Tony Waddington attacked me in the press, saying, 'Bowles is crazy. Somebody should go up to him and ask him if he's still a schoolboy. Did he lose his head? When things happen like that you wonder if he has one to lose. The man has real talent and skill, it's so silly to start abusing it. We've definitely decided to appeal against Pejic's booking.' So I'm off his Christmas card list, then!

The business with Pejic wasn't a one-off thing, he used to knock lumps off me every time we played against each other, so there was a bit of needle between us throughout my career. Mind you, Pejic was multi-talented. They say he once auditioned for the role of the Elephant Man, but he looked too frightening and he wasn't even wearing make-up!

I do have to own up to being very quick-tempered on the field, and Gordon was forever trying to get me to calm down a bit. However, I felt that sometimes my temper used to spur me on, and if I had mellowed I wouldn't have been the same player. I was a totally different person off the pitch. I also admit that when I am in a betting shop, I am like a lunatic. I lose my temper very quickly, but when I come out, it is all forgotten about and I am a different person.

In one way, that season was the end of an era. On 1 January 1974, we played Manchester United at Loftus Road, beat them 3–0, and I scored a couple of goals. Looking back now, it was a sad occasion for football, because, as it turned out, that was George Best's last game for Manchester United.

I have the greatest respect for him because he was the finest footballer I have ever seen. It is very sad that he was only twenty-seven when he stopped playing at the highest level. Although he continued to play – in the US and then at Fulham – a footballer like that needs the big stage to bring out the best in him.

In February, Ann decided that she wanted to move back to Manchester. This put a huge cloud over my future because the last thing I wanted was to lose my wife and family. I became unsettled and this came at a bad time for QPR, just before an FA Cup match against Coventry City.

Ann admitted to the press: 'The fact is I don't like living down here, it's too quiet. I want to get home to Manchester as quick as I can. I'm going at the weekend and taking the kids with me. I've never been happy living outside Manchester. We've had four moves in five years and what with three young children, it's all been getting too much. I don't think people realise what it's like being a footballer's wife. It's getting on my nerves. He gets all these invites, and the phone is ringing all the time.'

On top of all this – due to my gambling tendencies – I'd placed my wages in the hands of QPR and domestic bills were being sent to them for payment. I was receiving a limited amount each week for spending money. My marriage was in turmoil, my finances a shambles, but I didn't want to leave the club. QPR was the one thing that kept me going. I think the fact that I scored a last-minute winner in the cup tie against Coventry, proves the point!

As it happens, I remember that particular goal very well. It was the last minute of the game, and we were awarded a free-kick on the edge of the box. I took it and scored. Everyone thought I had swerved the ball around the wall but I hadn't: Gerry, at the last second, had pulled Coventry's Tommy Hutchinson off the end of it and I'd put the ball through the gap they'd left. The City players were, understandably, going mental, but everyone else thought that it was another bit of Stanley Bowles magic! There was one person in the ground, however, who had seen exactly what had gone on: England manager Don Revie. Later on, when I played for England in Italy, Don remembered that free-kick and wanted us to try it in Rome. We were keen, but the only trouble was we never got near enough to their box to give it a go!

During the 1973–74 season I didn't miss a game for QPR. I played in all 42 matches and finished top scorer with 23 goals in the league and cup. People had said that I wouldn't last half a season, but I proved them wrong.

I was a hard and competitive trainer because I knew that if you didn't train, you couldn't do it on a Saturday. I was very rarely injured, and the managers I played for have always complimented me on the way I turned out to play as much as I did. Ernie Tagg was delighted when I played 37 consecutive league games for Crewe in 1970–71.

At QPR, we already had the makings of a very good side, with a talented attack featuring Don Givens, Dave Thomas and myself. Terry Venables was still in midfield with Gerry and Mick Leach, Phil Parkes was becoming a top-class goalkeeper and Dave Clement had made the right-back position his own.

At centre-back, Frank McLintock was partnered by Terry Mancini, whose nickname was Henry. He was as bald as a coot. I'm not exactly sure what a coot is but I assume whatever it is, it lacks hair. Henry had as much talent as he did hair; he had everything else except ability. He could only kick the ball whichever way he was facing, and even then it wouldn't go where he wanted it to go. He was lucky to play in a good side, so he never had to do very much. The only player we had who was worse than him was Ernie Howe, a centre half who came to us from Fulham.

We were doing quite well, but the crowd used to slaughter Henry every week. He took a lot of stick, so one day, when we were playing Sheffield Wednesday in the League Cup, he decided, without telling anyone, to run out with a wig on, so he now had curly hair. When we kicked off, he wore it for a couple of minutes, and the crowd loved it. We won 8–2. I think Henry's wig got one of the goals!

The date was 6 November 1973, and from that day on, the attitude of the crowd changed towards Henry, and he became a comedian, a prankster, a cult hero who could suddenly do no wrong; even though he was still doing the same things, still kicking the ball whichever way he was facing!

The month before, Mancini – qualifying through parentage – had been picked for Ireland to play against Poland, who had knocked England out of the World Cup at Wembley four days previously. The teams stood in a line before the game, twenty-two proud footballers representing their countries, as the national anthems were played. Henry was standing next to Don Givens, and the national anthem was going on and on and on. So he turned to Givens and said, 'Their anthem's going on a long time, isn't it Don?' And out of the side of his mouth, Givens hisses, 'Shut up Henry – that's ours!'

Later on, after Henry had joined Arsenal, we played them at Loftus

Road. The game ended 0–0, but I'll never forget it. At one point, Arsenal had a corner, and all their big defenders came up into the penalty box. All of a sudden, as the ball came across, Phil Parkes jumped up and shouted, 'My ball, Henry!' So Mancini ducked, and Parkes caught it. Afterwards, Mancini said, 'Then it dawned on me that I ain't playing for this crowd no more!' It was not gamesmanship by Phil Parkes, it was just that he was so used to shouting: 'My ball, Henry!' Basically, Mancini fannied his way through his football career. Looking back, I can hardly believe he was in our side. We only got away with it because Frank McLintock was so good, and the team became a lot better once David Webb was slotted in alongside Frank.

Eventually we finished as London's top club – eighth in the First Division in 1974, coming on strong towards the end after a mediocre start. That was pretty good for a newly promoted team. We also reached the sixth round of the FA Cup, knocking out Chelsea, Birmingham and Coventry before finally being beaten by Leicester City 2–0 at home. We'd had a fair season that year, but more was expected, both from QPR and from me.

By this time Terry Venables was coming to the end of his Loftus Road stay. He was a decent footballer who made the most of his talent and it was pretty obvious he had a future in coaching. Terry was forever discussing tactics, formations and set pieces in training and most of what he said made good sense.

In addition to having a sound knowledge of football it was also clear that Terry had plenty of side deals going on in the background. Venners was a wheeler and dealer, a ducker and diver, he knew how to make an extra buck and liked nothing more than sealing a deal. Basically, Tel was a born businessman who had plenty of transactions going down at any given point. Quite often you had the feeling some of Terry's business dealings might not be totally legit but if that was ever the case Terry covered his tracks well because to the best of my knowledge no one ever caught Terry out.

I might have been Jim Gregory's blue-eyed boy as a player but Jim always had a lot of time for Terry as well. Jim admired his entrepreneurial spirit; maybe Terry reminded him of himself in his younger days. The two had a mutual respect for each other and would often be found in deep discussion, as Terry would often seek Jim's counsel before taking any business decisions.

I know Jim lent Terry a large sum of money somewhere in the region of £100,000 which I think he eventually let him have as a gift. Sadly Jim suffered serious illness towards the end of his life, Alzheimer's disease and gangrene. I was going to visit Jim shortly before he died and mentioned this in passing to Terry.

'I wouldn't bother Stan, Jim doesn't remember things anymore.'

'I bet he remembers that £100,000 he bloody well lent you!' I replied. A cheeky grin appeared on Terry's face.

Terry told me that he and Rodney Marsh had gone to visit Jim a couple of weeks earlier. The two former players talked to Jim patiently for about ten minutes while Jim, appearing a little agitated, struggled to get any words out himself.

Eventually, after fifteen minutes, or so, when a gap in the conversation presented itself, Jim struggled valiantly to express himself and finally forced out his first words, 'Will you two fuck off.' Terry said he and Marshie had to laugh.

Chapter 8

Three Lions on My Shirt

In March 1974, Sir Alf Ramsey picked me to play for the Football League against the Scottish League at Maine Road. I scored a goal in a 5–0 win. Alf was a man of few words, but after that game he said to me, 'I'll be seeing you soon.' And sure enough, a week later, I found myself in the England team for the friendly against Portugal, to be played in Lisbon's famous Stadium of Light.

Phil Parkes, my QPR team-mate, also made his international debut that day, and we had Leicester's David Nish and my old mate from Stoke City, Mike Pejic, as full-backs; Dave Watson of Sunderland and Colin Todd of Derby were centre-backs; Martin Dobson of Burnley, with Martin Peters and Trevor Brooking, were in midfield. Finally, there was Malcolm Macdonald, Mike Channon and myself up front. Liverpool and Leicester had drawn their FA Cup semi-final, and their players were not released for the England squad, and so six of us were winning our first caps. The other four were Dobson, Brooking, Watson and Pejic. The result was a 0–0 draw. It wasn't exactly a memorable match, but I had earned an England cap and I was quite proud of that landmark in my career.

However, less than a month after that game in Portugal, Sir Alf Ramsey was sacked. He had made history by winning the World Cup in 1966, and taken England to the quarter-finals against West Germany in Mexico in 1970, but now, after eleven years in charge, he had been sacked because England had failed to qualify for the 1974 finals.

My old mentor, Joe Mercer, who was now general manager at Coventry City, had taken over as caretaker manager of England, and he called me up to play in the home internationals – a traditional end-of-season tournament annually contested by England, Scotland, Wales and Northern Ireland.

We played our first game against Wales in Cardiff. Of the team that had played in Lisbon, only Nish, Pejic, Todd, Channon and myself were picked again. We were joined by Peter Shilton, Roy McFarland,

Emlyn Hughes, Kevin Keegan, Colin Bell and Keith Weller. I did reasonably well, scoring the first goal in our 2–0 win, with Keegan scoring the other.

The Derby County trio of McFarland, Todd and Nish always had the mickey taken out of them because they used to come to England squads in their club uniform of blazers with little rams on their V-neck sweaters and identical slacks. They were cliquey, never talking to anybody. Everybody else just dressed casually, and put on an England tie for the game. Cloughie's little lambs didn't dare mix with the rest of us for fear of being contaminated. I laughed then, but I didn't find it so funny later on when old big 'ead was in charge of me.

At this time I was under contract to Gola, the boot manufacturers. I got an extra two hundred quid every time I played for England in Gola boots. The sales rep used to come to the team hotel in the morning with a briefcase containing cash for a number of players, and he'd say, 'Here you are, here's your £200.' As an incentive, you used to get an extra fifty quid if a picture of you in a Gola T-shirt appeared in the paper, so I was always keen for a bit of that.

Then, later on, the Adidas rep came round touting for business, and someone said, 'The Adidas lads are getting £250.' So I went out and talked to the Adidas rep, and he said: 'If you wear these, I'll give you the same.' So, naturally enough, I said, 'Yeah, fine.' And he gave me two hundred and fifty notes, plus a new pair of Adidas boots. Gola boots had a yellow strip on the side, and Adidas had three white stripes. Christmas has come early, thinks me.

A bit later on, one of the other players says, 'Hang on Stan, you've signed with both. What are you gonna do?' And I said, 'For £450, I'll wear one boot on each foot!' Nobody knew what I had done till a few days later, but it obviously didn't go down too well when they found out. David Webb told me that Trevor Brooking tells this story in his after-dinner speeches. Webby reckons that it's the only decent story he's got and you could fall asleep during the rest of it!

The next game in the Home International Series was against Northern Ireland at Wembley. I have to admit that I was slightly worried that Joe Mercer had taken over – because of our past history at Maine Road. I didn't really know whether he had a grudge against me or not. The suspicion somehow stayed in the back of my mind, but Joe came out publicly and said that he had no grudge, so I had to take that at face value.

When we played Northern Ireland on the Wednesday it was 0–0 going into half-time, and no one had played really well. In the dressing room I overheard Joe Mercer tell Harold Shepherdson, the trainer, to take me off after ten or fifteen minutes of the second half.

I knew that – because of the way it was said – whatever I did during that time wouldn't have made the slightest difference; I was going to be substituted anyway. And that's the way it happened; I was taken off after ten minutes. Frank Worthington came on and made the winning goal for Keith Weller, his Leicester team-mate.

I made up my mind there and then that I wasn't going to go to Scotland for the third international. I was angry because I thought Joe should have taken me off at half-time; instead of trying to humiliate me – as I saw it – by taking me off after ten minutes.

I arranged for a friend to pick me up from the hotel, but I didn't tell Mick Channon, who I was rooming with, because I didn't want to upset him. Just before lunch, when the team was due to travel up to Scotland, I left the hotel. At the time I felt quite hurt; but perhaps, on reflection, if it had been another manager, I might have been able to accept it better.

In the evening I went to White City, which was the premier dog track in those days and the venue for the Greyhound Derby, which was always televised by the BBC on *Sportsnight* on a Wednesday evening. The White City had an electric atmosphere, and was usually packed with people from all walks of life, and it seemed that everyone knew everyone else. I knew so many characters there, and even if I ended up skint, I was assured of a good laugh.

Many people regarded the dog tracks as much inferior to the horse racing scene, but both sets of punters and bookmakers used to come to the track after a horse race meeting. It used to follow on naturally – a day and night circuit.

You'd get all sorts at the dogs. The comedian Frankie Howerd had a few dogs at the track and he and other celebrities could usually be found in the restaurant at the top of the steps. Ladies would be dressed up for a night out at a club later, and you would see plenty of glamour, as well as people who were destitute and down on their luck. I was with Brian Donoghue, a friend who had been in prison a few times for stealing jewellery. I lived with him and his wife for a while, a stone's throw from the White City.

Everyone would be crowded around the bars talking about the dogs, and trying to sell things to get money for gambling. The Whiz Mob, a band of seven or eight pickpockets, were always there. They used to work all the different racetracks as well as the big department stores. On top of that you would usually bump into the local thieves, who would be trying to sell jewellery and other trinkets. The going rate at that time was a third of the real value – and this was well known in the bars – so these guys were pretty popular when they came in.

I think it was this that I liked most about the White City: the cross-section of society. From the rich businessmen and celebrities right down to the lowest of the low – everyone seemed to be together. People were there for different reasons – socialising, gambling, selling, stealing or watching the racing – but for some strange reason there was a toughness, almost a decadence, that made it exciting. There was a real buzz about the place which I loved. As luck would have it, on this particular night, someone had spotted me at White City, and tipped off the *Daily Mirror*. A photographer, Harry Prosser, and Mike Ramsbottom, a reporter, turned up and began pestering me, asking me why I had walked out of the England squad. Obviously, it was big news, but I wasn't feeling particularly chatty, and told them on three occasions to leave me alone – or words to that effect. The two guys I was with – Brian and Micky Delaney – took great exception to this hassle, and were clearly getting the needle. As it happens, the press boys didn't twig, and they continued following us everywhere. In the end, Brian had had enough. Although I didn't ask him to do anything, he just whacked the photographer, who went flying down the stone steps, and crashed into the bookmakers. Brian shouted after him, 'And don't go down my pockets again!' Prosser just lay there scared shitless, accused of pickpocketing, and preparing for a quick exit.

Next day, not surprisingly, a big song and dance was made of the incident. The photographer claimed he had needed stitches and patching up. Naturally, the *Daily Mirror* went to town on it. The story was on the front page and they printed a big picture of Prosser that made it look like he'd been attacked by a pack of Rottweilers on crack. It didn't take a genius to work out that the photo had been touched-up in the darkroom.

The outrage over this little bit of nonsense soon died down when the papers moved on to the next trumped up story about some other poor bastard. Even so, as a so-called 'celebrity' it was hard to keep out of the papers. Every day and night I would have photographers and reporters around me: at the gambling club, my house, and anywhere I went socially. The sports reporters were mostly all right, because they could get what they wanted at the training ground, but the news reporters were just interested in getting a bit of dirt and making it stick. They used to pester Ann at home trying to get family photographs from her, but I'd marked her card early on and so she used to handle it pretty well.

In the early years I used to feel that it was an invasion of my privacy, but over the years I got used to it and accepted it as part and parcel of my daily life. Paul Gascoigne and, more recently, David Beckham, have received similar treatment, always being followed and harassed by reporters. I think I was able to handle it a lot better than Paul, probably because he has a different temperament to me. The Prosser business was the only incident that ever turned nasty in my career. I thought that it was entirely the photographer's fault; so street justice was called for and given.

Following my England walkout, I had a meeting with Gordon Jago at the Bush. The two of us strolled out into the middle of the pitch so we could have a quiet talk.

'I want you to go back to the squad,' he said.

'I'm not going back,' I said.

'Well, there's going to be big trouble over this.'

My attitude was that I didn't care how much trouble there was going to be – I was not going back. There were lots of reports in the papers saying that I had apologised, but somebody must have done it on my behalf because I never did. It didn't really matter though, because Joe Mercer was saying: 'There is no way that Stan Bowles will ever play for England again – not while I am in charge.'

It looked like there was no way back into the England team, but it didn't really bother me. As far as I was concerned I had shown that I was good enough to play for England. I had done something that they said I couldn't do, so I was now happy just to play club football. Luckily, all this happened in the close season so the furore had all died down by the time we reported back to Loftus Road for training at the end of June.

It was never announced that I had been banned from playing for England, but that is exactly what happened. I would still do the same thing today – because I felt humiliated that night. I thought that Joe had done it to teach me a lesson. Years later, Joe and I got back on speaking terms, but I have never forgotten that incident.

It wasn't unusual for me to go on the missing list throughout my career. Whatever came into my head, whether it was right or wrong, I would just do it. It was an impulse thing with me. Maybe I convinced myself that I was right, even when I was wrong. That is the way I felt, and that is the way people had to accept me. If they didn't, it was just too bad. My way might not have been the right way – but it was my choice.

I never set my stall out to be an England international. I just wanted to be a good footballer and play as well as I could for my club. When I look back, and see some of the players who got a lot more caps than me, sometimes I feel a little sad, but the feeling soon goes. I was lucky that I had a very understanding club: managers who took the good with the bad, and a chairman, Jim Gregory, who could read me like a book and was prepared to bend a little.

It was two years before I would be considered again for the England squad. In hindsight, I firmly believe that if I hadn't walked out, I would have had many more caps for my country. I was playing very well at the time, and they would have had no alternative but to put me in the side. Still, I am what I am and I don't believe I would've acted any differently even with the benefit of hindsight.

A couple of Greek sides were interested in me at the time. One was Panathinaikos, the other Olympiakos. The latter was part-owned by a casino owner in London who said that he would like to take me over there. A friend, Minos, who owned another gambling club off the Shepherd's Bush Road, introduced me to the Greek guy at a time when Olympiakos were struggling to find their form. Consequently, the owner was coming under increasing pressure from the fans. I was a big name and he thought that if I signed, it would create the right sort of publicity and reduce the pressure on him and restore his popularity. We had a few meetings over dinner and I believe a firm offer was put on the table. I kept them stringing along for a while but there was no way I was ever going to go to Greece.

The Spurs transfer was also still on the cards when Gordon Jago had an argument with Jim Gregory, and said he was leaving the club. It was blown up as a sensational resignation and the chairman had to cut short his holiday in the South of France and come back to sort out the situation.

During this unsettling period I was persuaded to join Gamblers Anonymous. A friend who had been going for five years asked me if I would like to go along with him, so I decided to give it a try.

I went along to an open meeting and found that the stories that people were coming out with were quite funny. You are allowed to laugh, as they encourage you not to hold any emotions back. So I sat

Top left Me at nine, refusing to wear daft hats, and (*above*) with Mum and Dad on a 1950s family holiday at Butlins; *top right* The model professional

Manchester life. Mowing the lawn, and (*left*) an early appearance for City

Opposite page from top left Back when Carlisle played in the Anglo-Italian Cup, June 1972 (Empics); An early mugshot at Loftus Road (Empics); A quick drink before the match; The 'Fab Five', Dave Thomas, Gerry Francis, Phil Parkes and Ian Gillard

Terry Mancini (no hair) *above* and Terry Venables, after we took Wolves apart, 4–2, October '73

Moving past Trevor Brooking, 30 Aug 1975 (Empics)

Opposite page A dummy takes out Bob McNab, 27 October 1973

Our day in court on 'motoring offences'. Is that a toilet seat around Don's neck? (Empics)

Another one hits the net

there laughing my head off. It was more of a comedy night than a meeting. My friend is still in Gamblers Anonymous now, so it must have done him good, but it was not for me. I only went that one time. Mind you, I bet I'd have no trouble giving up gambling if I wanted to! My mate gave up betting during those first five years, and to commemorate this achievement the people at GA gave him a tiepin, which seemed a pretty shabby return for five years of bet-free living – if you can call it living.

My pal Jim Davis, a former pro who didn't quite make the grade as a player with Crewe, fell off the wagon spectacularly in 1994 when he got a wind of a 'certainty' running at Haydock. He stuck £7,000 on it only to see it fall when five lengths in front going over the last. In fact the horse broke its leg and had to be shot. My pal would have gladly pulled the trigger that day. Jim the Fruit, as he was known, was a greengrocer by trade and he told me directly after he lost the money that he wandered back to his stall in something of a daze thinking of how he could possibly explain his missing life savings to the wife.

Apparently a little while later that day an old woman, with the inquisitive look of a rodent emerging from a drain, began to study, squeeze and scrutinise his King Edwards, tutting and muttering to herself at frequent intervals. This has the undoubted effect of pissing you off. She moaned about the quality, freshness and price of his potatoes and after a blunt exchange Jim eventually lost his temper, kicked the whole stall over, told her she could have the fucking lot for all he cared and marched out of the market leaving fruit and veg sprawled all over the floor.

I could fully understand his point of view. I'd imagine you have to sell an awful lot of spuds to make seven grand and the last thing you want to be doing is arguing over a few pence when you've just dropped seven large.

I suppose I must have seemed quite a strange sort of person to those who didn't know me. Gordon Jago did an interview in the press trying to explain to people what I was like, and how he used to handle the situations. He always used to stick up for me and, although he was mild-mannered, he had the knack of knowing how to get the best out of me. I still don't think he really knew what made me tick, but, to be honest, that makes two of us!

Gordon knew what he wanted from the football club, however. He continued to improve the side, bringing in David Webb from Chelsea for £120,000 in May 1974; and, in September, Don Rogers arrived from Crystal Palace as Terry Venables and Ian Evans went the other way. We also picked up Don Masson from Notts County, in December.

If I remember rightly, that was the year we played a pre-season tournament in Spain. Other than the heat, the thing that stands out most about that little trip was a little incident with the actor – Hollywood bad guy – Jack Palance.

Me, Webby and Johnny Hollins were standing in a bar, when we spotted him. John is a big fan, so me and Dave wound him up, saying, 'Go on, John, this is your big chance, mate!' Now, John is a bit on the shy side and he's the nicest, most polite person you could ever hope to meet, so it took a lot for him to go over and introduce himself. Eventually, he works up the bottle and goes over. 'Hello,' says John, 'I'm an English footballer, John Hollins from Queens Park Rangers.' Jack is sitting at this table with his wife and daughter. He doesn't say anything, he just stares at John with these big piercing eyes. John goes on, 'I'm a big fan of yours, really big. I've seen all your films.'

He then reels off a long list of movies that Palance has been in. The actor still doesn't say a word.

Johnny is sweating like mad. 'I just want to say what a great pleasure it is to meet you.'

Palance stares for a long time, then, at last, he speaks. 'Fuck off,' he says, without any emotion.

'Okay, Mr Palance,' squeaks John. He turns round and shuffles back to us. 'Nice guy,' he said, 'really nice.' Me and Webby are pissing ourselves!

Jack goes back to eating. A group of Yanks come up to him – they get the same treatment. He was exactly like his big-screen persona. All I can say is, it's a good job he didn't have a bleeding gun on him.

I also remember that trip for another reason. When we arrived back at the airport, we were standing around waiting for our suitcases to come off the conveyor belt. Next thing, this dirty great case comes wobbling round. It's so old that it must've been the one that Noah took on the Ark with him. It's covered in ancient 'Kiss Me Quick' stickers and is done up with dirty great big bandages to hold it together. We're pissing ourselves laughing – who the hell would own a piece of crap like that? Gerry Francis, England captain of the future, that's who. Talk about lifestyles of the rich and famous!

Round about this time, things began to look a little brighter for me on the England front. After a summer tour of East Germany, Bulgaria and Yugoslavia, Joe Mercer had relinquished the England caretaker manager's job after seven games in charge and Don Revie left Leeds to become England's new boss. Don went on record as saying that bygones could be bygones and, if it was proved that I had the necessary character, I would be reconsidered. In September 1974 he picked eighty-four players to attend a seminar in Manchester, and I was one of the players selected.

On the weekend of the seminar I was absolutely slaughtered by Mike Langley of the *Sunday People*. Now, a lot of people said he was a good writer, and sometimes his column could be quite witty. But Langley was always digging somebody out in his column and unfortunately, this particular week, it was my turn. I'd never met the man, even though I knew most of the journalists, and used to drink with them. In the piece, Langley talked about my England prospects and called me 'a moderate one-footer'. As hatchet jobs go it was a classic, a minor masterpiece in which he sliced me apart limb from limb.

It is worth reproducing the article in full, just to prove how much he had it in for me:

The Piccadilly Hotel, where Don Revie waits to greet 84 English footballers over the marmalade this morning, is 14 storeys of modernistic slab looming over the bus stations in the middle of Manchester.

You can't miss it. But I hope Stan Bowles does, just as he missed England's plane to Hampden Park four months ago. Am I mistaken in believing that the inclusion of Bowles affronts millions of patriotic, decent, ordinary fans, as well as threatening a clever public relations exercise with falling flat on its face?

Make no mistake, Revie's opening assembly as new England manager is principally a public relations job. He knows better than anyone that England doesn't contain 84 real international class players, but he needs the club support that Sir Alf Ramsey failed to generate. That's why Revie's net is spread so wide that it originally included an indignant Scot from Nottingham Forest. He has hauled in seven from West Ham. Presumably, the non-selected four are responsible for their being around bottom of the league. And he has invited seven men who have been sent off in the last 12 months, thus exposing all the hopes of a better behaved England as mere pious in the sky.

But why be so insensitive as to send for Bowles, who in his slight frame, symbolises nearly everything that mature spectators regard as wrong with today's game? Bowles is peevish, petulant, a baby when tackled, a squeaker at referees and a verbal provoker of opponents. At this moment the FA, Revie's employers, are considering whether to haul him before a commission for V-signing spectators and making filthy gestures at Luton players.

He is the league's No. 1 mug punter, and his associates on the tracks include gorillas who butted, punched and kicked two journalists when they were legitimately asking why Bowles had skipped furtively from England's hotel to White City dogs. I must admit that Bowles belatedly apologised to England, but his sorrow was somewhat diluted for me by a statement only three weeks earlier: 'I can't say I have any regrets.'

Revie will be in line for the title of arch-apostle of expediency if he thinks what happened in the past has nothing to do with him. The past is too recent for that risk. And, besides, the England team belongs to the nation, not to the manager, and Bowles betrayed us all. If it's any consolation to Revie, he won't miss much by discarding Stan. In world class terms, which is the test England must apply, Bowles is a moderate one footer with doubtful temperament. For me, he never looked an England player in his two and a bit appearances and my message to him this morning is: Do us a favour, Stan. Get lost again.

Who rattled his cage, then? There's a word for people like him – but I've never been particularly good at words, so I can't remember what it is. Mind you, I wonder how good a footballer Mr Langley was? I bet there's a word for that and all!

As far as the seminar was concerned, we arrived the evening before and had the meeting with Don the next morning. I was sitting around a table with Peter Osgood, Frank Worthington and Alan Hudson. Literally all the seminar consisted of was a team chat, like you would have in the dressing room on a Saturday. Nothing actually happened at the seminar other than a team talk; the general consensus was that it was a waste of time.

Chapter 9

Bush Ranger Bowles!

Once back at QPR, I fell foul of the rules by turning up late after the England seminar. Gordon told me there had been a lot of unrest among the Rangers players because of my behaviour, and something had to be done about it – I was suspended for two weeks. I missed the first two games of the season because of this, but played in most of the matches after that.

We had a very poor start to the 1974–75 season, winning only one of our first ten games, so Jim Gregory decided that enough was enough and sacked Gordon Jago. I was very unhappy when Gordon left the club, but I suppose he didn't know whether he was coming or going at the time. When Gordon was under pressure he used to get a badly bloodshot eye, and he suffered this for about three weeks. The strain seemed too great for him, what with me and the other players getting on to him. His head must have been bursting, and I think, in one way, the end came as a relief. When he left, he took over at Millwall and spent three years there before he eventually got a good job in America with Tampa Bay Rowdies, who featured a certain Rodney Marsh in their line-up.

In football, things moved quickly, and before we knew what was going on, Dave Sexton was appointed manager at the end of October 1974.

In his seven years as manager of Chelsea, Dave had led them to famous victories over Leeds in the 1970 FA Cup Final, and Real Madrid in the 1971 European Cup Winners Cup Final in Athens. After those heady triumphs, things quietened down at Stamford Bridge. Although Dave took them to the 1972 League Cup Final, things were never the same again. That great Chelsea side started to break up in early 1974, when Dave fell out with Peter Osgood and Alan Hudson. Sexton lost out, and he was sacked. Thirteen days later, he was hired by Jim Gregory. It proved to be a very shrewd appointment.

Of course, Dave had heard about my problems – everybody had! I had been transfer-listed in the September, following my suspension, and put up for sale at £250,000. Sheffield Wednesday and Derby were interested; but Jim Gregory used to chuck my transfer requests in a drawer, because he received them so often. The drawer was so full, it wasn't easy to close!

I scored in Dave Sexton's first four matches, so we got off to a very good start. Dave was saying in the press that he had no problem with me on the pitch, or in training, so that calmed things down a little.

In November, I had a couple of fights with two of the QPR players. One was with Frank McLintock. Frank had played for Leicester as a wing half in the 1963 FA Cup Final against Manchester United, and, of course, captained the Arsenal double-winning team in 1971. He had a tremendous career, and was already thirty-five when he joined us. Frank had terrible trouble with his ankles, so before training he had to go in a hot bath to get them warmed up. While he was doing this, we'd be out getting warmed up on the pitch. After half an hour, he'd come and join us.

It so happened that Don Shanks had just joined QPR from Luton, and this fracas happened on his first day with us. He was quite shocked, and I think he wondered what he'd let himself in for. We were playing seven-a-side and fifteen minutes into the session there was a massive punch-up between me and Frank. Don says he was looking on thinking, What's all this? Frank was a friend of his, and so, of course, was I. That was his first day at Rangers and he thought, What a nice friendly little club this is!

It's something Frank hasn't forgotten either. He remembers the incident this way:

I had a bad ankle. I had broken it when I had just joined QPR, and I was taking about ten pain-killing tablets a day, and sometimes it would really play me up, and I had to limp for the first ten minutes until it warmed up. It was annoying me that morning in a little seven-a-side game.

It was really quite painful, and Stan Bowles was in one of his moods. I think his dogs must have gone down the night before or something. He beat Dave Thomas, and Dave Thomas brought him down, so he said, 'The next person that does that to me, I'll sort him out!' I was hoping he'd get the ball, and he did get the ball, and I went in and clattered him. We started arguing, I dived on top of him, and put him down on the ground.

As I was doing it, I thought, This is bloody stupid, it's just a flash of temper. But as I went to get up, he bit my ear! I went berserk and flew back on him. It was Phil Parkes who pulled me off him. Phil was like a big bear, he was six foot four, and I found these big arms round my chest, my arms pinned to my sides, and my legs swinging in the air like a little kid.

I almost bit Frank's ear off, and he still ribs me about that to this day, but we are still the best of mates. I have to admit I've always been very competitive; I like to win and I don't let anyone knock me about. Although, if it had been big Phil Parkes instead of Frank, I might have kept my mouth shut!

The other scuffle was with Gerry Francis after we drew 2–2 at West Ham. I hadn't had a very good game and I was a bit sick about the way things had gone. In the dressing room after the game, I started kicking the practice balls around in a temper.

Gerry's father Roy was the kit man, who was responsible for collecting the balls, so he had a go at me. I told him to get lost, he told Gerry, who came looking for me. A bit of a scuffle took place and we squared up to each other. Eventually we were dragged apart. I suppose it was more handbags at fifty paces than a fight, but it could have turned nasty, especially for little old me! On the park, me and Gerry had a great understanding, but off it, we didn't have much to do with one another. Later on, we became good friends; so maybe he took to my fighting spirit. I must have been in a bad mood that night because I said, 'I'm never going to speak to Dave Sexton again.' I didn't mean it, of course. That was one of the few tiffs Dave and I ever had.

Some fans thought I was lazy, but I don't accept that. Rodney Marsh looked lazy – and he was! I may have looked it too, but I worked hard and was a lot quicker than I appeared to be. In the sprints, I was always up there: Don Givens and Dave Thomas would always be first or second, I would be third or fourth, and Webby would always be last. Frank, despite his dodgy ankles, was quite determined, so he was never last.

Don Shanks is often asked about the number 10 shirt: who was the best? Rodney Marsh or Stan Bowles?

According to Don, he had marked both of us when he played for Luton, and he reckons I was a street ahead of Rodney. He says there was just no comparison, and anyone who tries to compare us doesn't know what they are talking about. Don goes even further! He says:

Stan worked hard, could score goals in the air, and was a complete team player. He headed balls off the line, and he had so much skill, balance, finesse and an amazing touch. His mobility, that electrifying burst over thirty yards, was exciting to watch. Rodney didn't have those qualities. Rodney was literally the clown prince, whereas Stan was a players' player, and a world-class footballer.

If Stan had not had his particular lifestyle he would have got many more England caps, and would have been recognised as a world-class player. Anyway, to us, he was. He could do things that other players could only dream about. It was a pleasure to play with him, and I'm sure that many other people would say the same.

I couldn't believe that he was such a hard trainer and a conscientious professional, when the other side to his life was so reckless.

He was never interested in women so much as going out for a bet, or a pint in the pub. He never chased women although, obviously, women would have a look at Stan; but it didn't bother him at all. He used to show a lot of respect for his wife when it came to the attentions of other women.

I didn't even have to pay Mr Donald for that assessment! If you don't believe what an old rogue like Shanks has to say, Frank McLintock agrees with a lot of Don's views on Rodney and myself, and has his own ideas on my style. According to Frank:

Stan was a little bit unique. He was somewhat similar to Peter Beardsley in that he could drop deep, and come, and turn, and go straight at defenders, and wriggle past them. Also he had the ability, which I thought was a great asset, to know when to pass the ball, and when to go for goal himself.

I think he was more effective than Rodney Marsh. Rodney was a marvellous entertainer, but sometimes he would try and put it through your legs rather than put the ball to somebody else who could score a goal for the team. Stan seemed to have that great ability, like Peter Osgood, that he could take people on, but that wasn't the only thing in his mind. If somebody was in a better position, the ball would go to him. Stanley was a great entertainer, but he put the knife in when it was needed.

Dave Sexton understood him quite well. He thought the world of Stan, because he knew he was a great player. People ask me, when I do after-dinner speeches, 'Who is the best player that you've ever played with?' Well, Stan would rank with some of the best I've ever played with. He was a superb player at Rangers.

I never saw him looking as if he was playing on a bumpy pitch because every time the ball came to him, it just seemed to stick to him like glue. Off he would go, weaving his magic, past defenders, bending balls with the outside of his foot, just inside full-backs, and right into the path of wingers. He was a superb passer and dribbler of the ball, and could contrive things out of nothing; very often with Gerry Francis.

Gerry was another fine player. In fact, he was quite superb; but you didn't notice it at first. I remember watching the first game up at Sunderland when they had just been promoted. Dave Thomas was the man that caught my eye at first, because he was so energetic and could go from one 18-yard box to the other, and was a great crosser of the ball. But after I'd been with them for a while I could see the way Gerry and Stan linked up. They'd be coming to the edge of the box, and I would be behind them watching. I'd be thinking, Nothing looks on here. But then Gerry would just turn away to his left, and start to run across the box. Then, with the outside of his right foot, dink it round the corner, get the return from Stan, and play a quick one-two – and sometimes two one-twos – and have a shot at goal. They really could conjure up something out of nothing. They had an excellent understanding.

Stan would go down screaming at the slightest touch. Even if you ripped a plaster off him, you'd think he was having his leg amputated! But he only missed a few games in the four years I was there. He was kicked by everyone, but he was so slight, he could roll it. He was black and blue – often. We used to take the piss out of him because he was carried off on a stretcher so often. But he'd always come back on again. He was a character.

He used to take the mickey out of Don Shanks. He'd say: 'They only bought you to keep me company in the card school!' He took the mickey out of Don unmercifully, even though he was one of his best pals. His humour was quite cruel.

Jim Gregory indulged Stan, he loved him. That was his hobby: having Stan Bowles in the side. The chairman put a lot of money into the club, and that was his pleasure, putting Stan Bowles in the team. He'd occasionally threaten him, or even drop him. He was a hard guy, Jim Gregory, but he used to shell out money in readies to Stan on the side. Jim used to pay him bonuses for goals, which kept Stan on a leash a lot of the time. He knew how Stan ticked.

*

Stan Bowles

In December, due to another row over cash bonus, I was transfer listed once again, and Steve Burtenshaw, who had been a coach at Rangers, came in for me to join Sheffield Wednesday. This was the second time they had shown interest, and it was the second time that nothing came of it. I was put on the list for a month, and Dave dropped me while I was on it. As it turned out though, I missed only two games.

At the end of the season, after the second last game against Arsenal in April 1975, I had a row with Jim Gregory. It was genuine enough, but I knew that we would make it up within a couple of days.

But, for a bit of a laugh, I decided to 'officially retire' from football and did a story with a journalist called Brian Madley, whom I knew quite well. He was delighted with his 'scoop'. But things didn't work out as he'd planned: I retired on 20 April 1975, and came out of retirement on 22 April 1975 – five hundred quid better off thanks to the *Sunday People*. That was my revenge for some of the stories the papers had done on me. Brian Madley has never spoken to me since that day more than twenty years ago. I expect that when I genuinely retired, Brian didn't believe it. To this very day he's probably still waiting for me to announce it was a joke, after all!

Back then, the FA didn't get involved in making statements about this sort of publicity. These days they'd fine you, suspend you and probably have your balls cut off! Jim Gregory just suggested that I left it a couple of weeks before I played again. One of the papers said: 'Stan Bowles has gone for more walkabouts than the average aborigine.' This was probably true, but I always found my way back, and I've never owned a boomerang in my life!

In those days, the Football Association didn't have the sort of media profile that they do now. Back then, it didn't really matter – everything was pretty amateurish. However, the FA is still made up of umpteen nice old men from County Football Associations around England. They've got a nice little number just sitting on the FA Council – dozing off and saying 'yes' or 'no' when called upon. They are total amateurs who know sweet FA about professional football. They are now being found out because of all the media attention on the game. All of a sudden they have to come up with professional answers to hard questions. And they just can't do it because they're all nice little old men; chairmen of some small rural FA or somewhere and they have to deal with the likes of Rio Ferdinand and Roy Keane – people from a different planet as far as they are concerned. The poor old buggers just haven't got a clue!

I have said for ages that we ought to bring in more professional people who understand the game and know what they are talking about. For example, Bobby Charlton, who is now a director of Manchester United, has been knocked back so many times in his efforts to get on to the FA Council that he's probably given up by now. But he is just the kind of person we need on the Council – an intelligent, former professional, to sort out the octogenarians. They always resent the ex-pros, and are frightened to lose their nice cushy number. They are dragged out of the cupboard every two months for a meeting in London to decide the future of a top professional. It is ludicrous! They're not in touch with the professional game; they probably don't even realise that the game is professional. They're back in the days of Gentlemen v Players, long shorts and handlebar moustaches. It would be funny if it wasn't so bloody sad.

In June 1975, Ann filed for divorce. I rushed back from a pre-season Continental tour to try once more to save our marriage. After numerous pleas, she called off the divorce, and we were together again – for the time being anyway. It may not have been a dream marriage, but I wanted it to work.

Talking about dreams, the *Daily Express* did a spread once about sports personalities. Players were asked: 'If you weren't a footballer, what would be your dream?' I said that my dream would be to ride an Epsom Derby winner. Mr Donald jumped on this straightaway, and hatched a plan that would make us both a few bob.

There was a bloke called Henry Zeizel whom we knew quite well and we used to go to his club the Rheingold, which was named after his famous racehorse. I had arranged, with my agent, to do a picture spread for one of the Sunday newspapers, showing my dream of riding a Derby winner at Epsom coming true. Basically, the whole thing was one of our many stunts to earn money for gambling; and this particular scheme would earn us £500.

I had a reputation of not turning up, especially if I had been paid in advance. So, in this instance, we were told that payment would only be forthcoming after the event, which obviously meant there was no way out.

It was a misty early morning in June and we arrived at the Epsom racetrack at 6.45 a.m. I hadn't realised that my clock had that time of day on it!

I know jockeys are short fellows as a rule, but I must have borrowed the pants off the jockey with the smallest set of knackers in the yard. After a struggle I squeezed into his jodhpurs – which was no easy task – and my lunchbox looked surprisingly large, if a little lopsided!

A bossy woman with a head full of teeth appeared and informed me she'd let me have the 'mildest horse in the yard'.

All of a sudden, things go drastically wrong. The horse box appears in the distance. It was like one of those things you see in the Dracula movies – four wild horses in the front pulling the carriage. All you could hear was the creature inside going berserk, it was kicking the back of the box like a wild bull. This was one seriously pissed-off nag. According to Mr Donald, my face changed dramatically. It went from laughing and joking to tense and worried, the coloured drained out of it.

The people from the paper were supposed to get a nice tame horse, something that wouldn't be too difficult; the kind that you would see at a riding school for beginners, or pulling an old-fashioned milk float. Well, they opened the back of the box, and out came this horse like a pit bull on crack.

The stable lad leads out this big chestnut brown and when the beast claps its dumb eyes on me its mood changes from very annoyed to thoroughly pissed-off. It was a mare – I have this effect on females. The horse starts lashing out with its hind legs at the stable lad sending the poor boy flying. Then the animal rears up and starts acting like Jan Molby is going to mount it, and not the great Stan Bowles.

At this point I'm thinking, I'm not getting on that beast under any circumstances. I've seen horses like that do damage to experienced jockeys, usually when I've backed them.

Eventually, Don persuades me to see sense with four very persuasive words: 'Think of the money.' The woman running the show then asks me what level of rider I am. I had never even so much as sat on a rocking horse before and I was eager to convey my novice status to her in the strongest possible terms. I told her my level was zero. She nodded and told me to get on it as if she thought zero level was quite a reasonable standard to have obtained.

The idea was to jog past the winning post, where the photos would be taken. It sounded an easy way of earning a few quid.

We're both half hungover, but set to earn a couple of hundred notes out of it, so it seemed worth the trouble. There we'd been, standing by the rails, waiting. There was me with Henry Zeizel's racing colours on, a whip in my hand which I'm banging against my leg like the jockeys do, and flicking it up in the air. I'm thinking. This is easy! Shanks says he'll never forget my happy, smiling face.

Don couldn't stop laughing when the horse appeared, he was biting his arm to stop himself as I went totally white with fear. Shanks takes a deep breath, turns to me and says, 'There's nothing to it, Stan. Just get on and canter round the track!'

Then he just turned round and creased up with laughter.

'I can't get on that,' I croaked, my legs completely gone.

Shanks retired to a safe distance – about 250 yards away – hiding underneath the rails. I don't imagine he really thought I was going to get on this wild horse. He knew I'd never ridden a horse before, so to even get on it was insanity. Well, I got on the horse, and it took off with me hanging on for dear life. It was flying round the Epsom track and I was screaming like somebody falling from a great height. Shanks couldn't watch, he had his head buried in his hands. My agent became conspicuous by his absence. Doom and gloom – this looked like the end. What were they going to tell Dave Sexton: 'Your star player has just broken both his legs. He fell off a horse on Epsom Downs at 7 o'clock this morning'?

So, anyway, the horse eventually stopped and we were led back to safety. I was rigid with fear by this time. In the end, they decided that I would walk the horse past the winning post, and finally the photographs were taken. That was one day at the races we would like to forget. Shanks always says, that looking back, it was one of the funniest things he'd ever seen. But at least we got paid, and off we went to spend it at the dog track. Typical of Shanks that all he had to do to earn a couple of hundred was get up early in the morning – I had to risk life and bloody limb. It's a funny old game, like someone once said.

I missed the last match of the 1974–75 season, and the word was that a special board meeting was being called to discuss the matter. The reality was that a QPR board meeting, in those days, was Jim Gregory looking at himself in a great big mirror! There were no board meetings at Loftus Road. What he said, went – it was as simple as that.

Chapter 10 •

A Pain in the R's

As the new campaign began, Dave Sexton was convinced that we were heading for a special season. He really believed that we could win the League Championship. None of us had really thought about the title; although we knew that everything was coming together, and that we were all playing well. But Dave was adamant: we could be champions.

As a coach, Dave was forever on the lookout for new methods and he used to get a lot of his training ideas from Holland and Germany. One year, Dave bought a load of big yellow plastic dummies from Holland which you could line up as walls, or use as right-back, left-back and so on. It was quite comical – the dummies were better than some of our players! He sent them back in the end because we were all taking the piss. Dave and Gerry Francis were very close and would always talk about training. We would all go in and get changed, and I would see them still out there talking together. Gerry would take in everything that Dave said, whereas the rest of us would just have a laugh.

Dave was totally fascinated by the Germans, and every summer he used to take us to a place called Hennef – near Hamburg – a pretty little village surrounded by forest. We went there pre-season, when Dave was the manager, and played Borussia Moenchengladbach, Bayern Munich and other top German sides. They had a lot of good players, and we bumped into some of them in the UEFA Cup, later on.

When we were in Germany, we couldn't go into the town in the evening, because there was no town! The place we were stuck in was like a prisoner-of-war camp! So we would all go out at night to this place which was like a shed, and drink these big jugs of beer; except for Don Givens and Dave Thomas, who were quite happy with orange juice. Don Givens was a very good striker, but he didn't socialise much, because he was teetotal. I am told he was a bit of an alky at Luton, but after he joined us he never touched a drop. So he and Dave used to sit in a corner talking about gardening, or something.

Gerry Francis wasn't much of a drinker either. In those days he used to wear big platform shoes. I remember Terry Venables telling me about coming off the pitch after a game, and he and Gerry were the same height. Next thing, in the bar, Gerry's towering over him, and Terry's talking to his belly button! We all used to have a pop at Gerry over his platforms.

One night, on one of these tours, we were all sitting in this shed, sipping lager, and as bored as dead sheep, when me and Webby decide to have a bit of a laugh. As usual, Gerry is being Captain Sensible – strictly three or four pints a night. Me and Dave are having none of this, so we start lacing his drink with vodka whenever he wasn't looking. By the time they shut, about eleven, Gerry's pissed as a fart. Once we're outside, the air hits him and he's completely gone. We're a couple of miles away from where we're staying – a long walk home in the pitch black. Gerry can hardly stand – even with the two of us holding him up – and he's tottering round on these ridiculous high heels. We're dragging him along through the mud, he keeps falling down and we're miles behind the others. Me and Webby are knackered – it's worse than training! In the end, Gerry goes arse over tit into the bushes, his bloody great shoes peeking out of the hedge. Me and Webby think, Bollocks to this! and leave him there.

Next morning Gerry turns up for training covered in bruises and scratches, with a thumping hangover and no idea about what had gone on. He wasn't exactly up for it and finished last in the training run – he was probably still wearing his platform shoes!

In our 1975 pre-season friendlies, we beat the West German champions, Borussia Moenchengladbach 4–1, and also the Portuguese champions, Benfica, 4–2. The team Dave Sexton put together had a balanced look about it. Phil Parkes was a big guy and one of the best goalkeepers I have played with. He was very good at stopping shots, and when you were shooting at him point-blank, he had this knack of blocking the shot with his arms, and it would rebound a long way. A lot of keepers just parry it, but Phil punched it, so it sometimes went near the halfway line.

Dave Clement, our right-back, used to get forward quite a lot, because he knew that, in our side, not many people were going to lose the ball. So he could afford to keep going forward, knowing that he wouldn't have to run back all the time.

Frank McLintock, a passionate Scot who was always shouting on the pitch, was the key man at the back for us. We were playing a Dutch system at the time. As soon as the goalkeeper, Phil Parkes, got the ball, the two full-backs, Dave Clement and Ian Gillard, would push twenty or thirty yards on; the wingers in front of them would push up, and then turn inside; Frank would pull to the side, and get the ball thrown to him. If the winger came towards him and left our full-back, he would just chip it over the full-back's head to Dave Clement. If he stayed where he was, Frank would play it to Don Masson. I would give him a third option by coming deep. That's how we would start the move.

It was a sort of big circular movement, and we worked at that for a long, long time in shadow play. So we knew our own game very, very well. In England, it was unique. We sometimes played with two wingers; Don Givens up front; and me having a free role – like England are talking about now, having two wingers and a centre forward, and the other man coming deep; a complete rotational system. But you need eleven good players. Most of those players have to be good on the ball, because it breaks down very quickly if you're not comfortable in possession. Frank was assured on the ball; if the winger came to him, he could just float it over his head to Dave Clement, and set the move off. It was exciting stuff – for us and for the fans.

We couldn't wait for the season to begin, we knew something special was on the cards. Our first game of the season was at the Bush against Liverpool, who had just finished second to 1975 champions, Derby County. The Reds were a powerful team: Ray Clemence in goal; Phil Neal and Phil Thompson in defence; Ray Kennedy and Terry McDermott in midfield; Kevin Keegan and John Toshack up front.

It turned out to be a dream start to the season. We beat Liverpool 2–0, but the scoreline did not reflect the game – we should have won at least 5–0. Gerry's goal, a minute before half-time, turned out to be BBC TV's goal of the season. Emlyn Hughes was claiming that it was offside, but Gerry played two one-twos with Don Givens so quickly that it was impossible to tell. Anyway the linesman was on the spot, and Emlyn always put his hand up for offside – even if you were just coming out of the dressing room!

After the match, you could sense that the fans and the players knew that something exciting was happening. It was not just the 2–0 scoreline, but the way that we beat a side packed with internationals. We were literally taking the mickey by the end. It was also a great boost for Gerry, who was bidding for the England captaincy. We reckoned that if we could beat Liverpool, we could beat anybody.

We then drew at home to Aston Villa, and our third game of the season was at Derby County, who were the reigning champions. Derby, with classy international players like Bruce Rioch, Francis Lee and Charlie George, were definitely one of the best British teams of the seventies. They were playing on their new pitch, and Dave Mackay, their manager, was quoted as saying that our type of attractive, attacking football would bring out the best in them. Mackay likened us to Holland's 1974 World Cup side in the way we pushed forward, with everyone joining the attack. But I think he was using a bit of psychology on us – he really thought it would be a walkover; especially because we were without our two best defenders, Frank McLintock and Dave Webb, who were out injured.

Dave Sexton took a gamble by bringing in two youngsters into defence – Tony Tagg and Ron Abbott, both eighteen. Although we were a bit concerned, we knew that we could cover them. There was an air of confidence running through the team because we had eight or nine players firing on all cylinders at the same time. We didn't see it as much of a setback. We got an early goal, which helped to settle the two youngsters at the back, and from then on we took them apart winning 5–1.

I scored a hat-trick, and was presented with the match ball at the end of the game. I will always remember the stunned silence of the Derby crowd. They just could not believe what they had seen. The previous season Derby had beaten us 5–2 at the Baseball Ground, so the idea that we could go there with a depleted side and hammer them must have been unthinkable.

Dave Mackay criticised his defence, saying, 'How could they let in such sloppy goals?' But we had known that it would not be long before we hammered somebody, and it turned out to be Derby County. That 5–1 victory didn't surprise us, and there was no feeling of euphoria in the dressing room – we just knew how good we were.

Dave Sexton, as always in public, was very low-key about the result. He never bragged about our performances. That was how he was, all through his career. Privately, with us, he thought we had slaughtered them, and that it was a great result. The thing we had to do was to go on and prove that it was no fluke.

After the annihilation of Derby, the press started hinting that I should be given another chance to play for England. I had been in the international wilderness for eighteen months, since I had walked out on Joe Mercer, but I knew that it was only a matter of time before I'd get

Stan Bowles

another chance. People like Terry Venables and Gerry Francis were
saying publicly that I should be back in the England side.

In my private life I had settled down, although Ann still had the
desire to move back to Manchester. I was backing a few winners, which
always helps, and the general consensus of opinion was that I was
buckling down to the job. The press obviously didn't know much about
my private circumstances, but they liked me. I was the flavour of the
month again, and they launched a campaign to persuade Don Revie to
bring me back into the international reckoning.

During August we used to have a game on Saturday and one in
midweek, so our fourth game of the season arrived within ten days. It
wasn't too taxing physically because when we had midweek games we
didn't train extensively, just went through the motions and practised
tactical moves. Our philosophy was to try and win every game, and
that positive attitude continued throughout the season.

The fourth game was away at Wolverhampton Wanderers, whom
we considered to be an average side. It was end-to-end football; a
magnificent game full of flowing, positive moves played at an explosive
pace. It finished up a 2–2 draw. We played 'total football', and I think
our approach served to raise Wolves's game. We still had the two
'rookie' defenders playing and unfortunately, Tagg pushed John Rich-
ards over in the penalty area. Ken Hibbitt equalised from the spot. Don
Givens bagged both our goals. We missed the opportunity at Wolves
of going top of the First Division, but a draw was a decent result.

Our strategy was out-and-out attacking football. At this time, whenever a team attacked us we would immediately counter-attack. We
played a set pattern to a certain extent because that was the way Dave
Sexton wanted it, but with players like myself, Gerry Francis and Don
Masson there was a lot of room for doing our own thing and he
accepted that.

Masson and I didn't have a clue about defending, although Dave
would ask us to chase back whenever we could. Personally I found
this difficult, but Dave Thomas and Don Givens could run up and down
the pitch all day. Dave Sexton and I had a few arguments about this
'tracking back', as he called it. My idea was that I was up there to score
and make goals; but his attitude was that, if you lost the ball, you had
to get back, try to win the ball, or at least put the player off.

I tried to track back to the best of my ability but I wasn't very good
at it, and the players accepted this to a certain extent. Don Givens and
I had the occasional argument about him 'doing my running', as he

used to call it. But, other than that, nothing much else was said; after all, I was doing the rest of my job pretty well. In the following midweek game we entertained FA Cup holders, West Ham, at Shepherd's Bush. They were considered the aristocrats of the London scene – the sophisticated team. I feel that this was the game that changed the nation's perception of us from the young pretenders to an exquisitely skilled and adventurous side. Everything that we had practised in training came off, all our one-twos and tricks. One newspaper commented: 'Queens Park Rangers now sell more dummies than Mothercare.' The only part of our game that did not come off was the 1–1 scoreline, but West Ham were very lucky to go away with a draw. I hit the post and the bar, and we had goals disallowed. It could easily have been 5–1.

At that time, English football was in the doldrums with clubs becoming more negative in their play. It seemed that teams were more afraid to lose than wanting to go out and win. On top of that, the media, and just about everyone else were worried about the escalation of football hooliganism. Then highlights of the QPR–West Ham game were shown on telly, and it seemed like a breath of fresh air for people who loved the game. Everyone was saying that it was one of the finest advertisements for football ever seen on the small screen.

Our next match was away at St Andrews, and Dave was quite concerned about it because Birmingham City had handed us four-goal hidings on our last two visits. He was keen that we shake off the 'Indian sign' that they had over us for the previous two seasons.

The Birmingham match was watched by England manager Don Revie, and it turned out to be a poor game for us. We were subjected to heavy pressure for most of the ninety minutes. Dave Thomas saved us with a thunderbolt of a shot, and we were quite relieved to come away with a draw.

In midweek we travelled to Gay Meadow to play Third Division Shrewsbury Town in the second round of the League Cup. We thought it would be a difficult game because Shrewsbury were renowned for causing a few upsets in cup competitions. History tends to repeat itself quite a lot in football, and we didn't want any hiccups at this early stage of the season. They scored after only eight minutes and mounted a fierce assault on our penalty area which shook us out of our shell.

In the first half we had been trying to hit the front players too early, but we really came alive in the second half when we slowed down our build-up from defence through midfield. Once David Webb had equalised it was one-way traffic, and we won the tie quite easily 4–1. Alan Durban, the Shrewsbury manager, had to admit that we were a different class.

We then entertained Tommy Docherty's Manchester United at Loftus Road. Even though they were top of the table at the time, it was not the United of old because George Best and Denis Law had left the club. Docherty was rebuilding the side, bringing in players like Steve Coppell and Lou Macari. We beat them 1–0 and Alex Stepney, who made some brilliant saves, prevented the score being much higher. I missed a penalty and I can remember Alex Stepney laughing at me because I literally stumbled, and miskicked the ball, which bounced off his chest. He dived on the ball as the other players rushed in to convert the rebound. Tommy Docherty praised us after the game, mainly because we were producing the kind of football that reflected his vision of how the game should be played.

I was the official penalty-taker at this time. Every so often, we had penalty competitions in training between Gerry, Don Givens and myself, to decide who should have the job. Through most of my career with Queens Park Rangers that particular role was mine and I was confident that I could score from the spot every time. I would never hit the ball hard, but used to place it, usually low to the goalkeeper's right-hand side, and into the corner of the net. Basically, the goal-keepers knew where I was going to hit the ball – but most of the time they dived the other way!

A couple of years earlier, I remember taking a penalty at Luton, and Terry Venables saying to me, 'Don't place it in the left of the goal this time, put it in the other side.' But I had already made up my mind to continue as normal, and as I scored to the goalkeeper's right, someone from the crowd threw another ball on to the pitch. The referee insisted that the penalty be taken again because of the distraction. I actually pointed to the same side of the goal, signalling to the goalkeeper that I was going to score in the same spot again. For some strange reason, he thought I was trying to trick him; so I slotted it as usual, and he dived the other way.

Another piece of advice that Terry had given me before he moved on, was 'Why don't you make out that you are going to place it in your normal spot, and then whip it into the other side?' I practised this, but never felt comfortable, and would always revert back to my old style. Considering how many penalties I took during my career, the per-centage that I missed was very small indeed.

Our next game was on 20 September 1975 away at Middlesbrough, where Jack Charlton was the manager. I didn't know Jack, but he tried to sign me later in my career when he was manager of Sheffield Wednesday. It was reported in the press and I was asked to comment so I quipped, 'What division are they in?'

Maurice Setters, who was his right-hand man at Hillsborough, and later became his assistant with the Republic of Ireland, remembered that story. According to Maurice: 'Jack went mad. He said, "What does he mean, what division are we in?"' That was the end of that particular move!

We had to play Frank McLintock up front at Middlesbrough, because he had an ankle injury, so it left us exposed at the back, but Phil Parkes preserved our unbeaten record with a string of superb saves in a 0–0 draw. At the time we had quite a big injury list. Dave Thomas and Don Givens were out, that was two out of three strikers including myself. Although Frank was fucking useless up front, we didn't have any alternative for this game. We were down to the bare bones of the squad. Our first-team squad normally consisted of sixteen players and we had been lucky over the season to stay relatively injury-free up until this game.

Once again, we were lucky to come away with a point. Dave Sexton was very satisfied with the draw; he was quite prepared for a few hiccups during the season and a point at Ayresome Park was, he said, very encouraging.

I don't think any team relished the idea of going up to Middlesbrough, Sunderland and Burnley, places like that. Partly because the weather was often pretty bloody awful, and also because everyone knew that it was very hard to win up there.

Despite our injury problems, we still had players who could come in and do a job. Mick Leach, for example, was a very good utility player who could cover any position on the field. Although he wasn't very popular with the QPR crowd, Mick could be relied upon to make a contribution to the game. Our next game, at home to Leicester City, was his 294th league and cup appearance, which made him second only to Dave Clement, our right-back, in the rankings. Mick scored the only goal in this match which took us to joint top of the First Division with Manchester United – the highest position ever achieved in the history of the club. The feeling in our camp was that United would not last the pace. We didn't think they were quite good enough to win the League Championship.

It was Mick Leach's testimonial season and he scored again in the following game against Newcastle at home, which we again won 1–0. There was some concern, particularly in the press, that I hadn't scored for seven games, but throughout my career I had never regarded myself as a prolific goalscorer. Basically, I saw myself as a creator – the goals were just a bonus. However, this did concern a few people and Dave Sexton mentioned it to me once or twice, but I wasn't too worried.

I had played a part in both Mick Leach's goals in these last two matches and one report, on the Newcastle game, said: 'Bowles, all left foot and wheeling round two defenders like a human can-opener, slipped the ball to Clement. A prod forward and there was Leach lifting the ball beyond the valiant Mahoney.'

I never thought of myself as a human can-opener, but I wasn't a greedy or selfish player. I could beat two or three players at a time, but if there was another player in a better position I would give him the ball. To me that was just logical and sensible. I wasn't hung up on the glory of scoring a goal, like Rodney Marsh or Malcolm Macdonald.

After the game Gordon Lee, the Newcastle manager said in the press: 'I thought Phil Parkes made two great saves. Malcolm Macdonald had three goal attempts, not bad for someone who is not fully fit.' My comment in the press was: 'Malcolm who?' The reality was that Newcastle came and played for a draw like an away team would in Europe. We were a fast, attacking side with five or six players who could score goals. Even Don Masson, who hardly ever went near the penalty area, could score; and Frank McLintock chipped in with the occasional goal as well.

Teams were now putting eight or nine players behind the ball against us, and playing for a draw, so we now had to adopt a different strategy by trying to get behind their defence. We started using Dave Thomas a lot more on the wing; getting him round the back of the defence to cross the ball into the area. Dave would be the first to admit that he wasn't the most highly skilled player in our team, but he could fly down that wing and deliver excellent crosses.

So far we hadn't really had to use this tactic extensively, but against sides like Newcastle this was exactly what we needed. With so many men behind the ball, it was becoming increasingly difficult to break them down by clever passing through the middle of the field. Our opponents kept one player up front, and relied totally on the breakaway, so for most of the game it was one-way traffic. Teams were becoming wary of QPR, and didn't want the embarrassment of a 5–0 thrashing. We were still top of the league, but the attendances were quite disappointing – around 22,000 for a home game. Although, saying that, with Loftus Road being such a small ground, there was always lots of atmosphere.

We then went to Leeds, where we finally surrendered our ten-match unbeaten run. Leeds, managed by Jimmy Armfield, were still a very good side. They had many of the great players who were so successful under Don Revie: Billy Bremner, Norman Hunter and Paul Madeley; and they had a good goalkeeper in David Harvey, who had played for Scotland in the 1974 World Cup Finals in West Germany.

We were desperately unlucky at Elland Road because Frank McLintock made a terrible back pass which Allan Clarke latched on to and knocked in. I scored from the penalty spot, and we almost grabbed an equaliser in the last few minutes, but in the end we went down 2–1.

I wasn't an arrogant player, but I had so much confidence and belief in my skill, almost a feeling of invincibility. I gather that this is a feeling shared by many sportsmen when they're at the height of their profession. I taunted Allan Clarke in the media because we had clashed a couple of times in the game. I said, 'I can't understand him. He must know that I am a better player than he is, but he just can't accept it. I think he must be jealous.' This didn't endear me to Clarke, or to the Elland Road faithful!

On the Monday morning we had a post-match discussion – as we did every week. We all thought we played exceptionally well, and I was even more confident that we could win the title. What we had to do was to get back to winning ways as soon as possible.

Our next game was a League Cup tie against Charlton Athletic. I was kicked in the head in the first half, and went off, but returned after treatment to head the equaliser which set up a replay. This was unusual for me because I didn't score many goals with headers. I also hit the underside of the crossbar by swerving a free-kick round Charlton's defensive wall with only six minutes left.

However, that drawn League Cup tie against Charlton, a Second Division side, did us a favour by firing everyone up. When we played Everton at Loftus Road they didn't know what hit them and we produced probably our best display of the season. Our play was spectacular, we beat them 5–0, and, although I didn't score, I think it was one of the best performances of my career. Alan Hoby, a journalist I always respected, wrote: 'If Francis, Masson and Leach were the three musketeers of Rangers' triumphant midfield then Bowles was the team's swaggering D'Artagnan. I loved every moment of it.' I'll always remember that D'Artagnan tag with pride, it beats being a human can-opener!

Outside of football, things were going along pretty much as usual. Don Shanks and I, as already mentioned, used to go greyhound racing nearly every night. We had a couple of dogs at the White City stadium, and it was Don who introduced me seriously to the sport.

The last dog I co-owned with Don was bloody useless. The one we bought was the last of a litter. After a few races it soon became apparent why because I could run faster than that animal. If you go to a dog track and pick up the race guide you'll have a line about the form of the dog, like: early pace, wide runner or good middle pace. My dog's write-up was, 'Starts slowly – then fades'.

One day, Don turned up driving an ambulance. It had been lent to him by a friend who went to prison for a long time soon afterwards – so long that he is still there now. The windows were blacked out, and it had LONDON AMBULANCE SERVICE in capital letters on the sides.

For the next three years, until it broke down, we went everywhere in that ambulance – it became our trademark. We were stopped by the police a few times, but Don had his logbook and licence in order. It isn't against the law to own and drive an ambulance, although it is illegal to ring the bell, so I only rang it in emergencies; like when we were late for the first race at the White City!

We could often be seen flying through Shepherd's Bush, on the wrong side of the road, with me ringing the bell furiously, just to get to the greyhound track on time. It was like the Keystone Kops!

The day after we hammered Everton the papers were saying that I was a 'must' for England when Don Revie announced his squad the following day, for the vital European Championship qualifying match in Czechoslovakia on 9 October 1975. I put all the speculation to one side in order to concentrate on our League Cup replay against Charlton, which attracted over 31,000 spectators – their largest crowd for five years – to The Valley. Unfortunately, before the game I had one of my many arguments with Chairman Jim Gregory, and that put me in a sulk. It was one of the many times I had asked Jim for some money, and it was one of the many times he'd said no. So I wasn't in the happiest frame of mind before the game. I was anonymous until right near the end when I beat two or three players and slotted one home to clinch a 3–0 victory. I still didn't get any money off Mr Chairman, though!

I used to ask Jim for money to cover gambling debts but would often come up with a blank. However, I would always ask just in case he was in one of his benevolent moods. If he was, he used to give me the cash. He said from the start that he would hold a little bit back for me, money that was not in my contract but which came out of his own pocket.

It was fairly common knowledge that he did this on occasions, although the other players were not supposed to know. I certainly didn't tell them, but word got around. It was supposed to be strictly between the chairman and myself. Several of the players probably resented this, although some of them were on better wages than me. After the Charlton game the argument between Jim and I was forgotten, and this went on throughout the years, and eventually became a standing joke. We just carried on as normal. I reckon that 70 per cent of the time it was no, and 30 per cent of the time it was yes – but every time I was hoping to catch him on one of his 30 per cent days.

In the end though, Jim Gregory started to give me £200 in cash, every Monday morning – on top of my wages. Our basic wage wasn't very good, but, as I said, the win bonuses made it up. But in the end I wasn't even worried about my wages, because of that two-hundred quid, every week, which nobody outside the club knew about. I had to give my wife X amount out of my wages, but I never told her about my weekly bonus – that was my betting money, so it went straight to the bookie!

When Don Masson heard about my 'extra', he went knocking on Jim's door, 'I know Bowlesy's getting £200 on a Monday,' he said, 'and I want £200!' and Jim said, 'Fuck off! You can't play like Bowlesy. And he ain't getting £200 – he's getting more! But you're not as good as him, so you're getting nothing!' That kept poor old Don in his place!

Later, in one of his mischievous moments, Jim told a national news-paper that I had put in thirty-one transfer requests since I had been at the club. I arranged with a friend to publish in a rival tabloid that actually it was thirty-three transfer requests. Jim found this hilarious, and it was a talking point in the club for weeks after. We drew humour and strength from each other.

While this battle of wits was going on, our football was attracting good press. After the Charlton game, our next league match was away at Burnley. On paper, this didn't seem like a particularly tough game but, as I said previously about Middlesbrough, nobody liked going to these places. Burnley were a very workmanlike side but, even so, we were expected to win. Man for man we were on a totally different planet. But it didn't work out that way – Burnley hit us on the break and Frank Casper scored the only goal of the game, to knock us off the top of the league.

I read a report in the northern press the following day saying that we had played the best football they had seen from an opposing team all season. They way we were playing, it would probably have been the best they would see in any season! Technically, Burnley were far inferior to us, and we really should have hammered them out of sight. Looking back at our results later in the season, that 1–0 defeat was a disaster.

We were then back to the same old routine of a club coming to Loftus Road, putting eight or nine men behind the ball, and hanging on for a draw. This time it was Sheffield United. I hadn't been selected for the England squad in Czechoslovakia, and they were leaving for Prague a few days after we played Sheffield United. One comment in the press said: 'When the England footballers fly to Czechoslovakia tomorrow, one sad, desolate figure will be left on the ground curbing a desire to thumb a lift. Stanley Bowles, the class among the dross of a grey day at Loftus Road, has elected to fight for his place with England.'

However, my first priority was the success of Queens Park Rangers, and my stage was Shepherd's Bush. Anything else I treated as a bonus. If an England recall happened, it would be as a result of my talent and skill; certainly not because I was a model candidate.

Even Dave Sexton, never prone to making outrageous statements, was saying that I was worth looking at again; and he made moves to pacify the FA. I knew that this would be very difficult after my England walkout in May 1974. Some people thought that I would be very lucky to get another international cap, irrespective of how well I was playing.

I was working very hard in training because, basically, I enjoyed every minute of it. During the close season we used to do promotional videos, showing off our ball skills. Before he left, I did one with Terry Venables. We were keeping the ball in the air between us: on the feet, head, back of the neck, and anywhere else we could think of. I enjoyed these skill-related sessions and I liked working with Terry because he was also a very skilful player. Some players could have practised all year round and would never have that kind of skill. And we didn't just do tricks, we showed our skills on the park where it mattered most.

It made me smile when I thought of teams such as Sheffield United because their overriding objective was a 0–0 draw. When we scored, as we did in this game, I could see the bewilderment on their faces. I could see them thinking, What do we do now?

Their formation and tactics did not allow them to get a goal back, and these games would often finish with a 1–0 scoreline in our favour.

Once again, the newspapers were on my side. Even if I wasn't playing too well – which obviously happens from time to time – the papers would give me a favourable report. They started another 'Bring Back Stan' campaign aimed at Don Revie. He wasn't very popular with the press at that time, so this was another way of getting at him. Even so, I think they did like my style, especially as most clubs were moving away from skill to an emphasis on strength and stamina.

It was the same with the fans; if I was playing below par at the Bush, the fans wouldn't have a go at me, they'd prefer to blame someone else. The fans thought I couldn't put a foot wrong; even if I failed to control an easy ball they'd make an excuse for me, saying that I must have stood on some ice or something – even if it was in August! If I played a bad ball, they blamed Don Givens and Dave Thomas for not being in the right place at the right time. Don and Dave got quite a lot of stick, undeservedly, and they got very annoyed about it. I used to play on it a bit by using 'theatrical gestures', as the press called them.

Between 1974 and 1977 only a very brave man in the crowd at Loftus Road would have had a go at me. Rodney Marsh had enjoyed the same kind of rapport with the fans, and I am told he also used to play on it in the same way. After a 1–1 draw against Coventry we met Tottenham at the Bush, and suddenly the mighty Spurs were being classed as the underdogs. They had been renowned, a couple of seasons earlier, as being one of the most skilful sides in the First Division, but, in no time at all, we had overtaken them to become the best side in London.

We now had nine internationals in our team, which had blossomed within the space of seven or eight months. The England caps were Phil Parkes, Dave Clement, Ian Gillard, Gerry Francis, Dave Thomas, John Hollins and yours truly. The other two were Scotsmen, Don Masson and Frank McLintock.

The Spurs game was a bit of a stand-off and produced a 0–0 draw. I was interested to note that the press said that Ralph Coates was the most dangerous man on the pitch. It must have been an absolutely desperate game for Coates to be the most dangerous man on the pitch, since he was about as lethal as a parrot's fart. I actually played with him later on in my career at Orient, and I was amazed that he had somehow won more international caps than I had. How he ever got one cap was beyond me. Spurs had a few very ordinary players in their team, like the aptly named John Pratt (sorry John), and Jimmy Neighbour – a winger who was about as much use as an ashtray on a motorbike.

To be honest though, I never paid much attention to other players. One or two I thought were great, a few were crap, but mostly I didn't bother with the ones in the middle. It wasn't arrogance or anything, it was just that I concentrated on my game and – of course – other things!

As Frank McLintock says: 'You would seldom see Stan in the dressing room before 2.30. He was usually in the local bookies looking at the 2.30 race. He'd be in the vicinity, but not in the ground or in the dressing room. Stan was very relaxed, very laid-back, never gave a toss about anybody, never thought the opposition was any good. Sometimes he would grudgingly say, "Yeah, he's a good player," or "Yeah, they're a good team." But he didn't put people on a pedestal very often.'

After the Spurs game, to my great delight, I found out I had been picked for England in the crucial European Championship qualifying tie against Portugal in Lisbon. Finally, I was back in the England squad. Gerry and Dave Thomas were in as well, which made it even better. I reflected for a while on all of the problems and incidents that had stalled my international career, and breathed a heavy sigh of relief that I had been given another chance. Had I been a fool for following my own instincts and for being myself? Then I thought, No, who else could I possibly be but myself? Good or bad, brilliant or exasperating, I have to be my own man. That was the only way I could feel comfortable. I couldn't live out a charade, just to please the football establishment, or anyone else. I was – and am – me; take it or leave it.

On 11 November 1975, we played Newcastle United in the fourth round of the League Cup. This game was at home and, again, we were faced with three centre halves and ten players behind the ball. It was a little like playing against the Berlin Wall. I remember the Newcastle game in particular, because I was carried off in the 85th minute with a groin injury, which I had never suffered before. We lost the tie 3–1, mainly due to Malcolm Macdonald, who was the lone striker up front. Newcastle hit two balls over the top, Macdonald left Frank McLintock and Webby for dead and he scored twice. Frank and Webby normally covered each other, but in this game they didn't, and I can honestly put this defeat down to them. Sorry lads!

Although we were knocked out of the League Cup, we were setting our sights a lot higher and, in time-honoured fashion, concentrating on the League. I had to pull out of the game against Ipswich because of my groin strain, and anybody who knows me is aware that I never liked watching football. If I wasn't playing I would never travel away to watch the team perform. I'd only go to games if I was instructed to go specifically by the manager, who knew that I got bored watching football. In my absence we got a 1–1 draw at Portman Road, with Don Givens getting our goal. Obviously, if we were playing at home, and I had nothing else to do – like if the racing was called off – I would go. When injured, I preferred to either spend my time racing, or with friends in Shepherd's Bush or Hammersmith. Dave Sexton was quite good about this. He realised that just watching people play didn't turn me on at all.

One innovation in 1976 was the Fair Play table, in which we were second from bottom. But we weren't a dirty side. Okay, so we had more bookings than any other team, but half of these bookings came from my arguments with referees. Almost every time I swore at, or near, a referee, I was booked. Only once in my career was I booked for foul play, and it was well known that I couldn't tackle to save my life.

I always regarded swearing as an integral part of the game, and whether you think it is right or wrong, footballers will always swear. There were a few referees, like Jack Taylor and Gordon Hill, who would swear back and not take any notice. I was always quite happy when they were refereeing a game. I can remember one incident with a referee – Clive Thomas – who turned down a blatant penalty claim for us at the Bush, and I actually calmed the crowd down to stop them coming on to the pitch. Five minutes later, he booked me. I stopped him from getting a good hiding, but he booked me!

When I met Clive years later he said, 'Well, you said something obscene to me.'

'I say that to them all, it don't bother Jack Taylor and people like that, they've said a lot back worse to me.'

I once asked a referee, 'What would you do if I said you were a ****?'

'Obviously,' he said, 'I'd have to send you off straightaway.'

'What would you do if I thought you were a ****?'

'I wouldn't be able to do anything about that.'

'Well, I think you're a ****!'

Jack Taylor was probably the best referee of all. Not just because we swore at each other, but he was recognised by most of the players as the top referee. The FA issued a directive at one time to try to cut the swearing out of football, which I thought was ridiculous. If Jack was in charge, though, we carried on as usual.

Burnley were bottom of this Fair Play table – rightly so in my opinion. They had some vicious players who didn't care how they brought you down. When that happens, eventually you're going to get booked. With us, though, I can honestly say that our low position in the table was no reflection on our style of play. It was down to me and my big mouth.

I was even sent off a couple of times for using obscene language. It was known that I was quite bad-tempered on the field, and could be easily wound up, so people would play on it. Players would talk to me a lot, and try to get me angry, but most of the time it didn't bother me too much.

Gerry Francis, unfortunately, picked up an injury during the draw at Ipswich, giving Don Revie another problem. As it turned out, I wasn't fit enough to go to Portugal but Gerry recovered and captained the side, as he had done ever since scoring two goals in England's 5–1 demolition of Scotland at Wembley in May. Gerry and I would have loved to play together for England in Portugal, but my groin strain prevented that dream from coming true. The final score was Portugal 1 England 1 with Mick Channon scoring for England.

I was back in the side at the Bush on 22 November against Burnley, whose star player, Leighton James, was missing because of some personal problem. It wasn't a very inspiring match in which to make a comeback, but I got a simple goal on a cold, grey afternoon to win the match in front of our lowest crowd of the season so far, around 17,000. That victory put us back on the winning trail after the press had started to say that our title challenge was sinking, with three consecutive draws against Coventry, Spurs and Ipswich. We had slipped down to fourth in the table, so the win over Burnley perked everyone up again. We were back in contention.

I have to say, through all of this, that Dave Sexton was like a connoisseur of football. He was very in-depth and tactical, spoke to the players individually and tried to get you to play a certain way.

He loved players who could express themselves on a regular basis. He would tell the players to give the ball to me and rely on me to produce a bit of magic to swing the game.

Dave had a few systems that he liked to play. He would use the rotation system with midfield players bombing forward with maybe the centre forward dropping back into midfield – we were doing a lot of this. The full-back, for example, would be overlapping and someone would drop in to that spot so that the full-back did not have to rush back in to position. The defender would be encouraged to stay upfield and then ease his way back. This way of playing was a little bit different from the way most teams played in those days.

We created a lot of confusion in the opposing teams' ranks by operating this system of play. I would receive the ball at an angle and let it run to Don Givens. Don would then play it straight back to me, causing confusion, and then I would slip Don in again. It wasn't like your standard: ball comes in, forward holds it up and plays it off the way he's facing. Players would zip the ball in to me, I would touch it very faintly with the outside of my foot, I knew Don would be in the slipstream at an angle. I would then turn the defender and Don would knock it straight back in to me and we would set up from there.

Dave studied all of these moves and was a great tactician. However, one of Dave's weaknesses was that he could never understand the lifestyle of a player like myself. 'How can you be a gambler Stan? How can you be so good at training and be fantastic on the field, when the rest of your life is just bedlam?'

Dave really didn't understand how people like me could be professional footballers. My behaviour would immediately squash Dave's enthusiasm when he enquired as to why I couldn't be in the dressing room fifteen minutes before kick-off for a major game. I'm sure that Dave would have tried to put a stop to it if I was having nightmare games, but he just seemed to let it go.

Chapter 11 •

Championship Contenders

In our first fourteen games of that season we had won seven, drawn five and lost two – at Leeds and Burnley. We were playing better than ever, but the fact that we were drawing so many games was a bit worrying, and the way teams were deciding to play against us also caused us concern.

From mid-October to November 1975 the goals dried up, thanks to the attitude of the opposition. Visiting managers were doing all they could to spoil the games and suppress our attacking flair. Sometimes, opposition defences were so packed that I thought they'd employed the travelling fans at centre half!

Gerry Francis was taking a lot of stick following a bit of a barney with Mick Mills in the game at Ipswich, where everyone thought Gerry had tried to head-butt him. The press were questioning his right to the national team captaincy, and Ipswich boss Bobby Robson was saying that it was conduct unbecoming of an England captain.

In the incident, Mick Mills had gone in very hard and made a bad tackle. But I think it was a personal thing with Gerry. I don't think he had a lot of time for Mick Mills, either as a person or as a player, and if he didn't respect a player he would react in that way. If Gerry didn't like Mick Mills, I reckon he was a good judge of character – I never liked Mills either!

I played with Gerry for seven years and he was a fantastic footballer. He was very skilful, and he was also a great tackler who tried to win every tackle fairly, going for the ball every time. I never saw Gerry go over the top, but I have seen Mick Mills do it, and I have had arguments with him myself. Throughout a footballer's career you will always come across a Mike Pejic or a Mick Mills – you just have to put up with it.

Dave Sexton used to compare Gerry to Dave Mackay, the great Spurs half-back. Mackay was known as a hard man, a marvellous competitor, a great leader – but he was also skilful. I saw Mackay react many times in the same way that Gerry reacted that day. I think they had similar qualities. You very rarely found a footballer who was that tough, but also that talented. Even in those days – when there were a lot of great players around – those two qualities didn't often coexist in the same player.

Dave Sexton used to say that if you tried to intimidate Gerry you'd wish you hadn't, because he would never let you get away with it. Gerry was one of the most talented midfield players I've ever seen – going forward, or defending.

On 29 November 1975 we played Stoke City at home. This was a game we were all looking forward to, because Stoke were very similar to ourselves in their approach to the game – although not as good as us! Their manager, Tony Waddington, who had tried to sign me when I was at Crewe, had built a good, well-balanced side with Alan Hudson, John Mahoney and Geoff Salmons in midfield, Jimmy Greenhoff up front – sometimes with Terry Conroy – and Peter Shilton in goal. We knew Stoke wouldn't man-to-man mark me, so it would be a very open game. This suited me down to the ground, because whether I scored or not, I knew that I would make chances. It turned out to be a really exciting game. We beat Stoke 3–2 and we got the winning goal in the last minute through Webby.

If we were drawing and there was only a few minutes to go – as we could find out easily from the crowd – we used to throw Webby up front, because he was a big man and had a great presence. This was a regular tactical move, and Webby didn't need telling. He just used to forget about defence, push forward, and try and get the winning goal. Remember, our attitude was always to try and win the game. It meant that we used to leave ourselves a bit open at the back, but Webby came through on numerous occasions scoring some important goals each season.

At training Dave Sexton used to play Webby up front in practice games so that he would get an idea of what went on in our territory, rather than his own. He had a knack of being in the right place at the right time. We reckoned that the opposition wouldn't know what to do because Webby had suddenly appeared up front, and it might create a bit of space for one of us to nick a goal near the end. And yet, quite often, it would be Webby who got that goal.

Alan Hudson, another friend of mine, always said that he regretted that we never played together. Unfortunately, Alan got booked in this game for kicking the ball away in the penalty area with only seconds to go, and the press had a right go at him for this. Alan had the same problem as me: the slightest thing that he did wrong was picked up on by the press, and as he was trying to work his way back into the England squad it didn't go down very well at the time. In those days, something like that was frowned upon by the people that ran the game.

David Webb remembers our days together at Loftus Road:

Some of the things Stan used to do on the pitch were pure magic to watch. I was entertained playing in the same team. I used to watch him go up the line, firmly believing that the ball was out of play, but somehow he used to keep the ball going with a little shuffle, and then he'd do something amazing. His vision of the game was second to none. I used to find myself applauding and clapping some of Stan's magic moments because I knew that – as a defender – I would have been powerless to stop him; just as the opposing defenders were.

He was the most talented player that I ever had the honour of playing with. If we were up against it, Stan was a marvellous team player who would always stand his corner. He would be with you to the bitter end, helping out wherever he could. I was lucky to play against players like Best, Pele, Cruyff, Jimmy Greaves and many more, and you could probably name twenty world-class players in those days.

I wonder, in twenty-five years' time, how many players will be remembered in today's game. People will remember that a player played in a certain team, but not for his individual skill and talent.

That is why it is sad for people like Cantona, who would have fitted into the seventies' game perfectly. Cantona would have been one of the star players of that era. Players today are manufactured, and taught, at a very young age, that winning is the only reason to play football. And it makes me angry when I see junior team managers adopting this policy. Instead of allowing young players to go out and enjoy themselves, they talk about guts and commitment and letting the side down. They put too much pressure on young players to win, rather than allowing their talents to flourish naturally.

Stan used to show tremendous skill when we were under pressure. He would be the Lone Ranger up front, and if he got the ball he was able to give us, in defence, a breather. You knew he wouldn't give the ball away easily and this was an incredible asset to the team. It would give you a chance to reorganise if you were under the cosh. Somebody would have to kick him up in the air to get the ball off him, and he got us out of jail many times.

On a personal level I used to get on well with Stan although we were completely different characters. We had a rapport, a mutual professional respect. In a way we both wanted to learn about life outside football, and his upbringing made him like that. I was involved in business outside the game, and we had a wider view of life. A lot of characters he knew became acquaintances of mine, and we still see them today.

I remember at one time I was in financial difficulties and had to sell my Mercedes and I bought a little Triumph Toledo. One day I had to go into the City for some treatment, and I had my young daughter with me. Stan was training, and I asked him if he wanted a lift because I knew he was going to see Shanksy. So I dropped him off at Park Royal, and as he got out he gave my daughter half a crown, and said, ' 'Ere you are, sweetheart.'

I went into training the next day and told the players what had happened, and Shanksy told me that Stan had borrowed the half a crown for his tube fare. So he must have got out of the car, and walked because he had given his last few bob to my daughter. I've never forgotten that, and many people don't see that side of Stan. He would give people his last tenner, but unfortunately most people wouldn't give him their first tenner. I would never try to change him, he's got a lot of good points about him.

Before we played away at Manchester City, unfortunately I had another altercation with the chairman. I had asked for money to cover yet another gambling debt – Jim refused point blank. Consequently, on the Thursday I asked for a transfer which, on reflection, was probably not a good move. It upset the apple-cart a little bit and Dave Sexton left me out of the squad for Maine Road.

It was a typical spur of the moment thing which Dave got used to over the years. He just used to say, 'Stan, Stan ...' and that was it. I think he understood it to a certain extent. He had the firm belief by now that we were going to win the league and nothing, however traumatic, was going to stand in his way.

I was losing a lot of money at the time. I used to arrive late for games because I'd been gambling, and it was no wonder Dave went grey. But when I was on that pitch, that was my stage, and I was relieved to be out there. I used to love that ninety minutes, because I had no worries out there – apart from trying to win the game.

In my private life, away from the football, I never used to talk about the game. I wasn't interested, and this is probably why it has taken me so long to put pen to paper. Also, at the time, me and Don Shanks were leading something of a double life.

Me and Don lived together for about six months in Ealing. We had a nice place just off the Uxbridge Road. Our landlords were Irish, and we used to pay about £200 per month in rent. It's funny really that when you gamble the cash flow is never stable. One day you may have a fiver in your pocket the next day five grand – this to us was one of the exciting things about gambling. A lot of people wouldn't be able to stand the pressure, but when you have a job, and you know that money is coming in, you don't have to worry about it too much.

At this particular time we were on one decent meal a day – Kentucky Fried Chicken and Cokes. The landlord and his wife lived on the floor beneath us, and it was one of those houses where, if you turned on the tap, you could hear the water running through the building for thirty seconds or so, and everyone knew who was in the house at any time.

Anyway, the first month went by and Don was having a good run on the horses, and so he paid the rent.

'Right, Stan,' he said. 'It's your turn next month.'

'Yeah, that's all right, no problem,' says I.

The next month's rent becomes due and because Don has once again got a few quid, he pays the rent for a second time. I'm out of the game, short of money, so Don thinks, No problem, he's helped me out many times, that's what friends are for.

But, at the end of the third month he was totally skint, just couldn't bet a winner. Unfortunately, I was the same. So the landlord has asked us for the rent and we keep saying, 'We'll give it to you tomorrow ... tomorrow ...' We had put him in promise-land for about a week or two, and now he was getting worried.

'Stanley, it's your turn for the rent,' Don says. 'I've paid the last two months.'

'Oh, I'll pay him, I'll pay him. Don't worry,' I replied, a bit nervously.

'Well, you'd better tell the landlord.'

'Don't worry, if he comes up, I'll tell him,' I said, not intending to say a bloody word.

'Well,' says Shanksy, 'I'm not answering the door if he comes up.'

So, we crept into the house late at night, went upstairs and got into our beds. Then I decide I want to brush my teeth, so the water is coursing through the plumbing system and the landlord obviously heard this. Needless to say, five minutes later, we can hear him coming up the stairs, so we turn over and pretend to be asleep, because I am not going to open the door – definitely not. The landlord is banging on the door.

'Boys? Lads? Are yer in there?' he shouts. 'Stanley, are you there? Open up!'

'Stanley,' says Don, 'it's for you mate. I'm not bloody answering it. Go on, go on.'

'No, I'm not answering it,' says I, with my head under the bedclothes. 'Tell him to come back tomorrow.'

Trouble was, the man was obviously not going to leave. He carried on banging on the door, even louder. It got to the point where Don eventually jumped out of bed, put some clothes on, and went over to the door.

'Hello, who is it?' enquired Don, politely.

'It's the landlord here.'

'What do you want?' With that, Don opened the door.

'Sure, I'm looking for the rent,' he said.

'Well,' said Shanks, 'you'd better come in, and we'll all look for it together!' After that, things went downhill, and eventually we moved out. The landlord must have thought that we were going to try and flee the country for £200. He would have got paid, but when you're gambling you exist from day to day; you would pay him when you had it, which didn't always coincide with when he wanted it.

I remember gambling did have a direct effect on our football a couple of times. One Saturday, we had a few quid on Red Rum in the National. We were playing some team at home and the crowd had their transistor radios blaring behind the goals to check the football scores, or other big events like the National. Me and Don had fifty quid each at 9 or 10/1. During the game there is a bit of a lull, and they win a corner. There's a little boy with a radio behind our goal. Usually, when we conceded corners Don would stand on the goalpost, and I would be a little bit in front of him to the left, protecting against the fast ball into the box.

As we're standing there we can hear the commentary on the race, and they're about halfway, with Red Rum in the front rank. The ball comes into the penalty area towards us, so Mr Donald heads it out for another corner. I think they got about five consecutive corners altogether while we were listening to the race. I headed two of them out when I could have easily cleared the ball upfield. Red Rum won, and we carried on with the game – very happy punters.

There is a famous photo of me reading the *Sporting Life* at Loftus Road when the opposing team were taking a corner. It was my job to defend the near post whenever our opponents took a corner. At Loftus Road the pitch is very close to the crowd and I noticed one of our fans was holding a copy of the paper. I wanted to check if a horse I'd backed was running later that afternoon so I quickly grabbed the paper and began thumbing through it. The crowd roared with laughter thinking I wasn't bothered about the game. But I genuinely needed to know when the horse was running so that if it won I could cash my slip in before the bookie's closed.

The funny thing was when the corner was swung in I headed the ball upfield while still holding the paper in one hand and we immediately went up the other end and scored. I can't really imagine that happening in today's game, even if I did get a rollicking off the boss at the time. It was always my first duty to entertain the crowd and that's what I always aimed to do during my career.

Another time we had a couple of tips from the Dick Hern yard. A friend of Don's looked after a horse called Water Mill, who at one stage was actually favourite for the Derby the year that Henbit won it. Shanksy had £100 win, £100 win and a £100 double on Shoot A Line and Water Mill for the Oaks and the Derby. Anyway, the Hern stable won it with Henbit. Willie Carson didn't make up his mind who he was riding until the last minute, and obviously chose the right one, much to Don's dismay.

Going back to these tips, we had hot information on Water Mill for its first run at Newbury. The price was about 6/1 and Don, me and all the boys from the White City who used to come and watch the football matches, are on it. The race was scheduled to run at about 4.15 p.m. and we were playing a bit of a boring game although 2–0 up. I've got about £200 running up on this horse and Don's got three times that on it. All the boys have bet on it but we don't know that they are up there in the stands. Me and Don are on the pitch so we don't know the result.

So as we are playing, Don said, 'How do you think the horse got on?'

'I dunno Don, no idea.'

Suddenly, we looked up at the stands and saw all the lads from White City swaying from side to side, and singing 'Water Mill – Water Mill – Water Mill – Water Mi...ll!'

From then on we weren't worried about football! We've had it off, and can't wait to collect. As it happened Water Mill went berserk in the parade ring, threw the kid who looked after him, and knocked him unconscious. So the lad was in the first-aid room, and the horse has bolted, delaying the off. But the race eventually started, and Water Mill won at 6/1, going from 5/2 to 7/1.

Don's gambling often affected his playing, and it was quite a relief for him to get on the field. He was often glad to get out of the betting shop – watching it on television – and just go out and play. That was where my strength lay. I could come out of playing cards all night, or being in the bookie's for four hours – losing absolutely every penny I'd got – go out on to the football pitch and perform like I was Gary Lineker. Within a minute of the start of the game, I would be totally focused – delighting the crowd with my skill and commitment.

Unfortunately, I was often late getting into the dressing room before the start of a game. One time, we had a Saturday match and before the game we'd been gambling as usual. While I was a bit of a star, Don was just another player at the club, so he couldn't really afford to do what I was doing.

He had to be seen to be a bit more conscientious and organised. He'd leave home about noon and meet me at the ground at 1 p.m. The game was not until 3 p.m. and we were supposed to report at 2 p.m. so he'd go in, put all his kit on, and don his tracksuit over the top. Then he'd come up into the lounge to watch the racing on the telly.

I wouldn't do that, of course. I'd be up there watching the early racing with my coat on and a suit underneath. This particular day we had a big bet running in the 2.45 race. So the time passes. It's 2.00, then 2.15, and soon it's touch and go whether Don dare stay and watch the next race. I wouldn't get into too much trouble if I stayed; but Don might've got a volley from the manager if he did. But, knowing that he's got his kit on, and only has to put on his boots, Don stayed a little longer. Talk about preparation for a big game.

By now more people had started to come into the lounge. 'Aren't you playing today, Stan?' said someone.

'Yes, course I am,' says I.

'But it's half-past two!'

'Well?'

By now the room is crowded, and filling with smoke. No one would dare touch the television while the racing was on. If someone had tried to switch it off there would have been a riot. About twenty five to three, Don's bottle would go, and he'd say to me, 'I've got to go, I'll see you down there.'

So he would go down, take off his tracksuit with his kit on under-neath, and the boss would think that he'd been there all the time. Shin-pads on, rub a bit of oil over the legs, ready to go out on to the pitch. But at 2.45 I still wasn't in the dressing room.

Dave Sexton had this procedure where he would go around the players individually, and give final instructions: 'Right, your job today is such and such. I want you to do this. When he gets the ball put him under pressure right away, don't let him ... cut his supply off ... when we've got the ball on the outside, get yourself forward.' That sort of thing.

Anyway, he's gone round about seven or eight of the players, and Don is starting to laugh, because I'm the next player due for the pep talk. But Dave can't find me in the dressing room anywhere. He turned to Shanks. 'Don, where the hell is Stan?' he screamed.

'He's here somewhere, Dave,' says Mr Donald, shrinking back into the corner.

'Where is he?'

'I don't know. He's here somewhere, I saw him a minute ago.'

Dave looked in the shower area, in the sauna. 'Where is he? It's twelve minutes to three!'

Suddenly the door opened and I waltz in like Billy the Kid: long coat on, hands in pockets. Don's got his hands over his face, looking through his fingers, thinking, How's Stanley going to get out of this one?

'You wouldn't believe it,' said I. 'That fucking horse just got beat in a photo finish!' That was the only thing I said.

Dave was too outraged to speak. But it turned out all right. Within seconds, I got my gear off, went out and – in the first two minutes – scored a goal. We went 2–0 up in about ten minutes. Don couldn't believe it. He reckons he couldn't have done that, nor could any of the other players. They wouldn't have been able to switch on like that. Most players needed about an hour before the game, psyching them-selves up, and really getting into it.

According to Don, it just meant that I was a completely natural footballer and he wishes some of it had rubbed off on him. He says I never really appreciated just how good I was. He thinks that, during my whole football career, I was probably underpaid for the entertainment I was providing on the field. I deserved a lot more. Having said that, Uncle Jim used to look after his adopted son!

Anyway, getting back to that Manchester City game, the official story was that I had been left out for 'personal' reasons. A 0–0 draw put us back on top of the First Division in front of 36,000 supporters. It was the biggest open secret in town that I had been dropped because of my gambling. I was also known for getting around the drinking establishments in Shepherd's Bush and Hammersmith; although I didn't drink a lot in those days. My obsession was purely with betting. I would have a drink, but you would be hard pushed to find anybody who could say they had ever seen me drunk.

It would have been nice to go up to Manchester – my birthplace – because I could have stayed the weekend with family and friends, but I knew that I would have another chance later on in my career. I probably went out with Don, to the races, that weekend because he couldn't get into the side, so he wouldn't have travelled either. Don was a reasonable player but Dave Clement was playing out of his skin. Unless Dave suffered an injury, Don had very little chance of getting picked.

Basically, Don was a reserve number 2 for Dave Clement. He was also supposed to look after me. But I spent most of my time looking after him. I think Dave Sexton bought him to be a friend with me, somebody who might control me, but Don was just as bad as me. It was like the blind leading the blind!

With this particular game, and the good season I had been having, Dave knew that he had to get a result in Manchester to keep the fans and the press off his back for leaving me out of the squad. He said in the papers that the 0–0 draw was one of the best performances of the season. If we had lost at Maine Road, the fans wouldn't have blamed me for causing a hiccup in the championship race, they would have blamed Dave. So in the end the goalless draw was more of a good result for Dave than anything else. If we had lost that game I think that he would have come under intense pressure. Because of that scoreline Dave felt that he could not change the side for the next game, at home to Derby County, so Mick Leach kept his place. Mick had played the first four months of the season in the number 4 shirt. But when John Hollins came into the side, Mick filled in for me, Gerry or John, and even, on one occasion, for the usually super-fit Dave Thomas. Mick was a very useful player to have in your side, or on the bench.

Dave had told me privately that he was convinced that we wouldn't lose another game for the rest of the season which, coming from him, was an outrageous statement. You could understand it coming from some of the players, who had got carried away with the euphoria of the title chase – myself included – but for Dave Sexton to make this comment was quite staggering.

Normally, my transfer requests would last for only a couple of days. Sometimes I would ask for a transfer on Monday, and by Wednesday I would have forgotten that I even made it. Dave just let me and Jim get on with it. He would never get involved, otherwise he would have ended up tearing his hair out.

I always believed that, as a person, I was straight down the middle, and that if fifty per cent of the people liked me, then obviously the remaining fifty per cent probably would not. There is no in-between with me. People either like me, or they don't. It has been that way throughout my life, and I have no hang-ups about that. With Jim, with Dave, I think they both liked me, so I was very lucky there.

Although I was left out of the next game – at home against Derby, the 1975 champions – I was ordered to attend because I was in the squad. I didn't think that Dave would play me and I was right, but we got a 1–1 draw. I stayed until half-time, then left because, as I said, I never liked watching football and I'd only shown my face because I had to. The press were demanding my recall; but even if QPR had won 5–1, they would still have said the same. This shouldn't have influenced anybody – certainly not Dave – but eventually he backed down and included me in the next match, against Liverpool on the Saturday before Christmas.

This was a very big game for Liverpool. They had just won 4–0 at Spurs, and wanted revenge for the first day of the season, when we had thrashed them 2–0 at Loftus Road. They got it, beating us 2–0 and going top of the league.

We then had two games in two days – Norwich City at home on Boxing Day, then Arsenal at Highbury. It was very important that we won against Norwich City, because Highbury had never been a happy hunting ground for us in the past.

At the time, Norwich were a typical spoiling side – lacking flair and imagination but difficult to beat. As well as the win being crucially important, it was important for me to get back into the swing of things. I was marked by Dave Stringer, a renowned man-to-man marker, so I was quite pleased to score a goal. We eventually won the game 2–0. Normally, if someone is ordered to mark a player and they have no intention of going for the ball, there isn't a lot that you can do about it. But I managed to escape him a few times and got our second goal – Don Masson having scored the first.

Next day we went to Highbury to face an Arsenal side struggling near the bottom of the league. It was 0–0 at half-time, and then Alan Ball scored. Again I was man-marked, this time by Peter Storey, and I didn't see a lot of the ball. You do get a little bit annoyed when you are man-marked throughout a game, because no matter where the ball is – it could be two yards away – the other player isn't worried. All he is concentrating on is breathing down your neck; so it was very frustrating.

Tempers got a bit frayed and I threw a couple of tantrums. I had only one shot – tipped over the bar by Jimmy Rimmer – and was booked for an ungentlemanly gesture to a linesman – that was my afternoon. Eventually Arsenal hit us on the break, and Brian Kidd, who had joined them from Manchester United, hit a shot that normally Phil Parkes would have dropped his hat on; this time, though, it went through his legs into the net. So we lost 2–0 to a side that was 18th in the table. After the game there was an incident in the marble entrance hall at Highbury between Mad Mitch, my mate, and Mike Langley, whose article in the *Sunday People* had upset us fifteen months previously. Reporters used to hang around there waiting to talk to players when they came out of the dressing rooms on their way to the lounge.

Mike Langley remembers it this way: 'A group of us were standing around waiting to see who might be worth talking to. And a very beefy London yobbo grabbed me by the tie with his left arm. And there the matter rested. I was just thinking what to do if he started to throw a punch when Bowles came up and said, "Stop digging me out, Mike!" And that is all he said. Nothing else. I had never written about him since September 1974. He was still out of the England team and very annoyed.'

Too right, I was annoyed. The only reason he had been digging me out in the article was because it was 'my turn'. Most tabloid journalists are just paid to slag people off. They know hardly anything about the game, they're just shit stirrers. At Highbury, Mad Mitch wanted to chin Langley, but the security guys descended on him immediately. I sometimes wish they'd been slower off the mark! After the Arsenal game we dropped to fifth in the league. Then we were knocked out of the FA Cup by Newcastle after a replay. We had experienced a bad December and New Year, and it didn't help that we had to face Manchester United at Old Trafford on 10 January 1976. United were then second in the league and playing some excellent football.

They beat us 2–1, and I came off with an injury. This sparked another row with Jim Gregory who, unusually for him, had travelled to the match. Jim claimed that it was a 'moody' injury and refused to pay me my regular £200. After a blazing row, in which I – as usual – demanded a transfer, he gave in eventually and paid it. It was a close call though.

After the defeat in Manchester Dave Sexton called an urgent meeting. He emphasised to the players that we were entering the final stages of the season; and that we really needed a good winning run to have any chance of catching Liverpool and Manchester United. Dave cleared the air a little bit and everyone got together and decided to make an all-out effort to win the title. But, if we didn't get it together right away, we were going to run out of games.

We embarked on a ten-match strategy – planning to go out and win every game! It would have been one of the greatest feats of all time for the Chairman to take the title after he had built up the club from nothing with his own money.

Our next game was at home to Birmingham City, who had Howard Kendall in midfield, and a young Trevor Francis in attack.

Somebody must have been smiling down on Don Masson that day, because he scored the two goals that clinched our victory. Birmingham had a wild man in Kenny Burns who eventually got pulled off by his own manager, Willie Bell, for kicking John Hollins's head instead of the ball.

The removal of Kenny Burns did us a favour because, although Kenny was a hard man, he was a very good player, and had been playing out of his skin that day. The important thing was to get the win to put us back on track, and Dave was particularly pleased with those two points.

Soon after this I was offered a picture-shoot with a topless model by the *Daily Mirror*. There was £500 in it for me. Naturally, I needed the money, so I agreed to do it. A journalist friend of mine, Kevin Mosely, put me in contact with a fashion photographer, Kent Gavin. I didn't ask anyone's advice – which was probably foolish of me – but, when money talked, I always listened. So there I was, in the West End of London, a far cry from the prefabs of Manchester. I went into the studio and suddenly I started to worry. I'm thinking to myself, What the hell will Ann say? And then thinking, Fuck it, I need the money. I sat there for ten minutes, and the girl hadn't arrived, so I was ready to do a runner. Then, all of a sudden this glamorous dolly-bird walked in, and I thought, Bollocks, I'm staying!

We were there for about half an hour and had five or six snaps taken.

There she was, rubbing her tits on my chest, and I was thinking to myself, I've got the best pair of tits in London rubbing against me, and 500 quid in my pocket as well! Lovely!

However, that brief and relatively innocent photo-session caused a lot of trouble. With hindsight, I wish that I had never agreed to do the pictures, even though at the time it seemed harmless. The publication of that photo in the *Daily Mirror* was the last straw for Ann, and she finally decided to go back to Manchester.

So I said that I would again ask for a transfer, which came at a bad time for Dave Sexton. I had a meeting with Dave and Jim Gregory and we decided that I would go on the list for a month and, if nobody came in for me in the meantime, I would have to stay at QPR. If a northern club came in, I would be allowed to leave the club – if the fee was right. Privately though, I knew that Jim wouldn't let me go.

At this time, I was living in one of Jim's houses which he let me use rent-free. I remember one incident – which I do not think Jim knows about to this day – when I lived in his house in Neasden. There was this big greenhouse in the back garden. In those days, Dave Thomas was heavily into gardening and one day, when he was giving me a lift to training, he came into the house and had a look round. We went out the back. The garden was full of weeds and, in the middle of it, was this massive greenhouse.

'What are you gonna do with that?' he asked.

'Fuck all!' I said.

'I'll give you £100 for it.'

'Don't be silly,' I said, thinking, 'Mmm, a hundred quid.'

Dave was well into his gardening whereas I thought a Flymo was a can of deodorant.

I thought Jim might take umbrage if he ever found out I'd begun to sell his possessions but I thought that I could use the ton as speculative capital for a night out at the dogs. With a few wins under my belt maybe I could buy the glasshouse back with an extra few quid besides. This is the way a gambler's mind works.

The argument seemed irresistibly steeped in logic. I gave it a few more seconds' consideration before shaking hands on the deal. He returned some time later with a truck and I helped load it panel by panel, until all that was left was a large, flattened empty space where the greenhouse used to stand. There were a few discarded plant pots scattered around the lawn so to rid myself of any damning evidence I tossed them over the fence. My next-door neighbour was a green-fingered elderly lady whom I knew would appreciate the gesture. I was pretty considerate with things like that.

I lost the £100 on the first night, after just four races, and neither Jim nor I ever got to see the greenhouse again.

Normally I sign autographs for kids whenever they ask me. Even though this can tie you up for hours on end, it's part and parcel of being famous. But that night I was feeling bad-tempered after losing the money. I remember a fourteen-year-old kid coming up to me and asking for my signature. I said, 'Not now sonny, I've just done a greenhouse.'

The lad seemed to accept it was a bad time for me, nodded his head and trooped off on his merry way. Later, I felt guiltier about not giving him the autograph than about losing the greenhouse.

Jim Gregory did pop round to see me about six months later. I suffered a few anxious moments when making him a cup of tea. He followed me into the kitchen and looked out through the back window. He did a little double take at the big empty space in the garden and I almost could hear him thinking, Didn't there used to be something there? At that point I sidetracked him into a conversation on *Bonanza*, the popular Western TV series he was quite fond of. After ten minutes of pointless conversation the subject of the missing greenhouse was blissfully forgotten.

Mind you, I didn't always get it right. Jim gave me the option to buy the house for £12,500, but I didn't take it up. Eventually the bloody property went for about eighty grand, so I lost out there.

I would have gone back up north to a big club, purely to keep the peace, family-wise, but I knew that if a club had been interested, Jim probably wouldn't have let me know anyway. It would have had to have been Manchester City or Manchester United, which was almost a nil prospect. So I knew deep down that I was going to stay at QPR for quite a long time, and that suited me.

There was certainly some unrest with the other players again because obviously, being a high-profile player, I used to get away with quite a lot, and I suppose that they were getting fed up with it. The likes of Gerry, Webby and Frank were pretty good about it, but I could be 99 per cent certain that the quotes coming out in the papers, saying that I should not be forgiven, were coming from Masson and Givens.

The model involved in the topless photograph was getting a lot of hassle from the press. Sadly, she was involved in a very bad car crash and that ruined her career. At the time, the press tried to make out that I was having an affair with her, even though I had met the girl only once. The picture was taken and away I went – happy as Larry, with five hundred notes in my pocket. However, malicious gossip about an affair was causing the model and her boyfriend a lot of distress. But, that was the fault of the newspapers – it had nothing to do with me.

After my latest transfer request I was left out for the game at West Ham, which we lost 1–0. I was also dropped for the next game, away at Aston Villa, where we won 2–0 with goals by John Hollins and Gerry Francis. The Villa game was the fifth league match that I had missed; but the first time the team had won without me. So now the crunch was coming ... would I get back into the side?

But, as luck would have it, after the Villa game we had a testimonial match for Mick Leach, and the chairman told me that I would be playing. I don't think Dave would have picked me, even though I had been informed that I was being taken off the transfer list. The testimonial game was against Red Star Belgrade, who were regarded as a highly skilled side. Even so, we beat them 4–0. It was only a so-called friendly but it was a good game for me because I had a big hand in most of the goals. That performance got me back into the team. My main motivation was that I wanted to play, but Don Shanks and myself had placed a bet of £400 at the start of the season that QPR would win the title, so that was spurring me on as well!

I was brought back for the home fixture against Wolves. I didn't have a particularly good game, because I hadn't really been training over the previous ten days; anyway we beat Wolves 4–2.

I wasn't match fit, and James Mossop of the *Daily Express* summed it up quite well when he wrote: 'Brought back after a two-week absence, he was like a racehorse sent to the stalls straight from the paddocks – not really ready to race.'

One factor in our favour was that the winter of 1975–76 was relatively mild and dry. The Loftus Road stadium had been built on a rubbish tip, so there were serious drainage problems for many years. If it rained for a couple of hours, the water would just lie on the top of the pitch making conditions very difficult. Luckily, the weather that season was so good that the playing surface remained in excellent condition right through the winter months, and that suited the type of football we played. If it had been very muddy in December through February, we wouldn't have been able to knock the ball around as quickly and accurately as we did. A lot of our play was based on first-time touches, so a good surface was very important.

As well as being a very shrewd coach, Dave Sexton was a great student of form. He'd analysed all our rivals with a fine toothcomb: Leeds, Liverpool, Manchester United, Derby and Ipswich. Finally he gave a message to the press: 'We can make it, we can win the title.'

It was early February, and we still had thirteen games left, but our manager believed we could win all of those games. The first game after this announcement was away at White Hart Lane, and we simply took Tottenham apart. As I said, they didn't have a very good side at the time, but even if they had, I don't think they could have lived with us. We won 3–0, and the only surprise was that we didn't score six. Unbelievably, it was 0–0 at half-time, then Don Givens scored, and Gerry added two lovely goals. Spurs were attempting to play the offside trap; but on one occasion Gerry broke clear, with only Willie Young to beat, and he twisted and turned him so much that by the time they got to the penalty area, Willie had collapsed in a heap.

Being hammered 3–0 at home was a huge embarrassment for Spurs, really. In fact, Dave gave us a bit of a telling-off after the game for taking the piss out of them on the field. Don Masson, Gerry and I had been knocking the ball around, inviting them to try to get it off us, but they just couldn't do it.

To be honest, Don Masson and I didn't get on throughout my years at QPR, even though we respected each other as footballers. After Terry Venables had moved on, Gerry and I took over organising the free-kicks. Gerry was always full of ideas, just like Terry before him. Then, Don Masson came along – a Scot from Notts County – and said to us in training, 'I think I've got a better idea of how to do that.' Me and Gerry looked at each other and just carried on, ignoring Masson completely. He kept his ideas to himself after that.

Dave Webb was slow, but Don Masson made Webby look quick! However, Masson was so highly skilled that he could get away with it. He was stuck in the middle of the park, in front of the back four, and didn't have to do a lot of running. He just used his football brain to make the right passes. A bit like myself, really, but I was quicker than him – everybody was, even the groundsman.

After Spurs, we played Ipswich back at the Bush. On paper, this was quite an easy game for us, but being in second place in the championship race meant that nothing was easy at this stage. We were two points behind Liverpool, and had played one more game, but our run-in seemed a bit more favourable than the Scousers.

They had quite a few awkward games coming up, and we were playing as well as we had at the beginning of the season. In every game we went into, we felt that it was only a matter of time before we scored. This is what happened against Ipswich, although the goals were scrappy. John Wark scored a ridiculous own goal, trying to kick the ball away for a corner and smashed it into the roof of the net. We won 3–1; and although there wasn't a good goal among them, we did play some good football.

We were now 7/1 with Corals to win the league because Manchester United and Derby, who were on the same points as us, still had to play each other and, like Liverpool and Leeds, they had a lot of hard games coming up. The teams left for us to play were generally regarded as run-of-the-mill sides. Me and Don Shanks were going to take this price of 7/1 and lay a heavy bet. We would have done so if we had played the same number of games as Liverpool, but in the end we didn't take it because they had that game in hand.

After beating Ipswich, we went to Leicester and got an early goal. I laid the ball inside to Dave Thomas, who hit an unstoppable shot and basically the game was over – they didn't have enough up front to worry us. Mark Wallington, their goalkeeper, had a good game, keeping the score respectable. I remember Tommy Docherty saying that if Manchester United couldn't win the title, he would like to see it go to QPR from a football purist's point of view.

We were already counting on another two points when we went up to Sheffield United, who were bottom of the league and, although we were without Gerry, we had no excuses for a 0–0 draw. We were good enough to have thrashed the Blades, who were one of the poorest sides I had ever seen in the First Division – eventually finishing in bottom spot. They had only one decent player – Tony Currie – who came to play with us four seasons later. That goalless draw at Bramall Lane was very, very disappointing.

So, now we had the same points as Liverpool, but were behind on goal average. We knew that Liverpool had a difficult game to come at Middlesbrough, which, as it turned out, they lost 2–0. We went into our next game against Coventry knowing that we had to win convincingly.

It was one of the most exciting championship races for years, with five clubs at the top of the table in with a chance. Many experts believed that it wouldn't be decided until the very last kick of the season. After beating Coventry 4–1, we went two points clear at the top of the table, but were still worried by the fact that Liverpool had that one vital game in hand.

At this time, Gerry and I were playing the best football of our lives. We had this uncanny understanding, which is hard to describe – it was just there. He knew where I was, and vice versa. If you watched the games – forget about the goals – you would see three or four one-twos, and if you blinked you would miss them. Gerry could play the ball blind to me, and I could back-heel the ball to him knowing that he would be there. We could have played blindfolded at the time, and were enjoying our football so much that the crowd sensed that something historic was about to happen. Everybody in the club, including the chairman, was convinced that we were going to be champions.

I was so confident that, whether we were at home or away, I would be collecting my win bonus *before* the match.

'Are you sure, Stan?' Ron Phillips, the club secretary, used to ask.

'Course I'm sure, just give me the money!'

We were on about £150 a point at this time, but we had to be in the top three to qualify for this bonus. I found it incredible that this guy – a former army captain who could speak about eight languages – would believe our fairy stories, tales right out of Enid Blyton; but I suppose he had never met anybody like Don Shanks and myself. The poor man thought we were gentlemen!

We used to terrorise him, really. We'd go to the betting shop, get knocked out and run back up and try and draw Saturday's win bonus off him – even though we hadn't played Saturday's game yet. We used to tell Ron that it would be an incentive for us to play really well, and Ron would say, 'Oh yes, that's a good idea. £75, all right?'

'Make it £150 Ron, thanks very much.'

Don would say, 'Stan's really on top of his game, he's been training very hard, we'll win easily.'

As Don walked out, I would be behind the door, he'd give me half the money and off we'd go! Then later, I would walk in for a repeat performance. This would happen week in, week out – day after day, even! We were running up an enormous bill and probably owed him about a grand apiece. He was pulling money out of his pockets, the safe – the poor man didn't know where he was!

In the end he had to plead with the manager, 'Please, you've got to stop Stan and Don coming in here, you'll have to stop them, I can't deal with this any more.' But, we always found a way to persuade Ron to part with more cash.

Ron always used to listen to LBC on the radio in his office, and the door would be slightly ajar. So we'd wait out there for half an hour or so, and eventually creep in; because if the radio was on you knew he was in there. However, one day we had waited outside for over an hour and he hadn't appeared. The radio was on, so we thought he must be in. Don said to me, 'Where has he gone?' He couldn't get past us because Don was outside the door, and I was at the end of the corridor. So I start banging on the door but there was no reply.

Usually, Ron would say, 'Yes, come in.' So now we're getting a bit bold and Don gets down on one knee, trying to look through the keyhole, thinking, Hello, is he with the female secretary or something? But there's no one in there, and Don says he can see the curtains, in front of some long, sliding windows, blowing in the wind.

It turned out that he'd climbed out of the window, dropped down about ten feet to the pavement, complete with bowler hat and umbrella. God knows what he looked like when he was getting out of the window. He must have sprinted up to the station to keep well clear of us.

One day I went round to his house because Ron had the misfortune of living in Ruislip, where I lived. He hadn't told us that he lived there, because he knew that we would be round every night, but Don somehow managed to get the address out of the secretary. Ron used to take the money home with him, and if we'd done our money at half five and wanted to go to the dogs at half seven, we would be desperate. When Ron saw me at the door he nearly died. The poor man didn't have the will to argue; he just handed over the money, without a word. In the end, Ron would always give in. He was such a lovely man.

I did him one day for £200. I had arranged for one of my mates to wait by a phone ready to say that he was a journalist on the *Daily Mirror*. I went in to Ron, to ask for the money, and told him that I was doing an article for the *Daily Mirror* that weekend and would be getting a £200 advance. Ron rang the number that I had given him and he paid out on the strength of the reply.

That particular wind-up was a classic. I got my bloke to wait by the phone box in the Springbok, a pub opposite the QPR ground, and told him that he mustn't let anyone else near the phone. I said, 'Wait there, it will ring in the next ten minutes.' It did, and he played his part brilliantly: 'Yes, fine, that's all right, Mr Phillips. The cheque is on its way.' We laughed about that then, and still do now. Without Ron Phillips, God only knows how we would have managed.

*

Following our win against Coventry we then had to go to Goodison Park which, on the face of it, was a difficult game. In the end, we beat Everton 2–0, and it was easy enough. The next two games showed how useful our ploy was of pushing Webby up front near the end. We won 1–0 on both occasions, against Stoke and Manchester City, and Webby got both goals.

Going into April, we had five games left to play. We thought that the hardest game of all would be at Newcastle. There had always been a lot of needle between me and Malcolm Macdonald. He said in the press that they were going to beat us and stop us winning the league, etc., etc. On the day it was 1–1 until literally ten seconds from the end. The ball was played to me in the box and I hit it through the legs of three players, and the ball wound up in the back of the net.

The first thing I did when I scored was run up to Malcolm Macdonald and shout, 'What do you think of that, then?' That moment was captured by a press photographer. The photo was a classic, and you can see it today framed in the QPR reception corridor.

Before Newcastle could kick-off again the final whistle had gone, and we had actually overcome what Dave had regarded as a major hurdle. We thought that if we could keep going, we would win the championship by three or four points. We beat Middlesbrough 4–2 at home. Although at one stage they got back to 2–2, by the end we swamped them.

Then came the game against Norwich City at Carrow Road. We'd won eleven of our last twelve matches and drawn the other, which was a fantastic sequence, by any standard. There were now only three games left. We knew that we needed to win all three.

I was then on sixteen disciplinary points which meant that if I got cautioned again I would miss at least one of the last two games. Dave told me just to go for it, not hold myself back, or worry too much about getting booked.

Norwich scored first after twenty-six minutes when the ball was crossed into the penalty area and, for some reason or another, Dave Webb headed it to their centre forward instead of heading it away. The ball went straight to Ted MacDougall and he scored from a yard out. We managed to equalise through Dave Thomas just before half-time, but then Peter Morris and Phil Boyer made it 3–1 to them. We got an own goal, when defender Tony Powell lobbed the ball over keeper Kevin Keelan, but we couldn't equalise. So now, our destiny was no longer in our own hands.

This disaster left us with two home games – Arsenal and Leeds United. We wanted to win both, and end the season in style in front of our own fans and, more importantly, we still had a chance of the title if Liverpool slipped up. In the Arsenal game, Frank McLintock again scored against his old club; Gerry got a penalty, and we won 2–1 in front of over 30,000 spectators.

We faced Leeds, in the last match of a tremendous season, in front of a crowd of 31,002 – one of the largest that QPR have ever had. Dave Thomas scored his ninth league goal of the season, a very good strike rate for a winger. I scored my tenth near the end, and we won 2–1. The fans were ecstatic and some of the players threw their shirts into the crowd. We were unbeaten at home in 21 games: having won 17 and drawn 4. It was a very emotional day, and we had a big party afterwards. I can even remember Jim Gregory crying.

In the next day's *Observer*, Julie Welch wrote:

> *Rangers are still in the league championship with a chance, thanks to a scrambled but timely Dave Thomas goal and a moment of pure footballing excellence by Stan Bowles. Now they must munch their nails till Liverpool meet Wolves on 4th May, to know whether this tremendous season of theirs has been rewarded with the ultimate prize.*

Julie went on to describe how Norman Hunter had to return to the touchline after splitting his shorts, how Frank Gray had to go off injured, how David Harvey made a very good save from Gerry's volley, and how, after we had taken the lead, Phil Parkes had to make an excellent save from Duncan McKenzie. Then, she added:

> *Luck had turned, however, for the home side, and in the 82nd minute, McLintock spotted Bowles racing in solitude down the right and reached him with a pass of hair-splitting precision. Bowles collected, controlled and cut inwards with that priceless fluidity of movement; Francis gestured and beckoned, but in vain, for Bowles, choosing his spot, drove left-footed into a distant, billowing corner of the net; breathtaking.*

Needless to say, it was a nice feeling for me to score the last goal of the season at Loftus Road, and I was glad it was a good one.

Meanwhile, Liverpool were busy winning and closing the gap on us. The Reds had to play their last three remaining games against Manchester City, Leeds and Wolves. All things being equal the games against City and Leeds would have been tough matches, but because of Liverpool's European involvement these games had been rearranged for later dates. As it turned out Liverpool ran out very easy winners against Leeds and City. One reason for this was because Leeds' and City's season were over, effectively they had absolutely nothing to play for and this was reflected in their performances.

We then had ten days to wait because Liverpool still had to play Wolves. The BBC put on a special showing of this game, and Gerry and I went along to the studios at Television Centre, Wood Lane, with Ron Phillips. Sheila Marson, Ron's assistant, was also there.

As we walked into the studio, I suddenly realised that all the work we had put into the past year, all the sparkling football we had played, all the twenty-four victories we had earned in the finest season ever seen at Loftus Road, could be wiped out by ninety minutes of football which we had no control over.

We sat there full of apprehension. Were we going to win the title, or get pipped at the post? I knew that if Wolves lost it would be a long time, if ever, before we would get this close again.

We had reached a dramatic point where it was either glory or total disappointment, not only for ourselves but for the fans and everyone connected with Queens Park Rangers. Jim Gregory couldn't stand the suspense, and went on holiday to the south of France in his yacht, asking Ron to ring him with the result.

The players were on a £6,000 bonus, if we won the title. On a lighter note, Ron was hoping that Wolves would win so that I could pay back the £3,000 I owed him at the time. But it was not really about money. Gerry, myself – and all the others – wanted a championship medal.

Wolves were battling against relegation. If Wolves won and Birmingham lost at Sheffield United on the same night, Wolves would stay up.

Wolves took the lead through Steve Kindon, a nippy winger, and they held on until twelve minutes from the end. Then Kevin Keegan equalised. After that, news came through that Birmingham had drawn, so Wolves were down anyway. Wolves lost heart after that, and Liverpool scored two more goals through John Toshack and Ray Kennedy, making it 3–1. Liverpool were champions, and we felt devastated. After 42 games, and the finest league season in the history of Queens Park Rangers, we had missed the league title by only one point. This is how the First Division table looked at the end of a great campaign by QPR:

	Home						Away					
	P	W	D	L	F	A	W	D	L	F	A	Pts
Liverpool	42	14	5	2	41	21	9	9	3	25	10	60
QPR	42	17	4	0	42	13	7	7	7	25	20	59
Manchester United	42	16	4	1	40	13	7	6	8	28	29	56
Derby County	42	15	3	3	45	30	6	8	7	30	28	53
Leeds United	42	13	3	5	37	19	8	6	7	28	27	51
Ipswich Town	42	11	6	4	36	23	5	8	8	18	25	46
Leicester	42	9	9	3	29	14	4	10	7	19	27	45
Manchester City	42	14	5	2	46	18	2	6	13	18	28	43
Tottenham	42	6	10	5	33	32	8	5	8	30	21	43
Norwich City	42	10	5	6	33	26	6	5	10	25	32	42
Everton	42	10	7	4	37	24	5	5	11	23	42	42
Stoke City	42	8	5	8	25	25	7	6	8	23	26	41
Middlesbrough	42	9	7	5	23	11	6	3	12	23	34	40
Coventry	42	6	9	6	22	22	7	5	9	25	35	40
Newcastle	42	11	4	6	51	26	4	5	12	20	36	39
Aston Villa	42	11	8	2	32	17	0	9	12	19	42	39
Arsenal	42	11	4	6	33	19	2	6	13	14	34	36
West Ham	42	10	5	6	26	23	3	5	13	22	48	36
Birmingham	42	11	5	5	36	26	2	2	17	21	49	33
Wolves	42	7	6	8	27	25	3	4	14	24	43	30
Burnley	42	6	6	9	23	26	3	4	14	20	40	28
Sheffield United	42	4	7	10	19	32	2	3	16	14	50	22

To say that it was a sickening anticlimax would be the understatement of the decade. When the game finished, Gerry and I walked out. I asked him if he wanted to come for a drink but he just said 'No'. He was stunned, and so he went home. I went for a drink and drowned my sorrows in Shepherd's Bush, where I knew most of the people in the pubs. I just got very drunk, but that didn't take away the sick, empty feeling in my stomach.

In my view, it was the 0–0 draw at Sheffield United that cost us the championship. Everybody says that the match at Norwich, three games from the end, was the one which lost Rangers that title, but I am quite sure that drawing the Sheffield United game, where a win would have taken us clear of Liverpool at the top of the league, cost us dear. Psychologically, it would have made a world of difference. For Sheffield United, who were by far the worst side in the division that year, to hold us to a draw was unexpected and very damaging.

QPR supporters today still recall the Norwich game bitterly, and reckon that was the match where it all went wrong. They still hold the view that we lost the championship there and that Dave Clement lost it for us, but I don't go along with that. If we had won at Sheffield United, as we should have done, there would have been less pressure on us for the Norwich game, and I'm sure we'd have got a draw at least, which would have been enough.

The consolation was, that as runners-up, we had secured a European place in the UEFA Cup for the following season. Jim Gregory gave me three grand at the end of the season, even after all of our arguments, because he firmly believed that I deserved it. And, what's more, Ron Phillips never saw a penny of it.

An end-of-season trip to Israel had been arranged by QPR in the form of a holiday combined with a friendly match. At the time Hamburg FC were showing a great deal of interest in me, and when I got to the airport I made my mind up that I didn't want to go to Israel.

I'd been through a long season and I really hated flying. I used to have to have a Valium before I could travel. I had thought that it would be only an hour and a half on the plane, and when I found out it was a longer flight I didn't want to go. So I had a big argument with Dave Sexton at the airport. He was also losing his temper with the press and photographers, which wasn't like him at all. Part of the contract for our game with the Israeli national team was that an agreed number of our internationals had to appear.

Dave phoned Jim Gregory and said, 'Stan's not getting on the plane. Will you speak to him?' So I talked to Jim on the phone, and told him I was not flying.

Eventually, Jim came out to the airport from his home near Roehampton, and took me into a little room and said, 'Now, what are you doing? Are you going, or not?' And I said, 'I'm not going,' explaining that I had just realised that this was more a long-haul flight, not a short one. So Jim said, 'All right. Just tell them that you're not going, and pop round to my house this afternoon, and have dinner.' So that's what I did. Of course, because QPR was Jim's club, there was absolutely no comeback on me – it was bliss!

While I was at Rangers I used to get so many fan letters that we had to organise the Stan Bowles Fan Club. I found that I had admirers in eleven countries worldwide. It was the second largest fan club in England – number one was George Best. I always tried to devote as much time as possible to the fans, after all, they and their mums and dads paid my wages. The secretary of the Stan Bowles Fan Club, for the whole time I was there, was Marilyn Demmen. She remembers those days well:

> Stan never let me or the fans down in anything I asked him to do. He would come out of the dressing room immediately after training to meet the fans and have a chat, sign autographs, and present prizes to the fan club competition winners. I would send him large batches of photographs to autograph which was very time-consuming but he treated it as an important task.
>
> We would collect toys during the season and have collections around the ground. During the Christmas period we would take the presents to the sick children at Hammersmith and Charing Cross Hospitals. Stan brought other players such as Don Shanks, John Hollins and Dave Thomas, and would speak on the hospital's radio. We even visited the hospital once as a rodeo team dressed up as cowboys. I used to accompany Stan's children to matches on the terraces at home and away games.
>
> We had a lovely family atmosphere in the fan club. I compiled a periodic newsletter for the fans and Stan would include a message, usually about football and his family. The fans adored him.

I always used to write a bit in the newsletter. Here's an example of the kind of thing that used to go in there:

> *Hello again,*
> *Where is 1978 going to? We are already a quarter of the way through it and the end of the football season is getting nearer and nearer. The only part of that I like is the first month or so when I'm glad of the rest, but after that I get very restless and can't wait to get my boots back on.*
>
> *Aren't we doing well in the FA Cup this year? We really shut up the Rangers critics when we beat West Ham 6–1 as they had written us off right from the start. If we can get a result from Nottingham Forest in the next round that will really give them something to think about. You never know we may find our way to Wembley yet.*
>
> *As long as Rangers can keep putting a regular team out as we have done in the last few weeks and keep getting results, I can't see any way that Rangers can go down this season especially with the support we have been getting these last few home and away matches. Keep up the good*

work, but don't just cheer when we are a goal up, cheer right from the kick-off to the final whistle as this gives the team a boost.

I expect a lot of you have seen my son Carl at the Rangers home games. As I said in earlier letters it would not be long before he joined Andrea and Tracy. He's still a bit fidgety though but he does enjoy coming, I think mostly for the drink and sweets!

He's really proud of the tracksuit he received from you all and loves to wear it everywhere, even to school. I expect you have seen him in it, it's just like the team's with his full name across the back. You couldn't have given him anything better!

My family have now settled down well in our new home in Neasden and the three kids seem to like their new school. We have once again got a new dog and this time we hope to be able to keep her. Her name is Penny and she's a real nutter.

I know Marilyn has already thanked you for the toy donations at Christmas, but on behalf of myself and John Hollins, I would also like to thank you. It really was a lovely surprise to see the amount you had given and great to see the expressions on the kids' faces when they opened their gifts. You not only made John's and my trip worthwhile, but you gave something to those kids to help them on the road to recovery.

While on the subject of Christmas I must take this opportunity to thank you all for the lovely cards and gifts you so kindly sent to all my family, plus remembering my birthday on Christmas Eve and Tracy's on the 1st of February. Marilyn gave me, on your behalf, a hair dryer for my birthday and a radio cassette player for Christmas. I don't know how she works out what to buy me but it's always something I need or want.

Well I think that's all for now. For those of you going on holiday, have a nice time and enjoy yourselves.

Bye for now,

Stan.

A few weeks after the end of the season, I was put on standby for the *Superstars* competition. This was quite popular on the TV at the time, a sporty light entertainment series in which BBC viewers could enjoy the novelty of seeing famous athletes compete against each other in sports other than their speciality. The show was watched by an average of fourteen million people in 1976 in the UK, and the total audience worldwide reached over 300 million. If you made a fool of yourself on this show you did so in front of an awful lot of people. The competitors took part in shooting, swimming and weightlifting, among other things.

I let Donald talk me into it, and he masqueraded as my manager, as well as being in charge of my training ... such as it was.

The woman from the BBC advanced me five hundred quid, and I also managed to get £500 off Ron Phillips – I told him the BBC wouldn't give me an advance! So, I've had this cash about a week before the event, and the majority of it soon dribbled its way – with annoying predictability – inside of a bookie's satchel at White City, meeting up with other money that formerly belonged to me. So now I don't want to do the show. Shanks decides that the best way to go about it is to pop up to their offices in Askew Road, and try and get the other half of the fee off them. I'm in the car outside, while Don, in his role as 'manager', goes to do the business.

Once he's in the office, Don launches into his best spiel.

'Well,' says the woman from the BBC, 'can you guarantee that he'll be there?'

'One hundred per cent!' he said, lying through his teeth. 'I guarantee he'll be there. For another £500, I can definitely guarantee that.'

'Are you sure?' she said.

'Yes, you have my word,' said Shanks, solemnly. 'Stan is a professional.'

'That's a big relief,' she said. 'Because people were telling us that he's unreliable and he might not show up, and being on television and everything ... it's very important.'

'Don't you worry. I shall drag him there personally with my bare hands, if I have to.'

So she parts with the £500, and Don comes back to the car, waving the money in front of me. We both start cheering, 'Off we go, we've done 'em again!'

Anyway, the end result is it's Saturday night and we're at the White City dogs. It's 10.05 p.m. and the last race has just finished. We've got about three quid between us and we're going nowhere.

The following day we're supposed to be at the competitors' hotel in Aldershot. But we've got no car and there's no way we can get there.

'I'm not going,' says I.

'Whatever happens, I'll get us a car,' Don replies. 'I'll also get us £300 when we arrive.'

'How you gonna do that?'

'Just leave it to me, I'll do it. Just say yes.'

'Go on then, you get a car, and come and pick me up.'

Don heads off to see a friend of his who's got a café. The guy's got an old, beat-up Marina, which he lends to Don. It was so old the speedometer was probably in Roman numerals. About half eleven he arrives to pick me up, but I definitely didn't want to go. We argue for a while, we've got to be there by lunchtime, and already it's one o'clock.

'C'mon, I'll get us some readies when we get there,' says Don. God knows how, he'd even had to borrow a tenner to put petrol in the tank.

So we drove down to Aldershot in this pile of crap, and pulled into the hotel car park – thick black smoke spewing out of the exhaust. There are Ferraris there; James Hunt's got his car there; John Conteh's got a Roller; and here's Stan Bowles in a beat-up Marina! We're like the Beverly Hillbillies. So we parked it as far as possible from the reception area, and backed it up so that it didn't look too bad. We walked over, and the BBC bird comes flying out.

'Oh, thank God you're here. I got so, so worried!'

We both look at her. 'We're very lucky to be alive,' says Don.

'Oh dear, what happened?' she asks, genuinely concerned.

Don launches into a huge explanation – every word of it a lie!

'Well,' he says, 'I've gone to pick up Stanley, and gone round Shepherd's Bush Green – I don't know if you're familiar with that area – but, anyway, a United Dairies milk lorry has come straight at me, and I've gone through a shop window in my Jaguar. My brand-new Jag is a complete write-off. Can you believe it? I've had to rent this car for £300 and I just don't know what's going to happen next.'

'Oh, my God,' says the woman, really shocked, 'I'm so terribly, terribly sorry. Let me get you the £300 right away. I'm sure you'll feel better when you get changed and have a rest.' And off she scurries.

So we go into the hotel and they start kitting me out for the events. I've got to get the tracksuit, the swimming trunks, and all the necessary T-shirts.

'Look,' says Don, 'I have to train him, so you've got to give me the same.'

'Well, we have only a limited number,' they said, a bit doubtfully.

But Don is insistent, 'No, look,' he says, 'I'm his manager and I've got to have him out early in the morning, training, so I need the gear.' In the end they give in and we both get kitted out as proper competitors.

It's early evening, and we're meeting the other sporting 'heroes' for dinner – all megastars in their own right. We're sitting there and you've never seen so many people so serious about an event in your life. There's me and Don drinking pints of lager, bottles of wine, smoking cigars and anything that we can grab to eat – like it's our last day on

Earth. One by one they're all leaving, having nibbled on a cucumber sandwich and sipped a glass of mineral water. They're nearly all tucked up in bed by ten o'clock; but not Don and me, we're drinking large brandies till one o'clock in the morning and we're the only two people left in the room. We can hardly stand up – empty bottles all over the place, ashtrays overflowing. We're a two-man pissed-up tornado!

James Hunt had stayed for a while; he was a nice guy and we had a laugh together. Malcolm Macdonald was there as well. Don had played with him at Fulham and Luton, and he was a good mate of his, but I, of course, hated him.

The other assembled competitors included David Hemery, Jonah Barrington, J.P.R. Williams, Gareth Edwards and Brian Jacks. Brian was staying in the same hotel but was appearing in a later show. He went on to complete somewhere in the region of 50,000 dips on the parallel bars. Brian couldn't believe I wasn't taking the competition seriously and made several sneering comments in my direction. I didn't appreciate his remarks and I remember thinking that if he made his name in another sport – say as a jockey for instance – instead of being a British judo champion, I would have most definitely have had stern words with him and quite possibly punched him in the face.

At what seemed like five in the morning, we started the events. We had hangovers the size of Wembley Stadium. It was soon evident that Don hadn't really trained me as well as he should have done. The first event was the swimming and I can't even swim! Don had said, 'Oh yes, Stanley swam all the time in Australia.'

I don't know why he said that because I didn't even do a length. I doggy-paddled two metres in an extremely tight-fitting pair of black speedos. I stopped and was holding on to the bar, and my manager says, 'Obviously, something has gone wrong, he must have got some chlorine in his eyes or something like that.'

The lady sighed, and said, 'Oh, well it does happen. No problem.'

So I finished last of the four. Not a good start – and it gets worse!

The next event was the weightlifting so we go into the gym. I slide under a bar with weights attached to either end, take a deep breath and then for all my worth push upward. After seven or eight seconds I am slightly perturbed to notice that the bar hasn't budged.

The woman in charge runs over to Don. 'What's happened?' she asks, worried and a bit annoyed at the same time.

'Oh my God, he might be injured,' says Don. 'I didn't really train him for this, I was too concerned about his old back problem.'

145

'Oh, I do hope that he is all right,' she says – not for the last time.

That's it. I have to pull out of the weightlifting. Two down, five to go.

Next event was on the river: the fast canoeing. You just get pushed out and go as fast as you possibly can. Don is acting like my cox – not in the boat, but on the bank. There's about a thousand people there watching the event. I'm such a lucky fella in life that I've drawn gate four, which is on the outside, right next to the safety boat. As soon as the canoes are on their way the safety boat follows, accompanied by waves about three foot high. I'm in the nearest canoe, and I've only gone about twenty yards when one of these waves engulfs me and under I go. The only satisfaction gleaned from this event occurred just before I sank: Malcolm Macdonald was also struggling badly in second last spot. He had the temerity to turn around and laugh at me shouting, 'You're not very good at this are you, Stan?'

The current then unexpectedly forced my craft into his canoe causing us both to capsize. We bobbed up and down helplessly in our life jackets until the safety boat picked us up.

Don's up on the bank, laughing his head off, he thinks it's the funniest thing he's ever seen. I've swallowed half the river, am wringing wet, and can't really see the funny side of it. I'm in the river, bobbing about in my life jacket, and someone shouts, 'You all right, Stan?'

'Yeah,' I reply, 'I done well in the swimming, so I thought I'd swim every bleeding event!'

I dried out just in time for the next event which was tennis and I've been drawn to play J.P.R. Williams, who happened to be an ex-junior Wimbledon champion. I thought I was quite handy at this game having once had a couple of hours' coaching at a tennis club, and thought that this probably ranked me somewhere inside the British top ten. But I had no chance whatsoever; I don't think I even saw the ball. The match lasted a very short time: six love, six love, best of three – all over in the blink of an eye. My points tally is not improving very much, and I'm so far behind, the others have almost forgotten I'm still there.

Then it was the 100 yards dash – something I can actually do, even with a hangover, but I finish about fifth or sixth. Most of the competitors pulled out of this event with hamstring injuries. Unfortunately I was better over twenty metres than a hundred metres. Malcolm 'Supermac' Macdonald, who had just moved from Newcastle to Arsenal that summer for £333,000 won by a street in around eleven seconds.

Next event was the shooting. For some unknown reason, I played my joker in the shooting – which meant I'd get double points. Unfortunately, double nothing is still bugger-all.

The shooting proved to be a 24-carat gold nightmare. It all sounded so simple to start with; all you had to do was point a gun at a bloody big dartboard and fire. I'd seen John Wayne and Jack Palance do that kind of thing loads of times, and outlaws didn't even have a great big bull's-eye in the centre of them. The only problem was that no one told me that guns have a mind of their own.

It was like a scene from a horror film. The army instructor was as hard as nails, he could kill a bloke from two hundred paces, just by gobbing on him. He was strutting about like a peacock on heat, barking out his instructions. He'd done this thing loads of times – shown amateur dickheads what to do – but he hadn't come across the likes of me before! Everything had gone okay in rehearsals, even though I hadn't actually hit anything. But for the real thing – and I mean the real thing, we were using live ammunition – I was a bit on the nervous side.

The gun was on the table. Each time you had to raise it, fire and return it. Which sounds simple enough; except when the gun's got a hair trigger and you've got sweaty hands. I pick it up and the thing goes off. I've shot something, thankfully it's only the table. When the gun went off, the instructor legged it, and everyone else scattered – competitors, spectators and, quickest of all, Don Shanks. Everyone was laughing, but it was what you might call 'nervous' laughter. The table only had a little hole on the top of it, but if you looked underneath it was a right mess. There was a huge dark crater there, and I'm thinking, Shit, that could have been me. Everyone else is thinking it could've been them.

My second and third shots were at least aimed in the general direction of the target; although I didn't hit the protective wall, let alone the target itself. After the first shot the instructor disappeared and wasn't seen again. They never found the other two bullets either; they're probably still heading for Mars, even now! The last event was the steeplechase. Like many of the horses I backed, I quickly tailed off, although I did have the satisfaction of beating Malcolm Macdonald into last place.

The funniest thing about the whole affair was that the woman in charge, by this time, can't believe how bad I am – she just can't believe it. She probably thought, Mmm, well I can understand the swimming, a lot of people don't like that. The weightlifting, well it's possible you can put your back out. Tennis? He got obliterated by an excellent player. But as for running, canoeing and shooting – give me a break – this guy is one big embarrassment.

'I can tell you,' Don said to her, 'this has been one big experience.'

'You can say that again,' she said.

'I'll make sure that he is trained to the peak of perfection next year,' said Mr Donald.

She shook her head. 'Next year?' she said in horror. 'Next bloody year? There won't be a next year for you two ... goodbye, gentlemen!'

And that was the end of that little episode. I still hold the record for the lowest points ever recorded on *Superstars*. I scored a miserable seven points out of a possible eighty! I'm quite proud of that, really; though now I come to think of it, I should have shot Donald instead of the table.

David Hemery, a right miserable sod, who wouldn't give you the time of day if he were handcuffed to Big Ben, won the competition. At the award ceremony, Hemery was presented with a large ceremonial sword by the sponsors, the function and usability of which was unclear.

Mind you, there was a little piece about me in the paper a few days later, and that made me feel a little bit better. In an article headlined 'How to Stifle a Superstar' in the *Daily Mail*, Brian James wrote that he'd seen me juggling a football and it put the whole *Superstars* thing into perspective for him:

> *Bowles, a shy and gentle man, had seemed overshadowed by the big men and bigger personalities around him until then. Suddenly, he came alive, his skills gave him an instant new dimension.*
>
> *The penny dropped. Here, at last, was someone doing something at which he was supernaturally GREAT – not merely bumblingly GOOD. It was the lack of simple excellence that had been making this curious contest so dull.*

I'm bloody glad I didn't shoot Brian James!

The programme aired on 10 November 1976, and my performance, or lack of, is still talked about today. Quite recently I was asked to attend the new series of the event as a 'blast from the past'. Understandably, I expect my clip to be shown again, with me the clown in the *Superstars* circus but I'm not bothered.

They weighed me out another appearance fee, which I guess I'd never have got if I had come second last. I heard David Vine interviewed on the radio recently. He brought a smile to my face when the bespectacled presenter was asked who the best ever *Superstars* competitor was. Apparently, 'It was too difficult to call who was the best; David Hemery and Brian Jacks were up there, but, without doubt, Stanley Bowles was the worst ever competitor to feature on the show.'

Jim Gregory decided, eventually, to offer me a six-year contract; after I had turned down SV Hamburg. I was twenty-eight, and agreed to sign. I didn't even bother to look at it, because Jim had promised to look after me, and I knew he would. This contract, effectively, would have kept me at QPR until the end of my career, which suited me fine.

By midsummer, I had taken up with an actress called Jane Hayden. My marriage was on the rocks, and I met Jane at the dog track. She was with a friend of mine, Robin Askwith, the actor who starred in such films as the *Confessions* series (I'll talk more about him later). Robin was going out with her sister Linda, and Jane and I got on really well from the start. Linda Hayden, also an actress, was in several of the *Confessions* films and later married Paul Elliott, who produced the *Buddy* musical in the West End, and also *Run For Your Wife*, a stage spin-off from the *Confessions* films.

During the time that Jane was living with me, Ann came down from Manchester and caught us together in the flat. They had a major row, and I just went out and left them to it. I went and stayed somewhere else for the night and that, effectively, was the end of my marriage to Ann. It's funny that I met Jane – who became my second wife – at the White City dog track, but I suppose that's fate. Mind you, I spent so much time at the dogs that I wouldn't have had a chance to meet her anywhere else. The only other possibility would have been if she'd been a First Division full-back – then she would have only seen my back!

Chapter 12 •

The UEFA Cup –
A Bouquet of Barbed Wire

The 1976–77 season was about to start and Queens Park Rangers were in European competition for the first time in their history.

The four English representatives in the UEFA Cup were QPR, Derby, Manchester United and Manchester City; while Southampton – who had beaten Manchester United in the FA Cup final – were in the Cup Winners' Cup along with teams like Marseille, Hamburg and Anderlecht. Champions Liverpool were, of course, in the European Cup.

There were some tasty looking foreign teams in the UEFA Cup: three times European Cup winners Ajax; Juventus, who had most of the Italian national team in their side; Barcelona, with star man Johann Cruyff; Porto, and top German clubs such as Schalke 04 and Cologne.

Our league campaign opened badly. In August, we lost 4–0 to Everton at home, and 1–0 to West Ham at Upton Park. After that things picked up, as we drew at Ipswich, and beat two Midland clubs, West Brom and Aston Villa, at Loftus Road.

We knew that we would be playing more games than we had ever played in one season. Since we had only a small squad it was going to be difficult if we were hit by any major injuries to key players. Dave Sexton was naturally worried about this. We were a relatively small club, with limited resources, compared to some of the heavyweights we might have to play. Europe was an exciting prospect, a great challenge for us; but the further we went in Europe, the more our slender squad was going to be stretched to breaking point. It was a real concern.

September would be a big month for us because in addition to our league fixtures we were also scheduled to play the first rounds of the League Cup, and the UEFA Cup competition. We thought that we might have an outside chance of challenging again for the league title, but some players were now getting on a bit; Frank McLintock and Webby being prime examples. The feeling was that we definitely lost our best chance of championship success in the previous season. I think, to a certain extent, Dave Sexton had accepted this fact. On the positive side, Dave was very excited about playing in Europe, because he was a great admirer of European teams, especially, as I said, the German sides.

We were drawn against Cardiff in the first round of the League Cup on 1 September 1976 at Ninian Park. It turned out to be quite an easy game for us as we went 3–0 up fairly quickly, so it became a bit of a stroll. After this victory our form in the league improved dramatically, and we won three of our next four games.

The night of 15 September was when a little bit of history came to Loftus Road. We played the first leg of our UEFA Cup campaign against SK Brann of Bergen. They were Norwegian part-timers, and the home crowd of just under 15,000 reflected this. We were expected to go through to the next round with no problem at all. We were happy that we had missed the big sides – Ajax, Juventus and Cologne, in the first-round draw – and looked on this game as a perfect introduction into European football.

I hadn't scored a goal in the league in our first five matches, but felt that the European scene would be tailor-made for me to show the type of skill that everyone knew I possessed. I was also intent on turning on a bit of a show for my friend George Best, who, to mark the occasion, had come down from Manchester – where he was based – to watch the match. We strolled to a first leg 4–0 victory. I scored a hat-trick; oddly enough, none of the goals came from my left foot. The press were saying that the Stanley Bowles show was on the road again. I was happy to agree with their assessment.

The following week we successfully negotiated our passage into the third round of the League Cup by dispatching Bury 2–1 at the Bush. We were now in a strong position: improved league form and easy wins in two cup competitions. Dave, who had studied the European sides, reckoned we only had a couple of teams to worry about, so everything in the home camp was going well. We were full of optimism, and it showed in the way we were playing.

I was really hungry for goals now, and during our next game at home to Stoke, a 2–0 win, I scored what was probably the best goal of my career. I picked up the ball deep, beat three players, then sent Peter Shilton the wrong way. At the time, Shilton was regarded as the best goalkeeper in England, but he had no chance with that one. It might have been goal of the season, but the game wasn't televised. James

Mossop wrote: 'It was Stan in one of those vintage flashes, when instinct, speed and skill are fused together to produce sheer magic.'

It must have been a little bit special because both Dave Sexton and Tony Waddington praised me in the papers. They said that I went past Tony Bloor like he was a tailor's dummy. I never scored another goal that could rival that one. Renowned for my theatrical gestures, I actually conducted the applause from the crowd after scoring. You could do this quite happily in those days. The referees weren't like they are today, getting you away from the crowd as soon as possible to discourage any trouble. They'd turn a blind eye and have a bit of a smile.

Tony Roche said in the *Sunday Mirror*: 'The maestro of Shepherd's Bush conducts his own applause from Rangers fans. Next he'll be wanting a transfer to the Albert Hall.' I conducted the crowd for quite a while, milking it for as long as I could. I felt that I was playing really well at this stage in my career, and when I was in this mood I genuinely felt that nobody could stop me.

In the second leg against SK Brann we turned on a superb exhibition of football, played the Norwegians off the field, and won 7–0 over there. Looking back on it, although I scored another hat-trick – a bit of a rarity in European football – I could have scored six or seven if I hadn't been a bit too flash. A statistician told me that the British record for goals scored in a European competition was only ten. Since I'd scored six in two games, everyone in the camp thought that the record was definitely on. In league and cup matches I had, by this time, scored eight in eleven games, and the way I was playing I felt that there were plenty more to come.

Things were looking really bright, but, as often happens in football, we were soon sent crashing back to earth. The bubble burst when we played Arsenal at Highbury. Although Frank McLintock scored yet again against his old club – reminding them that they had sold him too soon – we went down 3–2. We then played Norwich at Loftus Road, and lost by the same scoreline. For us to concede six goals in two games was unusual, and very worrying. Dave decided that he needed to plug the holes in our defence, and we worked hard to right this sudden inadequacy in our play.

The scene was set for a trip to Maine Road, which was only the second time that I had been back to Manchester with QPR. I remember this game particularly because it was a really frosty day, and Joe Corrigan had one of his spectacular matches. We had tightened up our defence and, after those two defeats, were quite pleased to come away with a goalless draw. The City crowd were always good to me, being a local boy. I know quite a few of the supporters, and have never experienced any animosity up there.

After that it was back to European action. We travelled to Czechoslovakia to play Slovan Bratislava in the second round of the UEFA Cup. The main thing I remember about Bratislava is that it is a very cold place indeed – even colder than Carlisle! Slovan had been Czech champions in 1974 and 1975, were runners up in 1976 and, at that time, they had half the Czech national side in their team. Ondrus, the big defender, and Masny, a very skilful striker, were two of the finest players in the world at that time.

Czechoslovakia had knocked England out of the European Nations Cup the previous season. Gerry Francis and our left-back Ian Gillard had played for England in Bratislava that November, when the Czechs won 2–1, with Mick Channon scoring England's goal.

The Czechs had beaten an excellent Holland team 3–0 in the semi-final of the European Nations Cup, and played West Germany in the final in Belgrade in June, drawing 2–2 after extra-time. They won the penalty shoot-out after Uli Hoeness had sent his spot-kick into outer space. So Czech morale was sky high in 1976 and Slovan, who were experienced European campaigners, had to fancy their chances against a little club from west London who were almost European virgins.

In the European Cup, Liverpool were playing in Turkey against Trabzonspor, and Southampton were visiting Carrick Rangers in Northern Ireland in the Cup Winners' Cup. Most of the media attention was focused on QPR and the other tasty tie: Manchester United at home to Juventus.

In *The Times*, the interestingly named Norman de Mesquita was obviously looking forward to a fascinating contest. He wrote:

For two Rangers players there is a personal score to settle. Gillard's last game for England was in the same Slovan Stadium where he received much of the blame for the defeat by Czechoslovakia and Masny created havoc down the right flank. Gillard feels that much of the criticism was unfair and is looking forward to facing Masny again.

Masson played in the Scotland team beaten in Prague only last week and the opposition included five Slovan players, notably the captain, Ondrus, who was sent off after an incident with Gray. Masson says the

Czechs did not impress him greatly and he will be disappointed if Rangers do not achieve at least a draw.

As it turned out, the match was a classic. We had to come from behind and score three goals to get a 3–3 draw. I scored twice, and also hit the post, so I wasn't far off scoring three consecutive hat-tricks in the UEFA Cup. I was naturally delighted to have scored eight goals in my first three European games.

There was no doubt that Slovan were shocked by just how good we were. They had 40,000-plus hysterical supporters in the ground, had previously won every match that season, and had never looked in trouble in the game; but by the end, they were hanging on. This six-goal thriller was an excellent advertisement for English football, and our performance did a great deal to restore the reputation of English teams abroad. Frank McLintock told the press that it was the best we had played in the three years that he had been at Rangers.

Frank recalls, 'It was a fabulous match. I remember that their coach said we were more Continental than a Continental side.'

After my two-goal contribution, I was now beginning to think seriously about the goalscoring record.

We knew that the tie at Loftus Road, being a small ground where the crowd seemed to be right on top of the players, would not suit Slovan at all. Also, the Czechs were renowned as bad travellers. Away goals counted double in these matches, so they would need to get a 3–3 draw at least to survive. We looked forward to the second leg in London, in conditions that would be a lot warmer than an October night in Bratislava, where we had almost frozen to death.

I always maintained that I could trouble Continental defenders – even the Germans and Italians. They didn't know how to handle forwards who brought the ball up to them – they would just dive in. At first, even the Czechs marked me tight, but then they dropped back, giving me more space. I reckon that was a self-destructive move against my style of play. I was hoping that Don Revie was taking this into account after our showing against Slovan had been publicly ranked alongside Manchester United against Benfica in 1966, and Spurs against Milan in 1972.

We followed this performance with a league game against Sunderland, who had just lost their manager, Bob Stokoe. The acting manager was Ian MacFarlane, the former Carlisle boss who had sold me to QPR five years earlier, but we were still very good friends.

I think I was the last person that Ian wanted to bump into his first game on trial for the Sunderland managership. We beat the Mackems 2–0, and after the game Ian came into our dressing room, walked up to me and punched me in the ribs. My team-mates all lunged forward, ready to pounce, not realising that this was Ian's way of saying hello. I had to quickly explain that it was a private joke.

Ian told the press, 'I must be Stan's number one fan. He has as much skill as Rodney Marsh and a more committed attitude over ninety minutes. I'm sure, if he keeps at it, Don Revie will give him the chance he deserves in the England team.'

Gerry Francis's ambition was that we would both play for England together, and he also went public, saying, 'If I were picking the England team, I would have Stan in the side for the World Cup game in Italy, next month.'

Against Sunderland I scored a goal after picking the ball up on the halfway line. I beat a player, and made out that I was going to score with my left foot, and when he dived in I slotted the ball into the corner with my right foot. Even if I didn't score in some games, I could always be relied upon to do something out of the ordinary that would excite the crowd. That goal still gets an airing on TV to this day.

We then went to West Ham for the fourth round of the League Cup. They weren't the same side as they had been in previous seasons, so we expected to win. Billy Bonds was given the task of marking me, and Billy wasn't very subtle at the best of times. He got booked after only six minutes, and I'm surprised it took that long. Then Keith Robson had a go at me, and he was booked as well. Keith was a fiery player but didn't really have the talent to go with it, and he made a few reckless challenges on me. West Ham were trying to stop me any way they could.

I have to admit that I sometimes used to get free-kicks using a trick where I tripped myself up. The referee wouldn't be able to see it because it was always done side-on. This was a trick that Rodney Marsh had taught me, and I had perfected it. If you managed to do it right, it looked as though you had been cut in half. By this time a lot of players were getting booked because of tackles on me. Some didn't deserve it, but most of them were guilty.

We had a pretty comfortable 2–0 win against a poor West Ham side. Over the years I played against them I had never really rated them; they were a very average team. This victory took us through to the quarter-finals, and I increased my goal tally to twelve in sixteen games.

Don Revie attended the game. I think the press were surprised by how I kept my temper from boiling over with so many heavy and clumsy challenges being made on me. They were saying that I now had the right temperament to face the Italians.

I wasn't the only player who suffered at Upton Park. Dave Thomas was carried off in the first few seconds. The injury came about as a result of a move we had been practising in training. When we used to go pre-season training in Germany, Dave Sexton had this idea which would put the opposition under pressure right from the kick-off. Don Givens would tap the ball to me and I would pass it back to David Webb, who would immediately launch a forty-yard ball towards the far corner flag. The plan was that Dave Thomas was supposed to hare up the line and put the opposition full-back under pressure. In a pre-season game against Borussia Moenchengladbach, we used the ploy: Don passed it to me, back to Webby, forty-yard ball up the line, and immediately the full-back crashed into him and Dave's jaw was fractured in two places!

So when Dave came back to the team after his jaw had healed, we had suffered a couple of bad results. I said, 'Look Dave, son, you have heard that we are going back to the old routine whereby Don knocks it to me, and you run up the line as fast as you can.'

He said, 'You can fucking leave me out of that! If you're going to do that, you chase it up the fucking line yourself!' – Dave was quite an excitable character – 'The last time I done that the old jaw was smashed in two places!'

Anyway Dave Sexton abandoned that particular move in the end, but at West Ham the move happened without even thinking about it, and Dave Thomas, not being the brightest of players, just chased the ball. He probably remembered halfway down the right wing, but by then it was too late – he went crashing into Frank Lampard. We thought that he had broken his leg, but it was later confirmed that he had suffered a nerve spasm in a thigh muscle. Quite a few spectators, including Don Revie, were still making their way to their seats when this incident happened.

Dave Thomas's nickname was 'Ticer'. This was after his grandfather, a cricketer who, apparently, used to 'tice' the ball; meaning he 'enticed' it. None the wiser? Neither am I!

Anyway, Frank McLintock ran up to him, turned him over and said, 'C'mon Ticer, get up!' But there was no way he was going to move. He was carried off on a stretcher, and Eddie Kelly came on as a sub. Kelly, a Scottish midfield player, had joined us from Arsenal in the summer, and played a lot of games that season while Gerry Francis was out with a back injury.

Don Revie was about to announce the England squad to play Italy in a vital World Cup game. There were quite a few names being bandied about as possible strikers, but the main focus of media attention was Trevor Francis and myself.

In the *Daily Mirror*, under the headline, BOWLES IS A MUST FOR ROME, Harry Miller wrote: 'Stan Bowles, the most skilful player in the country, must be part of the action when England resume World Cup hostilities in Rome next month. There is too much at stake to overlook his outstanding ability yet again. Inevitably, there are those who will question the temperament of the QPR striker to cope with the torrid and intimidating atmosphere that will be generated by the Italians. But England's failure to demolish the Finns in Wednesday's stumbling 2–1 win has made the gamble one worth taking.'

On the Saturday before the squad was to be selected, we had a league game against Birmingham City at St Andrews and the press built it up as a shoot out between Trevor and myself for the remaining England place. I had, however, already been informed by our club secretary that I was in the England squad, so all this High Noon stuff didn't bother me at all.

I had the backing of the managers and England players alike, including Trevor Brooking, who joined the growing chorus of stars supporting my recall. He was comparing my finishing with that of Jimmy Greaves, one of England's greatest goalscorers. Don Revie was under pressure to introduce fresh blood into the side after the previous international, that unimpressive 2–1 win over Finland at Wembley. When the squad of twenty-six players was announced, Revie had chosen Brian Talbot of Ipswich, and myself, as the new boys. If selected, it would be my fourth cap for England after eighteen months in the wilderness.

Two days after the announcement we played the second leg of our UEFA Cup tie against Slovan. I was one goal short of equalling the European goalscoring record set by one of my idols – Denis Law, for Manchester United. We had already found out that the Czechs could score goals, so it was going to be an exciting night at Loftus Road.

We beat Slovan 5–2, but didn't win as easily as the scoreline suggests. The match could have gone either way, and Phil Parkes was voted man-of-the-match after pulling off a string of spectacular saves. In the thirty-seventh minute I equalled the scoring record, and the chants of 'Easy, Easy' were echoing around the ground. QPR had now amassed nineteen goals in four games in this competition; an incredible tally, especially as we had been playing all season without the injured Gerry Francis, who didn't come back until February.

In the *Sun*, Bob Driscoll described how Don Givens had scored from a long pass by Don Masson in the nineteenth minute; how Ian Gillard had shackled Masny; and how Givens had made it 2–0 in just over half an hour.

Driscoll continued:

> ... *We knew it would not be long before Bowles got into the scoring act. And three minutes later he rose unchallenged to head Rangers third, and his record ninth of the tournament. The second half was only six minutes old when Bowles glided past Nezhyba and raced into the box. He seemed to stumble as the defender chased but a penalty was given. And that gave Givens the deserved opportunity to complete his hat-trick ... But with two minutes to go another piece of Bowles magic set up the chance for full-back Dave Clement to make it five at the second attempt.*

On the same night Manchester United were beaten 3–0 by Juventus in Turin and went out 3–1 on aggregate, while Derby, at home to AEK Athens, scored twice through Charlie George and Bruce Rioch, but were beaten 3–2, losing 5–2 on aggregate. So QPR were now the only surviving British club in the UEFA Cup.

Around this time I had to attend Willesden Court to answer my wife's claim for maintenance payments. Being me, I'd pretty much ignored what had gone on before, so I was heavily in arrears, simply because I hadn't been turning up for the hearings, and summonses had been issued. It had reached the stage that if I failed to appear, I would be in trouble. If I didn't attend, a warrant would be issued for my arrest – then the shit would really hit the fan. I was not legally represented, though Ron Phillips had offered me legal advice through the club. I arrived at the court and started talking to a very attractive lady clerk. I was – honestly – asking for some legal advice, but she suggested that we go over to the pub for a drink. She said she would explain the situation, and advise me what my options were. Fair enough, I thought and off we went.

So I had a few drinks with this glamorous clerk – who looked more like a model than a court employee – and I was being offered plenty of advice and, as it turned out, a lot more as well. So, all of a sudden, I had my wife Ann trying to divorce me and claim maintenance; Jane – the girl I was living with – on at me to marry her, and now I had this clerk of the court in bed, urging me to leave both of them! Ironic, isn't it? I had spent months trying to stay out of court, and now I couldn't keep away from the place! My life has always been like that – a roller-coaster ride with no one operating the controls.

In the meantime, the Italians were so worried about me, that they were considering restructuring their team. Their manager, Enzio Bearzot, was really upset about me playing, and planned to include Gentile of Juventus – the Italian tough guy – in his squad to do a 'hatchet job' on me. In Italian, 'gentile' means kind and polite, so they got that one wrong then! It seemed as if they were more worried about me than Kevin Keegan or any of the English forwards.

Unfortunately, I picked up a flu bug, and was unable to report to Hertfordshire with the squad five days before the game. I was kept in bed for three days, and this played havoc with Don Revie's plans. It meant he had to delay naming the side, and my thoughts went back to a year before when I had to relinquish my place in the England team against Portugal because of a groin strain. I was praying that Don would wait a few days until I had recovered sufficiently to join the squad.

On the Saturday night prior to the game on Wednesday, I had a phone call from Don. He said that if I could get myself out of bed, I would definitely be playing in the match. I didn't need to be asked twice, so I got myself up – although I was still feeling very shaky – and went to join the squad. Don sent me straight to bed when I got to the hotel to keep me quarantined from the rest of the squad. That suited me down to the ground, because they were playing bingo at the time! They used to play stupid games like carpet bowls and table tennis to relax, definitely not my cup of tea.

On the day of the match, a headline in *The Times* read: SIGNS ARE THAT BOWLES WILL BE SENT INTO ROME'S ARENA OF FIRE. Norman Fox reported that while Don Revie may have brought me into the squad as an afterthought – or by public demand – he had probably not been too impressed by Stuart Pearson's performance for Manchester United in the two games against Juventus.

Fox wrote: 'The argument in favour of including Bowles, if only as a substitute, is that the Italians know him only by reputation. Also, as Mr Revie keeps insisting, England go to Rome as underdogs. If they manage to have some success in defensive tactics, Bowles is the ideal, skilful forward able to penetrate the Italian penalty area on his own. In two respects, then, he could be the crucial element of surprise, both in his selection and manner of play.'

The posh papers had given QPR a lot of credit for our European exploits so far, and the *Guardian* headline as we flew out to Rome was: CLEMENT GIVES LINK TO BOWLES – whatever that means! In his article, David Lacey suggested that Don Revie had been influenced by my performances against Ondrus and the rest of the Slovan Bratislava defence, and quoted Revie as saying, 'Bowles has played exceptionally well for QPR last season – and this season – and nobody has doubted his tremendous ability. I hope he plays as well for us as he does for QPR.'

In the same piece, Lacey wrote: 'The presence of Clement, who played against Italy in New York in the American Bicentennial Cup, could be important here. So often, Clement comes into the attack for QPR, sending Bowles wide on the right and moving inside for a return. But obviously his more important role in Rome will be to guard against the late runs by Bettega, who has a knack of coming in on the blind side for far post balls from Causio.'

Clearly, this World Cup qualifier was a very big game for both sides. It was as good as a group decider, as both of us had comfortably seen off Finland and Luxembourg – the other two teams in the group. Only one team from the group would qualify for the finals in Argentina, so there would be no prisoners taken. The Italians had only been beaten twice at home in fifteen years. The venue was the historic Olympic Stadium in Rome, where Cassius Clay, as he was known at the time, had become Olympic boxing champion in 1960.

When the squad arrived at the hotel we were told that we would have to remain in the hotel complex. We wouldn't be allowed out to take in the scenery, or roam around the streets because the Italian fans would probably try to lynch us. We arrived the day before the game, so there wasn't much time to acclimatise, but we were ready to do the job. We were confident and not overawed in any way. The team was a good one – an excellent mix of skill, experience and determination. If you look at the line-up, I think you'll agree: Ray Clemence, Dave Clement, Mick Mills, Brian Greenhoff, Roy MacFarland, Emlyn Hughes, Trevor Cherry, Trevor Brooking, Kevin Keegan, Stan Bowles and Mick Channon. Of them all, the player I most respected was Keegan. For an average footballer, he made the maximum use of his capabilities, and continued to do so for many years.

It seemed as if the whole of Rome had closed down for the game, and we arrived at the Olympic Stadium with our police escort several hours before the kick-off. The stadium was surrounded by a moat and there were hundreds of stone-faced armed police, with Alsatians that were barking like mad. It took me a while to work out why the whole thing seemed so familiar. Then I remembered: it was just like that time me and Don Shanks were nicked outside the Wimpy in Holborn!

When we went out on to the pitch wearing our smart England suits – to take in the atmosphere – we found that, amazingly, the stadium was nearly full even though it was two hours prior to kick-off. Huge banners were waving, and the Italian fans were not at all pleased to see us. I walked alongside Dave Clement who was looking round the terraces in amazement. 'Look at that lot!' he gasped. At that moment, Dave actually froze; I could see the expression of terror on his face. Suddenly, I realised that for some players this situation was a terrifying experience. Not for me though, I was loving every minute of it, and couldn't wait to kick-off. When you've been around some of the places I have, 80,000 mad Italians are all in a day's work.

When we came out of the dressing room on to the pitch the atmosphere was electric. The crowd were hysterical, and the first twenty minutes were played at a hectic pace, with Gentile following me all over the place, pulling my shirt and spitting at me – the usual Italian tricks. He stuck to me so tight that I had to dig him out of my shorts at half-time. We managed to keep the crowd pretty quiet for half an hour; but then Italy were awarded a free-kick on the edge of the penalty area. Antognoni's shot hit Kevin Keegan and deflected past Clemence, to give them a somewhat lucky lead. The rest of the game was close, with few openings made. But in the 77th minute, Causio crossed and Bettega scored with a diving header. It was, as they say, all over.

After they went 2–0 up the Italians, typically, shut up shop. I didn't get into the game until late on, when we had a couple of chances, but it finished 2–0. It looked as if England would again fail to qualify for the World Cup Finals, having not made it to West Germany in 1974.

Dave Clement was very upset, and I am sure that a few other players froze in that atmosphere. We flew back to England a couple of hours later on a charter flight. It all seemed to happen so quickly, without a chance to catch our breath. In the *Sunday times*, Brian Glanville wrote:

The most alarming feature of the English defeat, however, was that this was probably the best, or the least bad, team that Revie could have put out under the present circumstances. This meant, inevitably, that Stan Bowles had to be integrated within 90 minutes into a team which knew him not. He said to me after the game that he thought things were going well in the second half, adding that he was sure England would beat Italy at Wembley: 'I don't think they're a good team.'

However, whether I thought they were a good team or not, it was Italy, not England, who later qualified for the 1978 Finals, and they were the only team to beat Argentina in that tournament, winning 1–0 in their group game.

Glanville compared me to Causio, the Juventus right-winger, and argued that English football needed more individualism. He continued:

Causio, as the Italians themselves say, and as one saw clearly enough even within the context of this game, is a player who can alternate the brilliant with the bad. But at least he has the courage, as well as the supreme skill, to attempt the difficult, the supreme virtuosity. Bowles can do that too, but by and large we breed this out of our players. Our football for years has been a poisoned well in which individualism, the one quality which can unlock today's well-organised defences, is discouraged and despised.

After that little outing, it was back to business in the league. On the Saturday we beat Middlesbrough 3–0 at Loftus Road. The victory was soured, though, by an altercation I had with the Middlesbrough defender Willie Maddren in injury time. It happened right in front of the South African Road Stand, and I was sent off. Maddren alleged that I went over the top in a tackle, which is the worst crime that a footballer can commit. Not Guilty. I had never done this to any player in my life.

I felt that Maddren had made a meal of it, and the crowd agreed as they gave me a standing ovation when I left the pitch. I had a go at Maddren in the passageway to the dressing rooms, and Frank McLintock had to step in to stop us punching each other. I felt the accusation was a stain on my footballing career. Going over the top can cause a broken leg or more serious injury, so I was very annoyed with the accusation; it's something I just wouldn't do. On top of that Maddren's masterclass acting meant that I would be automatically suspended for the next league game, so I was not a happy man!

A week after the England game in Rome, QPR were preparing to play the side Dave Sexton feared most in the UEFA Cup campaign:

FC Cologne. As I said, Dave used to study videos of the German clubs, and always insisted that we played them in pre-season friendlies. His view was that FC Cologne were the best side in the competition – very sophisticated in the way they used to regroup in defence and break quickly in attack.

My goal in this game, with which I rewrote the record books, arrived with only fifteen minutes left for play. I had achieved another milestone in my career, breaking a long-standing British goalscoring record. We played brilliantly and destroyed the Germans 3–0 – putting some pride back into British football.

So, in the space of a week I had played against Italy in England's biggest game for three years; got sent off against Middlesbrough at the Bush; and broken a goalscoring record against Cologne.

The second leg in Cologne was previewed extensively in the papers, and Brian Glanville was no exception in the *Sunday Times*:

> *On Tuesday in Cologne, when they defend a three goal lead in the second leg of their third round UEFA Cup-tie, Rangers have the chance to keep alight the beacon they have lit for the British game. While the England team this season have lurched from one fumbling performance to another, first drawing, then winning, then losing without flair or style, Rangers have contrived to thrash some of the strongest teams from some of the most highly developed footballing countries in Europe.*

Glanville added that we had won our home games against Slovan and Cologne . . .

> *With football that was composed, adventurous, skilful and incisive. No player in the team touched the excellence of Stanley Bowles, while Dieter Muller, the centre forward who was a revelation in the European Championship finals, got hardly any change out of the 'elderly' central defensive pair, McLintock and Webb.*

He wondered why we were so poorly placed in the league, and quoted Dave Sexton as saying, 'We've deserved more than we've got. You never get what you deserve. You get what you fight for. A lot to do with it really is that the front fellows haven't been very prolific at all in the league, but they have in Europe. Every successful team comes as a result of someone hitting form up front.'

Glanville discussed our lack of domestic form, and the League Cup tie against Arsenal, saying:

> *Heaven knows that European players don't stand on ceremony; the man-to-man marking in Rome stifled not only Bowles, but Channon and Keegan as well, but in the Slovan and Cologne matches, Bowles never had the sort of treatment he received against Arsenal. Quite simply he was able to beat one man with his astonishing footwork, swerve and balance, but if he tried to beat another, more often than not he was chopped down. We all know what happens to most ball players as a result of that. If they haven't the resilience and determination of a Bowles, they simply stop trying to beat people, and lay the ball off instead; as so many dull coaches at every level want them to do.*

We had enjoyed the support of around 21,000 fans at Loftus Road, and now we were walking out into a Mungersdorfer Stadium packed with 50,000 Germans. We knew it was going to be difficult, even with a three-goal lead from the first leg. Dave Sexton's strategy was to leave Dave Thomas and myself up front and try to protect that lead.

As it happened, we broke away – thanks to a Don Givens interception – and the ball went to Mick Leach, who crossed low for Don Masson to score. We went 1–0 up after only four minutes. It was a good job that Masson scored the all important away goal, because after that it was like the Alamo! We were imprisoned in our own penalty area, trying to stave off an unremitting German bombardment.

Cologne had some good players like Heinz Flohe and Wolfgang Overath in midfield, and they started to turn it on. People think Beckham hits a nice ball but believe me, when I tell you Flohe was an absolutely sensational player. He had the ability to send crosses in like rockets and this caused pandemonium in our ranks.

Muller equalised after twenty-four minutes when a shot was blocked by Webby and rebounded to him, then left-winger Lohr quickly made it 4–2 on aggregate. Next, Weber headed in from Flohe's corner. We were still 4–3 up but it looked like hard work. Worse was to follow when Lohr spat at Dave Clement, who punched him, so Dave was sent off. Down to ten men, we were really up against it.

At half-time Dave decided just to leave me up front and to concentrate on trying to hold the fort, because if Cologne scored another two goals we would be out, and, from the way the first half had gone, that looked a distinct possibility. Early in the second half, Muller scored his second with a header. The pressure grew even more intense, and how we held on with ten men I'll never know. We were on the wrong end of a 4–1 drubbing, and very lucky to win on the away goals rule.

On the night, the manager had been proved right: Cologne were a very good side. Nobody in England had given us a pounding like we absorbed that night. I have to say that Webby, Frank McLintock and Phil Parkes saved our bacon over there; without them, Cologne would have scored ten. Some of our players seemed to bottle out, and disappeared from the proceedings. Dave, though, was very pleased with the way I held up the ball, when it was whacked out of defence, and gave our hard-pressed defence a breather. I was naturally good at this particular aspect of the game.

Dave Sexton commented: The great thing for us was that we were able to stop them scoring at Loftus Road. So that, anything we could do here was important. I thought Cologne could score three against us here. I thought they played well to retrieve the goals. Of course, we had the additional problem after half-time of playing with only ten men. Thanks to good defence and the goalkeeping of Parkes, we were able to hold out. It was a wonderful achievement for Cologne – a great fightback.

I knew that as soon as I returned from Cologne, I would have to travel to Manchester for a court hearing and explain why I hadn't been keeping up my maintenance payments. I was already £600 in arrears, and they were going to decide whether to give me a 28-day jail sentence or not. Jim Gregory provided me with a good counsel; because he knew that this time it was serious. As I travelled north to Manchester, I thought about the possibility of being sent down. That would have been a huge stain on my character. On the other hand, I reflected, I knew most of the people in Strangeways anyway, so I suppose it wouldn't have been too bad!

My lawyer managed to get the maintenance settlement reduced, but it didn't really mean much, because I couldn't afford to pay. I owed QPR money; had huge gambling debts; and was totally insolvent. A committal order was made by the magistrate, but he said it would be suspended as long as I paid off something off the arrears. It wasn't really in the interests of either party for me to go to jail. I had to pay £150 off before Christmas, and then £15 a week off the arrears, plus the monthly maintenance payment. If I missed any of these payments I would go to prison.

Of course, they couldn't take it out of my wages. I was so much in debt, I didn't have any wages left for the next year. The order was made in December 1976, and I wasn't due any wages until 1978!

The players got six tickets for each home game, and I always gave these to my friends. Sometimes, I got extra tickets from other players who didn't need them, but there were times when I needed thirty or forty tickets. These were put on my account with Ron Phillips, and deducted from my non-existent wages. Even though I wasn't due any wages, I would always say to Ron, 'Don't worry about it!'

I was also still in the love triangle: the ex-wife was trying to extract money from me; my girlfriend wanted to marry me; and my new 'legal' lady-friend was trying to advise me. After a long weekend with the clerk of the court, I finally convinced her that I was innocent. We used to go to a pub in Hammersmith called The Raven, in Goldhawk Road. They had a hotel there, Terry's, where I would get a room for nothing because the owner was a QPR supporter.

This girl had a motorbike, and I thought she was a nutter, she could be really weird at times. I went to her house one night, and when we were in the bedroom, she said, 'D'you want to see my dad? He's in the wardrobe.' I wasn't sure what to think. She opened the door of the wardrobe, and took out an urn with her dad's ashes inside!

Having beaten Cardiff, Bury, West Ham and Arsenal in the League Cup, we were lined up, in February 1977, to play a semi-final against Aston Villa. It turned out to be a long, drawn-out affair.

We drew 0–0 at the Bush, then 2–2 in the second leg at Villa Park, in a cracker of a game. After that match there was a doubt about the venue for the replay. It was decided that the two chairmen would toss up to see if the venue would be Villa Park or Highbury. Jim Gregory and the opposing representative, who was about seventy years old, went into the boardroom.

Jim said, 'Toss up, then.'

So they tossed a coin.

'Heads,' calls Jim.

As the coin bounced on the floor, the Villa representative saw that it was tails. 'Villa Park, then,' he said, well-satisfied.

Jim was having none of it though. He held up his hand and said, 'Hang on a minute, I said heads it hits the floor.'

So, to my surprise, they had a re-toss, which we won, and the game was played at Highbury. It does seem unbelievable, but it's a true story; the Villa bloke must have been senile.

So we got the home tie that we wanted in front of 40,000 supporters but playing in London didn't help us because we got stuffed 3–0, with Brian Little scoring a hat-trick. It was probably a bit of poetic justice but I had no complaints. We were outplayed on the night.

In between the first and second Villa games, I played for England in a friendly against Holland at Wembley. But just before that, I had another game back home in Collyhurst – one that wasn't reported by the press.

When I was selected to play for England, I was supposed to report for training on the Monday morning. My boxer mate from Manchester, Brian Barlow, ran a Sunday pub team for The Fountain. On the Saturday I said to him, 'I've been picked for England, Brian.'

'Fucking hell, Stan,' he says, 'what an honour that is.'

'What's this game you're having tomorrow?' I asked him.

'Well, it's not for you, Stan, really.'

'Ah, go on, I want to play.'

'You can't play,' said Brian, 'don't be so bloody stupid!'

We said no more about it, but on the Sunday morning I turned up at the pub with a pair of plimsolls in my hands.

'What the hell are you doing?' demands Brian.

'I'm playing,' I said.

The game took place on hard shale at a place called the Red Rec, in Collyhurst. It was a pretty dangerous surface. Brian just said, 'Get out there on the wing, Stan.'

When the game started I was playing around with the ball, scrapping and messing about. Everyone was trying to kick me, but they all ended up on their arses, and I was laughing merrily to myself. I came off at the end covered in shit and dust. I loved the whole thing. They all chipped in to pay for my train fare on the Monday, so that I could report for England. I know that these days, a footballer would be wrapped up in cotton wool before an international match, and wouldn't get the chance of doing something like that. Mind you, if I was playing now, I'd give it a bloody good go.

Brian reckons that I am expensive to go out with. He used to earn big money and one particular night he had £1,800 in his pocket – in our early days together when beer was one and threepence a pint. We went to a club for a drink, and when we came out he hadn't even made a dent in his wad. We then went upstairs to a gambling club called McCawbers and Brian ended up having to borrow a tenner to get home. The best part about it was that he didn't gamble. He reckons I'm the worst card player he's ever seen in his life. He's probably right!

With the dizzy heights of pub football pushed to the back of my mind, it was time to concentrate on the international version. The team that Don Revie had picked to play Holland was: Ray Clemence in goal, Dave Clement, Kevin Beattie of Ipswich, Dave Watson and Mike Doyle of Manchester City, Paul Madeley of Leeds in defence, with Brian Greenhoff of Manchester United and Trevor Brooking of West Ham in midfield, and Birmingham's Trevor Francis – who was only twenty-two – up front with Kevin Keegan and myself. Joe Royle and Stuart Pearson had been in the original squad, but there was no orthodox centre forward in the team that turned out at Wembley.

The men in the orange shirts were a lot better than Italy. Although they only beat us 2–0, they really tore us apart. They had five of their great 1974 team: Cruyff, Neeskens, Krol, Rep and Rensenbrink. Jan Peters, a 22-year-old midfield player, scored both goals after pinpoint passes from Neeskens.

The papers, for once, didn't slaughter England. Instead, they heaped praise on the Dutch. The *Sun* headline was: THE SCARLET PIMPERNEL! SUPERMAN CRUYFF PUTS ENGLAND TO SHAME. In his report on the game, Brian Woolnough wrote: 'Johann Cruyff left millions of soccer fans gasping as he masterminded Holland's 2–0 win over England at Wembley last night.'

In *The Times* it was: RAGGED ENGLAND OVERWHELMED BY DUTCH FLAIR. Norman Fox reported: 'For those in a crowd of over 90,000 who had come through the rain to study at this night class, the Dutch masters gave immediate instruction. There was clarity and character, controlled speed and imagination; all this unfurling, even in the early moments. Cruyff stood back, for a time, to take a deep look at it all from among his own defenders, but such is the gangling stride and brilliant foresight of the man that no door was ever closed to him.'

After the game Don Revie said, 'The Dutch were just magnificent, especially in the first half. There is no point in kidding ourselves. We just couldn't cope. It was a lesson in control and passing and not giving the ball away. It was not just a lesson to the England international side but to all of English football. This was one of the best international performances I have ever seen.'

I respected Don most of all because he was the first manager to make sure England internationals got paid a decent amount of appearance money. It's incredible to think that with all the money in the game, the players were paid an absolute pittance.

Don managed to raise our appearance money to £200 per player and I was delighted about this until Emlyn Hughes almost put a spanner in the works. As Don announced the good news to the assembled players Crazy Horse pipes up in that falsetto voice of his, 'I don't need to be paid a penny to put the three Lions on my chest, boss.'

Well, all the lads in the dressing room fell silent and for one horrible moment I thought they were collectively going to waive their match fees in a ceremonial show of loyalty. I replied quickly, 'In that case Emlyn I'll have yours,' and the guilt-edged silence exploded into laughter. The other players were, in the main, greedy blighters much like myself.

On the domestic front, things weren't going all that well. We'd been knocked out of the FA Cup by Manchester United in the fourth round, beaten 1–0 at Old Trafford, so the UEFA Cup was all we had left. Our quarter-final tie was against AEK Athens, the Greek club who had beaten Derby earlier in the competition.

In a profile of Dave Sexton before the game, in the *Sunday Times*, Brian Glanville said he hoped we could continue to play the progressive, entertaining football we had produced against Slovan and Cologne. He talked to David Webb, who said that Sexton would make a good England manager: 'Because he wouldn't have to manage, he'd only have to coach. He's so superior in his teaching, and he could put it over in a matter of days.'

Sexton talked about his interests in music and poetry, and told Glanville that, 'The thing about football is getting a framework in which fellows can express themselves, but you can win, as well. Poets do with words what a good trainer can do with players.'

So, on 2 March 1977, we played AEK Athens, and, once again, we did well. Gerry Francis, who had been much missed, was now back in the side. He scored two goals from the penalty spot as we won 3–0. I collected my eleventh goal in European competition for the season, extending the record even further.

The Greek manager had said in the press after the game that the referee had been very biased towards us and that I had scored an offside goal. He implied that we had bribed the referee with gifts and money. They moaned about the penalties as well. Generally, they were a bit pissed off about the whole thing!

In the directors' box things had got very heated. Jim Gregory had welcomed the AEK Athens officials in traditional hospitable style, exchanging gifts, kissing each other on the cheeks, and all that business. But by the end of the match the two lots of club officials were squaring up to each other, as the Greek contingent got very excitable. Jim threw them all out of the box.

Jim always had a couple of handy looking pals hanging out with him. They may have been middle-aged and had a lot of money but it wasn't always like that. Jim and his mob all started off as working-class lads who lived on their wits and had plenty of history when it came to having a rumble. One Greek official's parting shot to Jim was, 'When you come to Greece we will slit your throat.' Jim replied, 'I've got news for you. I'm not going to Greece. Now fuck off!'

A couple of days after the game, I started to receive death threats in the form of letters at the ground. There is a large Greek contingent living around Shepherd's Bush, and I suspect this is where the letters came from. Basically, they were saying that I shouldn't go over to Greece for the second leg; if I did, I would be killed. It didn't bother me that much because there was no way that I would miss the return leg, I had made up my mind about that. I handed the letters to Dave Sexton. Dave was concerned because he knew how volatile the Greeks were, especially in their own country. Incidents of bribery in the Greek game were rife, so much so that it had been brought up as an issue in our Parliament.

As we arrived at Athens airport I was singled out and handed a large bouquet of flowers, which was the Greek tradition. The press were calling it a bouquet of barbed wire because of the threats to my person; like saying that I would have my legs cut off – which wouldn't be fatal, but would be a bloody nuisance when it came to trying to beat defenders. The secretary of UEFA had ordered a special observer at the game, and warned that any crowd violence would endanger AEK's future in European competition. I accepted the flowers gracefully and took them to the hotel. We were soon informed that we were banned from going outside of the hotel complex. It is one of my regrets that I've been to all of these countries – despite a fear of flying – and often been unable to venture outside. But that was the business we were in, and we had to accept it. At least we had a private beach where we could relax, and join in watersport activities if we felt so inclined, which, of course, I didn't. The *Superstars* fiasco was still fresh in my mind!

Unfortunately, Gerry had picked up a hamstring injury and Dave

Thomas and Dave Clement were also out, so a major part of our team was missing. Once again, we had to contend with a very hostile capacity crowd of 35,000. The fans were throwing huge rotten apples on to the pitch even before the game started. Perhaps they'd run out of flowers. When we arrived at the ground in the team coach we came through a narrow entrance near to one of the stands. The Greek supporters were up there in the stand pissing down all over us, this was our welcoming party, and right away you got the feeling that this was going to be a long couple of hours.

I had to time most of my runs down the wing using the linesman as a human shield. After a while the crowd ran out of apples and began tossing tomatoes at me. After you've had big hard apples chucked at you for a full fifteen minutes, it makes for quite a pleasant change to have squishy tomatoes hit you. The referee was obviously terrified of the crowd, and we expected fifty-fifty decisions to go against us. There were a lot of incidents that the Greeks would not have got away with playing in the English game – I think one of our players is still buried by the halfway line! We ended up losing 3–0 after a late goal, so we had to settle the tie by penalty shoot-out. The pitch resembled a bountiful orchard without the trees.

How do you take penalties in front of 35,000 mad Greeks? Don Givens took off his boots in the centre of the pitch and tried chopping his leg off, so I don't think he fancied taking one. We had to draft in people like David Webb, who had never taken a penalty in his life. I scored our first, and on it went; with a couple of misses for either side. I felt really sorry for Peter Eastoe – who definitely didn't want to get involved – and, unfortunately, he missed. It went to sudden death. Don Shanks had come on as a sub and slotted his penalty away in the bottom corner, but Webby's shot was saved by the Greek keeper. We were out of the UEFA Cup.

This was the signal for thousands of crazy Greek fans to come swarming over the fences like ants, and run on to the pitch. We sprinted off as fast as we could, even Webby did it under ten seconds! If we had been caught, I shudder to think of the consequences. It was very disappointing, because we knew we were the better side, but with three of our best players missing we had struggled. We had gone down fighting, but that defeat in Athens was very hard to accept. It was one of the most disappointing moments of my career because we missed the chance to play Juventus in the semi-final. I would have loved another crack at the Italians.

171

Frank McLintock remembers the night, too. He says, 'The Greek fans were unbelievable during the game. They were really, really worked up – well over the top. One of them kicked his foot through the back of the dug-out where Dave Sexton and the others were sitting. It was real hysteria. I think there might have been a riot if we had won. I was so gutted, getting beat. I was hoping to reach another cup final at thirty-seven. That would have been a great thing for me.'

Our season was now, effectively over, because we had no chance of winning any honours in the domestic league, and our cup runs had come to an end. Dave Sexton told us that he was highly delighted that we had gone so far, and had some tremendously entertaining games along the way. Dave was a very genuine man, and very much a player's manager.

On 19 March, the Saturday after the penalty nightmare in Athens, we travelled to play Bristol City in a league game. It had been raining quite heavily for a few days, and there was a heavy frost the night before which left the pitch soft in some places, and hard in others.

During the game I had a running battle with a bloke called Gary Collier. Eventually, a couple of minutes from the end, I lost my temper. I chased after him, but as I set off on a hard patch of the pitch, into a soft, muddy bit, my right foot stayed in the ground. Unfortunately, the rest of me carried on, and I broke my leg in two places *and* dislocated my ankle at the same time. My foot was pointing in the opposite direction. The pain was agonising and I was screaming my head off as I was carried to the side of the pitch.

In the pandemonium after the final whistle had gone, I was left lying on my own in the car park, while the physio disappeared to get the doctor. There I was on a stretcher for fifteen minutes, on the verge of hysteria and suffering from shock. The Bristol supporters were walking past me, thinking that I was acting because I had a blanket covering my legs, so they couldn't see the extent of my injuries. They were spitting at me and hurling abuse. I was in excruciating pain, worse than anything I had ever experienced – before or since.

Don Shanks remembers better than me what happened after this because I was on the verge of passing out. Don, who always keeps sight of his priorities, recalls the most frightening day of my career:

Now, bearing in mind that you don't want anything to go wrong – because we had to get to White City for half past seven in the evening –

Stanley goes out and breaks his leg in this game, two minutes from the end. That's typical of the man.

There was a big panic going on, and Dave Sexton said, 'Well, Don, you're his best mate. You'll have to go back with him.'

I was dying to bet a dog in the 7.30, so I didn't want to go back with him. 'There's nothing I can do is there?' I said. 'What can I do? Hold his hand, Dave? What d'you mean?'

'Well, take his clothes, you've got to take his clothes,' said Dave.

'Dave ... look ...'

'Go on, Don, take his clothes, go with him.'

So the manager and Stan's best mate travel back in the ambulance. Because Stan was the number one player, Jim Gregory had said, 'You can't operate on him in Bristol, he's got to come back to see my personal physician!'

So I'm sitting in the back with Stan and this ambulance is going about thirty-five miles an hour, trying to cause a major accident down the M4 motorway. I'm thinking, This is fucking lovely, this is!

It's guaranteed the dog that I wanted to bet has bolted in at 6–1. I was dying for a drink, and we were coming up to the services. So I said, 'Dave, tell the driver to pull into the Services, so I can go to the toilet, and grab a sandwich and a cup of coffee.'

'Yes, Don – good idea.'

Stan is delirious in the back. They have only given him a few pain-killers and he is in absolute agony. I said, 'He'll be all right, leave him there for half an hour.'

Stan's eyes were rolling in his head. We left him in the ambulance on his own, while I rang to put a bet on and we all had something to eat. As we get back to the ambulance, I put my head round the door to see how he's going. 'Did you want anything, Stanley?' He must have been delirious as he did an excellent impression of a dog with rabies when I asked him that!

We got back to Charing Cross Hospital late in the evening and were told that Jim Gregory's personal surgeon, Tony Catterall, wasn't going to operate until the Sunday morning. I was taken to the fifteenth floor and put in a private room. It was just like being in a hotel: television, phones and everything to make you comfortable. The only medication that was allowed was paracetamol, and they wouldn't touch my leg until the surgeon had seen the extent of the injury. The nurses, who were in and out of my room every fifteen minutes all night, were fantastic; making sure I was as comfortable as a footballer with a broken leg can possibly be.

On the Sunday morning, I had the operation, which apparently took six hours. When I eventually woke up, the first face that I saw was Lynn Frederick, the wife of film star Peter Sellers. I opened my eyes, and thought I'd died and gone to heaven – what with this beautiful lady standing over me. Peter Sellers was a patient in the next room, and Lynn had come in to see how I was progressing. Peter was having trouble with his heart.

A couple of days later my kids came to see me, and I asked Lynn if they could go and meet Peter Sellers, because they were big fans of Inspector Clouseau in the Pink Panther films. When they came out of his room they said, 'That's not Inspector Clouseau, Dad!' Peter Sellers was so ill that he looked nothing like the man my kids had seen in the films.

I was in hospital for two weeks and I was drinking champagne, having a bet and using the phone. I was having parties every day in there, it was like a five-star hotel. Louie, a Greek friend, used to bring me a dinner every day from his restaurant in Charlotte Street, so I was being looked after very well indeed. He was a member of the Magic Circle and he taught me quite a few card tricks. Within a few weeks I was in a walking plaster, so when I left hospital I was able to get around as normal, but I knew that I wouldn't play for the rest of the season.

Before the season had kicked off, I'd made a bet with Malcolm Macdonald about who could get the most goals in the season, and he scored about twenty goals more than me. When he said, 'Give me the money, Stan,' I said, 'Fuck off, it's not my fault I broke my leg, the bet's off.' So Malcolm never got paid, but I don't think he was too bothered about it. We'd bet on league goals only, if we'd included cup goals, my eleven in the UEFA Cup would have made us level on twenty-nine apiece. I really shouldn't bet!

I kept in touch with the surgeon who fixed my leg because I thought that he had saved my life. I still have the steel plates in my leg to this day. They were supposed to come out the next season but, because the team was struggling, Jim Gregory persuaded me to put off the operation. So nearly thirty years later I still have them, and I'm waiting for Jim to give me the OK to have them out!

On the lighter side every season QPR used to enter the *Evening Standard* five-a-side tournament. It was a knockout competition played every year between all the league clubs. The eventual winners would play something in the region of five or six games in one night. It was a popular competition with both players and fans, and although the players did everything they could to win, the competition was generally regarded as a bit of fun in contrast to the pressure-cooker atmosphere of league matches. The tournament was held annually at Wembley and televised by the BBC.

We usually fielded a strong side. Phil Parkes was a big enough obstacle to navigate a ball around in a full-size goal, let alone the considerably smaller five-a-side net. Our outfield players would usually comprise of Dave Clement, Gerry Francis, myself and the lively Dave Thomas.

We played a free-flowing passing game with good movement off the ball and that meant we were a very difficult team to beat. In fact, during the seventies we won the tournament three times with me winning the player of the tournament award on a couple of occasions.

The tournament organisers would present winners' medals at the end of the evening and a trophy to the player of the tournament. I've never been one for collecting medals, caps or trophies, which is something of a regret now as I realise these things can be readily converted into cash. Whenever I won something I would usually give it away to someone who valued it more than me, usually the fans who had bothered to travel down to cheer us on.

I vividly recall throwing a medal into a crowd of QPR fans one night after we'd won the five-a-side competition. I lobbed the shiny little medal high into the night air and watched it wing its way inexorably towards an elderly, bespectacled man draped in a QPR scarf. The fellow was cradling a thermos flask in his arms like it was a newborn baby. When he saw the medal plummeting towards him he dropped the flask to the ground and excitedly cupped both hands waiting for the medal to fall into his grateful clutch.

I looked on as the poor fellow completely misjudged the flight of the medal and watched as it landed painfully on his balding head. Before the medal hit the deck the old man disappeared under a whirling mêlée of arms and legs in a fight scene reminiscent of a Tom and Jerry cartoon. A mass of fans steamed toward the prize intent on grabbing some bit of memorabilia to take home with them. Eventually, they picked themselves up like dazed rugby players buried under a collapsed scrum. The old man was the last person to get up with his glasses twisted across his face, a huge bump on his bonce, the thermos flask smashed into pieces on the ground, and the medal nowhere to be seen.

All the players were in hysterics because he did look quite a comical sight but my heart was in my mouth because at one stage I thought the old chap might have copped it, and I'd have been responsible for his demise. The papers would have had a field day with that story. 'Stan Bowles Kills Pensioner!' I ran over to him, dusted him down apologetically, and handed him my player of the night trophy. His face transformed into a huge smile revealing four teeth in varying states of decay, randomly positioned in his mouth. He kissed me full on the lips by way of thank you. I recall he smelled strongly of Bovril.

One year we played some really great stuff en route and were scheduled to meet Leyton Orient in the final. I had a good friend who was known by all as Jewish Dennis. In those days bookmakers offered odds on who would win the competition and Dennis had backed his team, Leyton Orient, for a grand at 8/1. Jewish Dennis always carried a large fold of cash on him and liked to bet, which in my book are two good reasons for liking anybody.

Dennis had made most of his money through operating on the wrong side of the law, he was always in and out of prison and when he was out he was usually up to things that would put him back in, if and when caught. Dennis was an expert forger who had made a small fortune through chequebook crime; he once asked me to write down my signature, and within a few minutes he could write it better than I could.

One of his mate's greatest coups was forging Peter Noone's signature – the lead signer of popular songsmiths, Herman and the Hermits. Evidently, he popped into a bank in Shepherd's Bush, forged Noone's signature and left with forty grand of his money, ten minutes later. Not bad for a morning's work.

Apparently, the bank manager called Dennis's mate into his office. He thought about scarpering there and then but held his nerve and calmly walked into the room at the back of the bank, half expecting to be greeted by the law. Instead, he was handed the £40,000 in cash, offered a warm handshake and told that *No Milk Today* was one of the manager's favourite songs. The manager simply didn't want to hand over the money in front of anyone else in the bank, just in case 'any undesirable types' were present. As far as I know, the bank eventually had to stump up the money due to this gross negligence and so neither Peter Noone nor any of the Hermits lost out financially.

Dennis approached me and suggested that if I 'were to go hooky' in the final he would see me right for a grand. At the time my fee for the night was £100 so I was rather reluctant to turn him down. We were five down before the first half was over. In the second half I livened myself up a bit and scored a cracking individual goal. I ran over to the goal, picked the ball out of the net and shouted loudly to the lads, 'C'mon we can still do this.' We eventually lost 5–1. A puzzled Gerry Francis said to me afterwards, 'I don't understand it Stan, you played brilliantly all night apart from that last game, I suppose you must have been tired.'

As far as league football was concerned I was never, ever, approached to throw a game or even heard of anyone who had been. I would never have considered taking a bung even if I had been approached, because I had too much respect for the QPR fans. The five-a-side competition was a bit of friendly fun while the football league was all-important. Mind you, if some big money had been offered and I was skint, well, you never know.

Chapter 13 •

QPR 1977–78 –
Shackled with Shanks

I returned to football, after my broken leg, in July 1977 in a pre-season tournament in Belgium. The opposition included the likes of Bruges and Derby County. By this time, Dave Sexton had left to manage Manchester United and Frank Sibley had taken over at the Bush. I scored in my comeback game against Derby, and eventually we won that tournament. It all looked good but, unfortunately, me and that man Mr Donald got into trouble again.

We'd been to a friend's bar, got drunk, had a laugh, and gone back to our hotel wanting to get more drink. Trouble was, the Belgian hotel staff wouldn't serve us. Admittedly, it was about three in the morning.

So Don says to me, 'I bet you a tenner that I can get a brandy.'

'All right, you're on,' I replied, keen as ever to make a few bob.

Next thing, Don just collapsed on the floor and started shaking. Then he says to me, 'You've got to say to the bloke when he comes, "Quick! Get him a drink!"' So that was the deal. Don had had it all planned.

As expected, the waiter came running up.

'Get him a drink!' I cried, 'a brandy, or something. Quick! Quick!'

The waiter thinks that Don's dying, so, a couple of minutes later, he comes over, gives him the brandy and Don drinks it, then jumps up, hands him the empty glass and says, Thank you very much, goodnight!'

Off we go to bed, laughing our heads off, with the man looking at us in amazement. Fifteen minutes later, there's a knock on the door. 'We don't want any room service, thank you very much,' says Don. Another knock on the door, we say nothing. A couple of minutes pass, then we hear the sound of footsteps retreating down the hall. We've no idea who was knocking, but they've gone so it doesn't matter. Me and Shanks fall into the sort of sleep that only the truly drunk experience. Next thing, I think I'm having a nightmare; I can hear mad dogs barking. All of a sudden people are pounding on our door, like it was the bailiffs. The pounding got louder, and the dogs were barking and scratching against the door.

'Stan,' Don says, 'there's someone at the door for you. It's certainly not for me.'

Anyway, we wouldn't open the door and I was sheepishly saying, 'Go away, we don't want any room service tonight, thank you!'

By now this had gone on for what seemed like five minutes and they're really hammering at the door.

Then, someone shouts out, 'Police, open the door! Otherwise we'll shoot it open!'

'What have you done?' Don asks me.

'I've done fuck all,' I replied. 'What have you done?'

'What do you mean, what have I done? I've been with you all night!'

By now it was becoming quite obvious that we had to open the door.

'You open it,' says Don.

'If somebody's got to open it, you open it. You're not worth as much as me!'

'Fuck off!" says Don, unimpressed by transfer values, 'I'm not open-ing it.'

So we're lying in our beds. It's like a scene from *Gunfight at the O.K. Corral* – except all me and Don have to defend ourselves with are two continental quilts!

'Okay,' I shouted. 'Don't shoot! We are going to open the door.'

So in the end, Don ran to the door, opened it quickly and dived back into bed. The police had been standing outside for six or seven minutes, they've got the right needle and the dogs are barking fer-ociously. I'm in the bed on the far side, Don's nearest to them. In they charge.

'Right!' they shout. 'Get your clothes on, you're coming with us!'

'I'm not going anywhere,' said I, cowering under the covers.

But they're not about to take no for an answer.

'Get your clothes on and come with us! Otherwise we'll set the dogs on you.' By this time, Don's already up and dressed. He's got his passport in his pocket and ready to go, while staring at one of the dogs who's looking at him, ready to pounce. But I will not move out of bed.

'If he won't get out of bed, shoot him in the ankle!' said one of the cops. This doesn't sound like a good idea, but still I won't move.

'C'mon Stanley,' says Don, getting anxious about the possible sight of blood. 'Get out of there. Let's go and sort this out, it's obviously a mistake. Something's gone on that is nothing to do with us.'

'No, I'm not moving.'

So then our manager Frank Sibley is called up to the room with the hotel manager, to try to get something sorted out. But the police won't budge, they're insisting we've done something wrong, and they're taking us to jail. One of the policemen had a lead on this dog that you can let out so far – or reel in. These dogs are like two wild tigers, and the fella's let it go close up to my ear.

'All right, leave me alone,' I said, finally. 'I'm getting up . . . I'm getting up.' I jumped out of bed, with my hair all over the place, and put on my shirt, ready to go.

'Stanley, put your jacket on,' says Don.

'I don't want a jacket. C'mon let's go.'

As we went down in the lift and out to the entrance we knew that we were in trouble. Parked outside was one of those Volkswagen police buses with the sliding doors at the side. Frank Sibley was there as we were about to get in.

Dogs are barking; armed police are crunching along the gravel, looking very stern. They must think we're international terrorists, or something.

'What the bloody hell have you done?' said Frank, looking terrified. 'C'mon, you've got to tell us.'

'Frank, we've done nothing, honest!'

'Have you smashed someone up in a bar or something? What have you done?'

'Frank, we haven't done anything!'

Frank definitely didn't believe us. You could tell that all sorts of things were going through his mind – drugs, bank robberies, murder even. He's thinking, How am I going explain this one to the papers.

We're not worried at all. But, when Frank tries to get into the van and they slam the door on him almost breaking four of his fingers, we knew something was wrong. He's standing there screaming as the van just sped off with us in it. Now we are in the back with the dogs, and it looks as if, at any moment, anything could happen. They took us out of the van and led us off to this big, imposing police station – it looked like Gestapo Headquarters! As we walked through the door, Don says to me, 'Any moment now we're gonna get it.'

And he was right. They started pounding us with clubs, smashing us about the head and body, and all we can do is laugh. What was going to happen was going to happen, so we just had a bit of a laugh about it. Don was saying, 'Oh, lovely, Stanley, shall we book up here for a holiday next year? It's just lovely here!'

I'm in hysterics, even though they're knocking the crap out of us. Of

Dumped on my backside against Spurs (*above*) but getting away from Leeds'
Trevor Cherry (*below*), Norman Hunter lurks in the background (both Empics),
and the celebrations after the match (*over page top*, Getty Images) . . . all scenes
from the season we should have won the League . . .

. . . but Dave Sexton accepts the Loudest Jacket of the Year Award

Left Letting Malcolm Macdonald know that I had just scored the winner

Opposite page from top If only I could get at those England caps . . . scenes from an international career (*above and right*): taking on Claudio Gentile of Italy (Empics); (*bottom*) a friendly against Holland (Getty Images)

Taking on a young Alan Hansen, at home to Liverpool (*above*); doing the odd bit of defending at a corner, at home to Aston Villa (*below*, both Empics)

OFFICIAL
COLOUR

20p

SOUVENIR

FOOTBALL LEAGUE DIVISION ONE 1978
QUEENS PARK RANGERS
v.
LEEDS UNITED
SATURDAY APRIL 29th K.O. 3 p.m.

QPR

**Presented with the Player of the Year Award by
the Irish branch of the QPR supporters' club**

The boys are back in town

Seemed like a good idea at the time . . .

'Quick, the bailiffs are coming . . .'

Robin Asquith was a guest at my wedding to Jane

Days at Orient (*right*) and Forest, (*below*; Empics) with my mate Charlie George prior to the UEFA Super Cup Final against Barcelona

(*Anti-clockwise from top*)
The never-ending tussle for the
no.10 shirt; never thought I'd
be back, but recently I was a
guest at Carlisle; with Hannah

course, this just makes them even angrier and they lay into us even more.

They took us down in a lift, wherever we were heading must have been down near the earth's core because the journey took about a minute. There was even time enough for two or three more punches on the way down. We got to the bottom eventually and there were a couple of fellas and a woman waiting there; armed with big truncheons and guns – faces like The Terminator on a bad day.

'So,' says one of them, banging his truncheon on his hand, 'you two think you are playboys, no?'

Probably, we thought, but didn't say anything.

Then he asked me for my passport.

'I ain't got my fucking passport,' I says, reasonably enough. That wasn't the correct response, apparently. I was slammed up against the wall, feet dangling six inches off the ground.

Comedian, eh?' says he.

Don starts to make a move. Bang! Across his back with a truncheon. That puts paid to Don's rescue bid. They take off my shoes and socks and start bending my toes back. This is bleeding agony – 'Chopper' Harris was never like this, I'm thinking, screaming like a pig that knows what's for Sunday breakfast.

Don doesn't look all that confident any more, especially when they get the shooters out. At this, Shanksy pulls out his passport. 'I think you'll find that in order,' he says, smooth as you like.

I'm like hanging on a cross up there, getting pounded. In the end, they put us in adjacent cells. There is nothing in the cell except a concrete slab apparently for sitting or lying on. But we could still talk to each other.

'It's nice here Stan, isn't it?' says Don.

'Yes, lovely thank you, Donald! I said.

'This is your fault.'

'Stanley, it's nothing to do with me,' he said.

I didn't believe a word of it. Wherever Shanks is, trouble's just behind him in the queue.

By now, we've been there about three hours and Don suddenly wanted to go to the toilet. So they sat him in this tiny room, where you had to bend in double to get in. Literally, you couldn't move upwards or sideways. They left him sitting there for about forty-five minutes; he couldn't breathe, and thought he was going to die. He kept banging on the door but they paid no attention.

'Somebody, open this up!' Sweat was pouring off him, he was running out of oxygen. Eventually they let him out, and he lay down exhausted on his comfortable concrete slab in the cell.

About six o'clock in the morning the day staff came on duty, and Don got talking to this guard. He says to him, 'This is a big mistake you know, it's not right; we've been beaten up!'

'Would you like a coffee or hot chocolate?' asked his jailer.

'I would, yes. Very nice, thank you,' says Don.

So the guard let him out of his cell to get the hot chocolate, and while I'm sitting there Don thinks he'd have a laugh. Because I didn't know he was out of his cell, he decides to wind me up a bit. He walks past my cell door, drinking hot chocolate, and looking through the bars. As soon as I saw him I jumped up like a wild man, nearly crying.

'What are you doing? What's going on? They can't let you out without me!' I shouted, hanging on to the bars.

'I've told them everything,' says Don, smiling sweetly. 'I've been released.' I think I nearly fainted.

All of a sudden a buzzer's gone off, and someone grabs him and puts him back in the cell. Ten minutes later they took us up to see the fella who runs the jail. I demanded an apology; 'I've never been so badly treated in my life! Why has this happened? How can you do this?'

We are sure it's a case of mistaken identity. But it's 6.30 in the morning; we're absolutely knackered, been smashed up a few times, and so by now we couldn't care less.

'Tell us what we are supposed to have done,' I said.

'Last night, when you went back to your hotel, you pretended that you were in need of hospital treatment. When you went up to your room after a night of drinking, the porter called an ambulance, and when you call an ambulance in Belgium, if it isn't used, you get taken to jail and dealt with severely.'

So while we were staggering up the stairs after Don's prank, and he's copped a tenner, the old boy has rung for an ambulance, saying a man has collapsed. The ambulance has come round, they've come up to the room with the straitjackets, but we've told them to go away. Ten minutes later the police arrived. I remember Don saying, 'What are those straitjackets for, mate?' It was like *One Flew Over the Cuckoo's Nest*. Afterwards, when we had been released, I said, 'You've won easier tenners than that, Don!'

As it happened, Derby County were staying in the same hotel and it turned out that Stuart Webb, their secretary, blabbed about the incident to the press and we became newsworthy yet again. Still, that turned out good for us because when we came home we negotiated a newspaper deal for two or three grand. Don thought it was quite hilarious as I got most of the stick and yet it was all his fault. Typical Shanks!

I know it sounds hard to believe but just before I went on that trip to Belgium, Ann and I were reconciled. After all the trauma and court cases, we were going to try and get back together; mainly for the sake of the children. Jim Gregory offered us a flat above one of his garages in Wembley – rent free – to try and get myself sorted out and back on an even keel. Jane and I had split up, but, as it turned out, it was only a short reconciliation. Before I knew where I was, I was back with Jane again. The papers were having a field day, it was like a roundabout. Ann went public in the *News of The World* when we were back together, saying, 'Other women had better beware if anyone else comes into his life. I won't be running to Mum like I did before. I'll stay and fight.'

It was all my fault really because I'd kept in touch with Ann by phone, and finally she gave in and came back to me. People might say that I was a bastard; but we had been in love with each other since she was fifteen years old, and we found it very difficult to be apart, but, unfortunately, even more difficult to live together. It is one of those love stories that will never end. I know that, and I think she does too. Looking back, I didn't give Ann a very good life but I hope that she will forgive me. That knowledge is something that I have to live with, and all that we can do is get on with the rest of our lives the best way we can.

On 20 August 1977 the new season began but we knew that the halcyon days were over. Frank McLintock had gone to Leicester City and Dave Needham had been signed from Nottingham Forest as a replacement. Dave Thomas had been sold to Everton for £200,000, and Webby played only a few more games at the start of the season, before following McLintock to Leicester. So, one of the best English club sides in recent history was breaking up. When great teams break up like that they can never be re-created, but they are always remembered and talked about over the years. I was very lucky to have been a part of that classic side. But I knew the great days were over, we were on the slide. Teams had got to know our style of play, we brought in a few younger players to replace the more experienced guys that had moved on, but they took time to settle in.

Towards the end of the season we were battling in the relegation zone, and only managed to survive by the skin of our teeth. The game that swung it for us was against Arsenal – who were FA Cup finalists – at the Bush, on 11 April 1978. The old partnership won it for QPR – me and Shanksy; the two scallywags. We both scored in the 2–1 win. This victory was the turning point for our new manager, Frank Sibley, who was under a lot of pressure at the time. After the Arsenal game we had six games left. We won two, drew a couple 0–0, and stayed up, missing relegation by one point.

Away from the game I used to mix with celebrities and pop stars, as well as my slightly dodgy connections. In my early days in Manchester I was introduced, by Joey Leach, to Phil Lynott of Thin Lizzy. I was seventeen at the time and our friendship lasted until his tragic death in 1986. We didn't have much in common on the football front because Phil supported Manchester United. He was well into the London scene before I moved down there. I lost touch with him after leaving Manchester City, but when I moved to QPR we met up again, and picked up on our friendship.

I used to go to most of Thin Lizzy's concerts at the Hammersmith Palais. Joey and I enjoyed Phil's gigs, but neither of us wanted to be in the limelight, so we used to say, 'Don't pick us from the audience, please.' But Phil would do it anyway and we would get really embarrassed.

He would say, 'I wrote this song for my best pal, Joey Leach, where are you Joe? And another great friend of mine is here tonight, Stan Bowles.' We used to hide our faces in our hands, but the spotlight would come down on us, and we couldn't avoid it. Every time we would curse Phil for doing it. We used to get a great kick out of watching him perform; as Phil did watching me play football.

By this time, Phil was heavily into the drugs scene. Most of the pop stars I met were doing the same – it seemed part and parcel of their lifestyle. I went to parties at Phil's house, and to London's exclusive nightclubs with him. He introduced me to Pete Townshend, and later on, Julian Lennon – who were also well into drugs in those days.

Back then, Joey was in the music business. He was manager of the Drones, a punk group that he lost a lot of money on. I'm not surprised. I saw them in a club in Manchester once, but I didn't stay very long. They were so bad that they made the Sex Pistols sound like the Beatles!

Joey was also very friendly with Phil's managers, Chris O'Donnell and Chris Morrison, who were keen Queens Park Rangers supporters.

We used to spend time in recording studios in Dean Street, Soho, where people would go down into the basement for some privacy. I happened to walk in one day and somebody was having a line of cocaine on Mick Jagger's latest master tape! Phil used to like me being around; and I suppose that, in a way, I was one of his heroes. The feeling was mutual – he was one of the most exciting rock performers I have ever seen.

Phil asked me for one of my football shirts to keep as a memento; so I gave him my QPR shirt and, in return, he gave me a Johnny the Fox T-shirt. He used to wear my number 10 shirt a lot when he went out socialising. That made me very proud.

Phil used to have a go at us regularly for gambling – losing all our money on the dogs, horses and card games. He used to say, 'Why are you doing all of your dough? I would give you anything you could possibly want. You've both got so much talent, but you just throw it away!'

He offered us the rights promoting T-shirts and all the other Thin Lizzy merchandise; a lucrative business which was probably worth more than the ticket sales for his concerts. But we were too busy enjoying ourselves, and too disorganised to get involved in any long-term business commitment. In hindsight, we could have earned millions of pounds had we taken Phil up on his offer.

Later on, I introduced Joey to Maurice Clarke, of EMI Records, who looked after Cliff Richard, Frankie Vaughan and Dorothy Squires. Joey would take up a bottle of Dom Perignon every time he visited Maurice's office. Maurice was in the MOR department – middle-of-the-road music – and Joey managed rock bands. He told Joey that if he could find a middle-of-the-road band, he would sign them up straightaway. So Joey was pretty keen to keep in Maurice's good books.

In the studio there were always celebrities coming and going. People like Oliver Tobias, Johnny Rotten and Rod Stewart – all fans of his music. At the time, one particular girl used to come to the studio quite regularly, looking for a music story or a celebrity interview. She worked for a pop magazine and her name was Paula Yates. She was a punk at the time, and Phil was a major rock star. She was attracted to Phil but he wasn't really interested, so she ended up with the next best thing – Bob Geldof!

Many times, when we were in Phil's company he would recite words of songs he had written, and say, 'What do you think of this one?' There would be no music, just the lyrics, and I wouldn't take too much interest. I'd just say, 'Yeah, that's good, that is!'

Two of his greatest songs were written as a direct result of his friendship with Joey. Phil's management had asked Joey to supply them with three limousines for the group plus Phil's entourage. At the time, Joey had connections with a car dealership and he bought three Daimler cars, which had come from a funeral directors. There were six cars available, and a friend of Joey's asked him if he could buy the other three. Joey had paid cash for the first three, and did a deal with his mate that if he bought the others he would sell one to Joey for a cheaper price. A sum of £5,000 was agreed for this car and Joey gave him a cheque.

But when he received the car he wasn't happy with the state of the engine, so he stopped the cheque and gave the car back to his friend. The police got involved because his friend had bought the car under false pretences, and had given Joey's cheque to them as part-payment. The law were saying that he was involved in the scam to rip this car dealer off – trying to obtain cars by deception. Of course, this wasn't true, but Joey had a difficult time explaining it away. He had to prove to the police that Thin Lizzy had actually ordered the cars from him to put him in the clear.

At the time, Phil was in Los Angeles, working on a single with Bob Dylan, when Joey phoned him up and said, 'Phil, you're going to have to send me a letter stating that you ordered these limousines because I've got the police threatening me with a charge of deception.' After a while, Joey had to ring again, because the letter hadn't arrived. Joey said, 'Phil, I'm still waiting for this alibi statement.' The next thing we knew was that Phil had written the song 'Waiting For An Alibi', which included lyrics about gambling, Joey and bookies – all based on this particular incident.

Phil's mother, Phyllis, was a great storyteller and a good listener, if you had any problems that you needed to talk through with someone. We all used to call her Aunty Phyllis – she was a lovely lady, like a guru of the showbiz world. She was a second mother to us all; even George Best would talk over his problems with her. We used to go round to her house in Chorley-cum-Hardy for a late drink. The house was like a Victorian parlour complete with bar, and many showbiz stars who were in town ended up in her company. People like Lionel Blair, Tommy Steele, rock musicians, and professional footballers were her friends, as were the criminals from the Quality Street Gang.

Joey and I would go to the Portland Lodge, a club in Manchester city centre frequented by the local villains. Afterwards, we'd pile out into a Rolls-Royce; with three sitting in the boot of the car, two on the wings, and the inside crammed full of showbiz pals – still carrying their champagne glasses. We would then move on to the Cabaret Club. How we didn't get stopped by the police, I'll never know.

Some of my friends had a run-in with the police and were away at Her Majesty's pleasure. When they returned to Manchester Phyllis spoke to Phil on the phone, and – among other things – said to him, 'The boys are back.' Not long after that Phil wrote 'The Boys are Back in Town' – one of his greatest songs. The song appeared on his 'Jailbreak' album in 1976, and became a big hit in Britain and the USA. Phil had an incredible knack of writing songs from observing people and life in general, and it seemed easy for him. He used to say, 'I think of people I know, and the songs just come to me.' I found that quite astounding.

Phil also went on to write a song about another infamous character from Manchester named Jimmy Donnelly, alias 'Jimmy the Weed'. I'd been friends with Jimmy the Weed since I was about fourteen years old. He used to have a pub in Manchester called The Brown Bull, and Phil was so friendly with him that he gave Jimmy a gold disc, which Jimmy hung on the wall of the pub for all the years he owned it. A song from the album was dedicated to Jimmy and was actually called Jimmy the Weed.

Jimmy the Weed is also mentioned in a book by Eric Mason, one of the London underworld's most feared and respected figures for over thirty years. His own brutal code of honour earned him the friendship of the Kray Twins. In this book, *The Inside Story*, he dedicates a chapter to Manchester and the Quality Street Gang. The Barlow Brothers in Manchester had a big feud with Jimmy the Weed – which is still going on to this day. Jimmy shot one of the Barlows in the leg. In revenge, they bashed Jimmy over the head with a hammer. I knew both parties. I think that they keep well away from each other now, but it is probably still simmering.

Phil was a phenomenally talented musician but, sadly, drugs started to take over his life. One evening, I went with him to Twickenham Studios – owned by Pete Townshend – where he had to do some recording. I could tell in the limousine that he was high on drugs – by the time we got to the studio he was well out of it. He went into the recording session and ten minutes later came out, and said, 'Fuck it, we're going.' We went down to Tramps club.

Phil used to reckon that Pete Townshend was a shit guitarist, and I respected his judgement, although I used to like The Who. Because of Phil's opinion I ended up not liking Pete Townshend.

There was a lot of talk about drugs in football, as well. In 1978 a big scandal erupted when Willie Johnston – who had been randomly dope-tested in Argentina during the World Cup competition – was found to be positive. He was sent home immediately in disgrace. Bob Driscoll, a reporter from the *Daily Star*, asked me for my comments and if I had taken drugs or knew of anyone who had.

'How much money are we talking about?' I said. I was, as usual, skint at the time.

'A monkey,' he said.

A monkey is slang for £500.

'Give me a grand,' I said, 'and I'll tell you anything you want.'

So I invented a story that I had taken drugs – just to get the money. I signed the confession without reading it properly, which made matters worse. The *Daily Star* said: 'His startling disclosures are the biggest blow to English football since the notorious bribes case thirteen years ago.'

Inevitably, shock waves went through the football establishment; the FA were absolutely furious. I had to immediately state publicly that my interview had been misconstrued; in effect denying everything. When I told Jim Gregory what I had done, he just started laughing and told me to leave it to him. Ron Phillips issued a statement which calmed things down a little. The ironic thing is that, although I was supposed to be one of the wild men of soccer, a drink satisfied me and I wasn't into drugs at all. I know I shouldn't have done the article – but a thousand quid was a lot of money in those days and I couldn't resist the temptation. Thankfully, though, the earthquake eventually subsided. Once again, though, it was a close run thing.

During the early part of 1978 Frank Sibley and I discussed a change of role for me on the pitch. Because of all the hammerings that I had endured over the years up front, it seemed a natural progression for me to drop back into a midfield position.

What's more, I felt that the quality of my passing and the way I could read a game, were ideal qualifications. My skill gave me the time to visualise a pass before the ball arrived at my feet, and I firmly believed that my passing game was second only to Glenn Hoddle, and, perhaps, Tony Currie.

I was able to adjust my natural talents very quickly to the switch and settled in almost immediately. I was given a free role during a game, and our defence would try to find me with every ball out of our penalty area. I was able to create the play, and, when the opportunity arose, push forward into scoring positions.

After playing only a dozen matches in this new position, I was called up by Ron Greenwood for a game against West Germany in the resurrected England B Squad. Ron had been quite complimentary towards me, saying, 'I have watched Stan play in midfield for Rangers this season and I have been very impressed. He has proved that he has both vision and touch.'

As it turned out I wasn't picked for the actual game – the position went to Tony Currie of Leeds. Ron said that Tony was more experienced in the role, but, even so, I still thought I had a chance to stake a claim for the full England side.

Obviously, I was still very interested in scoring goals for QPR, but my natural game involved a lot more than that, and I was able to create my own time on the ball in this new position. Fortunately, I had the knack of finding space on the park. Everything seemed to be going great. Then . . .

At 6 o'clock in the morning of 18 April 1978 – only hours before I was due to join the team for the trip to Nottingham Forest in a league game – the police swooped on my house in Neasden. They had a warrant to look for traveller's cheques and jewellery which had, allegedly, been stolen from Heathrow airport.

Their 'visit' was part of a simultaneous operation in which thirty addresses in the London area were raided. Apparently somebody had put my name in the frame, and they nearly knocked the front door down. My kids were thrown out into the street, and our home was ransacked. They went through every drawer and wardrobe; under the bed, and in the back garden – they even looked in the fridge! They started digging up parts of the garden, mind you, I was quite happy for them to do it – saved me a job! The search carried on until about 8 o'clock in the morning. Then they said, 'We've finished for now. You might hear from us again, or you might not.' Very nice!

I didn't have a clue what they were talking about, but I knew it was obviously big, because the Serious Crime Squad were involved – along with Scotland Yard's Flying Squad and the Fraud Squad. As it happens, something like £300,000 had been stolen from Heathrow over a six-month period. Obviously, I was totally innocent, and was subsequently cleared of any involvement in the crimes being investigated. They tore the house to bits, but saying that, I've had builders in that have made a worse mess!

The whole thing hardly put me in the right frame of mind for a football match in Nottingham later in the day, but, as usual, I just got on with it. Even so, we lost the game 1–0.

Frank Sibley was also in the process of fining me £300 for accumulating twenty points for bookings throughout the season. This was an internal policy, and the fines and match bans were dished out automatically. I managed to plead successfully for leniency and ended up with a one-match ban. I think the club imposed the fine to keep the FA sweet, but I never paid it. How could he get £300 out of me? I wasn't due any wages, because I had already had the money advanced by Ron Phillips and had spent it all long ago.

In May 1978 we avoided relegation by one point, and after that the club went through a period of uncertainty, with managers coming and going. Frank Sibley was replaced by a caretaker manager – Alec Stock. He was a lovely fella who had managed Rangers from 1959 to 1968; but he was now getting on a bit.

There was an air of decay and disappointment at the Bush. I knew the dream was over.

Chapter 14

QPR 1978-79 –
Under the Doc

In August, the team flew out on a pre-season tour of Holland, but I refused to go because, during the summer, Jim Gregory had publicly declared that there was no money available for new players. The team had broken up, and we were deteriorating rapidly. Jim had said that this would happen if we didn't win anything in the 1977–78 campaign.

The pressure had obviously got to Frank Sibley, who didn't really have the ability to handle people's problems on a day-to-day basis. He stepped aside and returned to his coaching position – and Alec Stock took over as caretaker manager. Frank was always much happier as a coach than a manager.

Jim Gregory had put millions of pounds into the club over the years without any tangible success. It was all coming to an end, as far as he was concerned. The only reason I was still there was out of loyalty to him; I knew that I would really miss him if I left the club.

However, I was getting fed up with the struggle; week in, week out. It was probably the wrong thing to do, but I made it known publicly that I wasn't going to Holland. I made it clear that it wasn't about money, but about football. No matter what anyone thought, I still wanted to be successful in the game, and I knew that I wouldn't win anything if I stayed at QPR. The team wasn't good enough and – besides the fact that I didn't want another season struggling against relegation – the most important issue was that I couldn't see the QPR team improving in the long term.

I handed another written transfer request to Jim. He understood the reasons behind my decision and knew that this time it was for real. We both knew that my days with QPR were as good as over. If I stayed, all I could envisage was playing Second Division football for the next few years and I couldn't live with that.

There was really only myself and Gerry Francis who were carrying the torch from the good old days. Most of the other senior players had been replaced by youngsters. Phil Parkes was sold to West Ham in

February 1979 for £565,000 – a world record for a goalkeeper – and things began to look pretty desperate. The only young player to come through was Clive Allen, who'd been at the club since he was a kid. The others really didn't make much impact at all.

In the 1978–79 League Cup we beat Preston North End and Swansea City, but then, in November, we played Leeds United at Loftus Road and went down 2–0. In January, when the third round of the FA Cup came along, we were drawn away to Fulham, where we lost 2–0. This meant that by January 1979 our season was over. Worse was to follow; we were relegated from Division One, finishing third from bottom – on only twenty-five points – and we joined Birmingham and Chelsea in the drop. I scored only one goal in thirty league games, and Gerry scored only twice in thirty-one league games. Grim days for a partnership that had hit the heights only three years before.

Caretaker manager Alec Stock was soon replaced by Steve Burtenshaw, but the turmoil continued right through the club. There was speculation that I was being set up for a move back to Manchester City, in a straight swap deal for Mick Channon. But I knew that this would be impossible because Malcolm Allison was back at Maine Road in his second spell as manager: I was bloody sure he wouldn't take me back! Anyway, City, at that time, were overloaded with midfield players. They had Asa Hartford, Gary Owen, Paul Power, Colin Viljoen and Colin Bell, so there wouldn't have been room for me, even if the move had been on.

Joe Mercer, however, had stated that both he and Malcolm had failed to handle me properly, and that he had rated me as highly as Francis Lee and Mike Summerbee. He said, 'I still regret that we had no choice but to give him his cards. He was magic, he played teams on his own.'

Near the end of the 1978–79 season, the media were jumping on the bandwagon proclaiming: 'The Stanley Bowles era at Queens Park Rangers is over.' Steve Burtenshaw was also saying this publicly, and had dropped me for the away game against Bristol City on 3 April 1979, using me as the scapegoat for a run of bad results. He said that I was like a racehorse who was ready for the knacker's yard. I told Burtenshaw that, if I couldn't get a place in a team of average players, it was time to pack it in at the club. He wasn't too bothered; he wanted to bring in more young players and mould his own team.

By then I really couldn't visualise playing for QPR again. I felt that I had done my best for two seasons, and had put everything I had into the club's fight against relegation. At the end of the previous season

Jim Gregory had given me a big bonus for my loyalty and effort, but, as I said, it wasn't about money as far as I was concerned.

Round about this time, there was growing interest in me from several top American clubs. Tampa Bay Rowdies, managed by my former boss Gordon Jago, were heading the queue. Philadelphia Fury and Detroit Express were other clubs showing interest – at a fee rumoured to be around £300,000. Gordon spoke to me about a move, saying that I would be a sensation over there. Problem was, I definitely didn't want to live in America, and that was the end of it. George Best and Rodney Marsh were playing over there, and the package offered was fantastic, but to me the North American Soccer League was a non-starter. It just goes to show I've got some things right in my life!

That year I played only once for QPR in the last eight games of the season, but still I didn't leave. At the time, I was going through a very unsettled period all round. My divorce to Ann finally came through in July 1979, and I had no idea where my football career was heading. I was in conflict with Steve Burtenshaw and, once again, my whole life seemed to be in limbo.

The Football Association had introduced a new Freedom of Contract agreement, and Gerry Francis was able to negotiate his own transfer following the expiry of his contract with QPR. Gerry joined Crystal Palace, reuniting him with Terry Venables, and our magical partnership, which had spanned seven seasons, dissolved. I suppose it was inevitable, but when it happens it hurts because it's almost like losing one of the family. I think that Gerry felt the same way:

Stan and I clicked straight away after he joined the club, and throughout our playing careers together we had a tremendous understanding – it was virtually telepathic. Stan really brought out the best in my play and I would like to think that our partnership helped his career also.

I can honestly say that he was easily the best player that I ever played with. He had tremendous ability, and one of my regrets is that we never played at international level together. Another is that Stan didn't achieve more England caps.

There would certainly be room in the game for Stan today. He was a player with great vision and touch. He had that ability to go past people, and score goals almost at will. I am glad that I had the opportunity of playing alongside him, particularly from 1975 to 1977, when we had an exceptional side.

I always found Stan a happy-go-lucky person and he hasn't changed at all to this day. I used to say to him that his football career wouldn't last for ever, and that he should plan for the future. But Stan lived on a day-to-day basis, and you couldn't change him.

I was invited to his house for a meal one evening after training. Ann cooked a beautiful meal, and we all sat down at the table. Just as we started eating, a knock came on the front door. In came the bailiffs and took the television, three-piece suite, dining-room table and chairs; and anything else they could lay their hands on. We ended up with the dinner on our laps, with no furniture left in the room. You never knew from one day to the next what was going to happen with Stan.

In May 1979 Tommy Docherty became manager of the club with a brief to start a rebuilding operation. On his first day, he agreed to transfer-list both myself and Dave Clement.

Docherty had bought and sold thirty-five players for more than £3 million pounds in a hectic twenty-month reign as manager of Derby prior to joining QPR, and he was renowned for bringing in young players and getting rid of more experienced professionals. The reason for this, in my opinion, was that he could frighten youngsters, whereas he had trouble controlling experienced players, who knew what he was all about. He preferred lads who were trying to make their way in the game, and would do anything he told them to without question. He wanted 'yes'-men – 'yes'-boys really. The likes of Stan Bowles – a 'piss-off mate' man, if ever there was one – wasn't for him at all.

When Tommy came to QPR he didn't speak to us on a one-to-one – only as a group. Those players whom he feared would upset the apple-cart were destined for a very short stay. His plan was that the proceeds from the sale of Dave Clement and myself – added to the £500,000 still outstanding from the transfer of Phil Parkes to West Ham – would give him ample funds to carry on his big-spending habits. I believe Tommy had no loyalty to anybody in the game, and he often said, 'I only tell the truth when a lie won't do!'

I would rather let Colonel Sanders look after my chickens than put any trust in him. He was as good as his word, and his word was no good.

The Doc was trying to raise £1.5m to spend on his rebuilding pro-gramme during the summer of 1979, and nothing was going to stand in his way. He was blaming my transfer request on Steve Burtenshaw, saying that Steve had agreed to let me go prior to him coming to the club. This was his cunning way of keeping in with the QPR fans who would, naturally, be looking for someone to blame once I left.

I'll never know whether Jim Gregory agreed with these moves or not, because you could never get the truth out of Tommy – something he will admit to himself. So I would get one story from Tommy and a different one from Jim. I have to say, that having known both of them for a number of years, Jim was marginally more trustworthy than Tommy, but there wasn't a lot in it!

So, after all this speculation, Dave Clement was finally sold to Bolton for £170,000 in June; and Gerry joined Crystal Palace. However, at the start of the 1979–80 season, I was still there.

Docherty had signed Tony Currie from Leeds United for a club record fee of £400,000. Tony was an Edgware lad who had played for Sheffield United and Leeds; and I was really looking forward to playing alongside him. I thought we could build a partnership that would revitalise my game. In the past few years, I had climbed the same mountain half a dozen times with the same club; and everything was going stale. I desperately needed a new challenge, and felt that Tony could help me put the enthusiasm back into my game.

Tommy Docherty believed that the number you had on your shirt didn't matter; so I lost the right to wear the number 10 shirt. He didn't realise that, at QPR, the fans expected that shirt to be worn by someone special. When he gave it to some of the other players early on in the season, they soon got rid of it. They couldn't handle the pressure of being expected to do something out of the ordinary, simply because they were wearing the shirt that Rodney and myself had made famous. Fortunately for Tommy, Tony Currie took the shirt and wore it throughout the season. I didn't mind Tony having it because he was a great player.

I started the season still playing in midfield, but more in the middle of the park because Tony was a right-sided player. We immediately fitted into midfield very well together, and I started to enjoy playing with him. I was playing in the number 7 shirt which Dave Thomas had worn so successfully in the club's heyday.

Tony Currie and myself were both creative players, and Dave Mc-Creery, an Irish lad who had played for Manchester United under Docherty, was the terrier, so it was a good blend. McCreery's job was to win the ball and give it to me, or Tony, to create openings.

From 8 September 1979 to the beginning of December we lost only one out of thirteen games – away to Sunderland – so we were in full swing and enjoying the sweet smell of success once more.

However, on 8 December 1979 I played my last game for Queens Park Rangers. Wrexham provided the opposition. During Tommy's reign at the club I had come to like him, but only because he used to make me laugh. He was a bouncy character, and his little anecdotes used to have me in stitches. But, in my opinion, he didn't know a lot about football. It must have been his opinion, too, since he left the coaching to Frank Sibley! Mind you, he had his own style of management and charisma; could motivate players, and always had a joke up his sleeve.

Docherty used to get involved in training sessions, where I would take the piss out of him: 'Come on fatty, get it off me!' His rotund figure would come chugging towards me at full pelt, which was quite slow. When he got near me I would slip the ball to one side to sell him a dummy and invariably he would end up on his arse, admittedly a fairly sizeable landing pad. Poor ol' Doc used to follow me round the ground puffing away like an aged, overfed Jack Russell trying for all his worth to get the ball off me. He would come diving in because he was quite fiery, and I would just slip by him. I certainly sold him a few dummies on the training ground, and used to taunt him. These antics delighted the other players, although they didn't dare show it, until he was out of sight!

Tommy admits he didn't have it all his own way when he joined the club:

I found Jim Gregory quite difficult to get on with. He handled the money in the club, and ran it as if it was a business. I was trying hard at the time to bring in new blood but if Jim didn't fancy a player I recommended, he wouldn't be signed. This was a big problem for me. However, I did complete a few good signings like Chris Woods to replace Phil Parkes for £200,000 and of course Tony Currie. Also Derek Healey, the youth team scout, had found some brilliant talent in Clive Allen, Paul Goddard and Gary Waddock who were coming through the ranks.

Stan, of course, was a wonderful player and a model professional. He was never late for training and was a quiet, unassuming lad. He was certainly the best player I have seen, and would be worth twenty million pounds today. I was sorry to see Stan leave the club and I know that Jim was too. Stan was like his favourite son after all the years they had been together.

So, there you go then!

• Chapter 15

Nottingham Forest – Communication by Rumour

My departure from QPR – when it came – was sudden, and my new team was a big surprise.

One day, out of the blue, I got a call at the gambling club in Shepherd's Bush from Ron Phillips. He told me to give Jim Gregory a ring, urgently, at his offices in Roehampton. To my surprise, Jim informed me that Nottingham Forest had come in with a £250,000 offer for me and asked if I wanted to go and speak to them. Fair enough, I thought, and said okay. Ron Phillips would make the arrangements, said Jim, and I should go to Loftus Road straightaway to get ready for a trip to Nottingham the same evening.

It took me a few minutes to collect myself and gather my thoughts, as this was an emotional moment. Then I composed myself and began to calculate exactly what my cut of the transfer proceedings would be.

At the time, Forest were the reigning European Champions, and had been League Champions and runners-up the previous two seasons, so I was amazed that they wanted me – as was everybody else!

When Ron Phillips and I eventually got to the boardroom at the City Ground, the only person there was assistant manager, Peter Taylor. He told us that we should wait for Brian Clough to arrive, and, by the time he turned up over two hours later, I was getting quite pissed off. The chairman, Geoffrey McPherson, also arrived, although he seemed totally unaware of what was happening. It was obvious that neither Brian nor Peter had told him that they wanted to sign me. This was the way of things at Forest when Cloughie ruled the roost.

The first thing Brian said to McPherson was, 'We're trying to sign Stan Bowles.' I can remember the chairman's head seemed to drop back against the wall, and he went as white as a sheet. He muttered 'Oh ... my good God!' I thought he was going to have a heart attack. Eventually though, he stopped shaking and we started to discuss the details of the contract. Ron Phillips just sat there, without saying a word all through the proceedings.

In the end, it all came down to me having a conversation with Jim Gregory on the phone – there was no way that I'd sign without his blessing. I was happy with the package offered, particularly with the bonuses, and with the cash under the table! I was also promised £10,000 by Jim as an ex gratia payment – all above board – for my services to QPR. We spoke for about ten minutes on the phone and he said, 'I don't want you to go, but it's a big club and a good move … considering your age. If you want to take the money, I'll leave the decision up to you.'

At the time I was quite impressed with Brian Clough and Peter Taylor. On top of that, Nottingham wasn't too far from Manchester, so I decided to sign on the dotted line. On the face of it a move to Nottingham looked an attractive proposition as I had completely exhausted all my credit facilities in London. Jim's view was that if I was going to sign I might as well do it there and then. He would take the backlash from the fans.

Ron and myself travelled back from Nottingham the same evening without saying much. When we got back, I went straight to Maunkberrys, a club in the West End, where I explained the transfer to a few of my friends. Most of them couldn't believe it.

I was to move to Nottingham within a few days and would be staying – all expenses paid – for three months at the Albany Hotel. After that, I would have to find my own accommodation. The transfer was being supervised by Tommy Docherty, from his hospital bed in Stockport Infirmary! He had been travelling back from London to Manchester and had had an altercation with some Manchester United supporters, who had been singing the well known verse, 'Who's up Mary Brown?' – a reference to his affair with the club physiotherapist's wife which got him the sack from Old Trafford.

Tommy, being a bit fiery-tempered, had made the mistake of answering the fans back as he got off the train and they beat him up quite badly. The Doc later told us that he had been bound to a British Rail trolley by United scarves and pushed with some force down an escalator. It is common knowledge in the game that you don't answer opposing football supporters back, but unfortunately, Tommy couldn't keep his mouth shut. That was one little mess he couldn't talk his way out of. The lads at Loftus Road had a good giggle about it when the story was splashed across the front pages and one brave soul even tied a United scarf to one end of the club stretcher. It wasn't me but everyone assumed it was. I was more than happy to take credit for the deed once I'd left the club.

At the time I moved to Forest, the reigning European Champions were struggling. They had suffered four defeats in their last five league games. They needed to justify their position as champions and they had what I thought was an exciting midfield role waiting for me. Peter Taylor summed it up by saying: 'It really needs only three words to justify our interest in Stan Bowles: he can play. When we have played against him we have always admired his ability, and had to cater for it. He has class, his control is superb, he distributes the ball well, and he scores goals. He will be used in midfield, going forward, and he will give us more time and space.'

It all sounded so promising, but unfortunately, it didn't quite work out that way. Their plan was for me to play a left midfield role with the sole purpose of feeding the ball to John Robertson on the left-wing. This was totally alien to me – I was left-footed, but I had always previously operated from the right side. I felt totally awkward on the left side, coming in on my right foot. On top of that, I was the monkey to Robbo's organ grinder.

I think that, tactically, Cloughie was a bit naïve. If he had done his research properly he would have found out that I always operated from the right, coming in on my left. In previous seasons he had bought players and changed their playing patterns – Kenny Burns being a prime example – so he planned to do the same with me. The trouble was, it just wasn't on.

This strategy wasn't mentioned to me when I signed for the club – only when I started playing, and I was very unhappy with the arrangement. Arguments between me and Cloughie started almost immediately.

I said, 'There's no way I can do this, I have to play on the right.' But as far as he was concerned, I would play where he wanted me to – or not at all. My complaints didn't alter his thinking one little bit. I was actually dropped for one game, and played in the reserves on the right. But then when I came back into the first team, he put me on the left again. So I started, very early on, to question everything about my move to Forest. I spoke to Peter Taylor many times, and he used to say, 'I understand, and I'll have a word with him.'

I had only known Cloughie for a short period of time, but had already realised that nobody could make him change his mind. As well as that, I was surprised to find there was very little opportunity to practise any tactical moves. In fact, there were no tactics at Forest! Training consisted of walking alongside the Trent three times a week to a public park, where we had a warm-up, and then an eight-a-side game which was occasionally attended by Cloughie and Taylor, usually when Peter wanted to take his dog for a walk. The dog, Bess, even attended team meetings! Kenny Burns used to stand on it when Taylor was not looking, and make it yelp.

Their arrogance showed when Peter Taylor said: 'He [Stan] has the talent to command as much respect as John Robertson, Trevor Francis and Garry Birtles, and he will slot in straightaway.'

Unfortunately, football isn't as simple as that, and it was a big mistake on their part. Cloughie had seen me play only for QPR against Forest. Peter had done a little bit of research and knew I played on the right but he was overruled.

Fred Reacher, later chairman of Nottingham Forest, has since said: 'Brian had previously stated that we needed someone in the side with flair and excitement to complement the current squad. He was quite happy to take the gamble with Stan because if it helped us to win the European Cup again, irrespective of how short the period was, it was money well spent.'

Forest were not looking at me as a long-term prospect, only to fill a specific role in their team which had arisen with the sale of striker Tony Woodcock to Cologne for £650,000 in November, 1979. They had no loyalty to me and I found this out pretty quickly, but by then it was too late. A few weeks into my contract, Cloughie explained again to me that when my period at the Albany Hotel had expired, I would have to get a house up there. I wasn't too happy with this, and told him so.

'You cockneys are all the same,' he shouted at me, in the middle of the argument.

'Excuse me,' I said, haughtily, 'I was born and bred in Manchester!'

Cloughie didn't like that at all – he didn't like anyone trying to get the better of him – so we didn't start off on the right foot. He also thought all footballers were thick. I wasn't having any of that, so I told him I had four O levels and three A levels. This was a bit of an exaggeration really, because all I'd ever got at school was a star and a tick! My bragging didn't go down too well with the boss, seeing as he had no formal education himself and was a bit sensitive on the issue.

My first game for Forest was in the second leg of the European Super Cup against Barcelona, who had won the Cup Winners' Cup by beating Fortuna Düsseldorf 4–3 in the final. We had won the first leg 1–0 at the City Ground, and I was pitched straight in for the second leg in front of 120,000 supporters, in the magnificent Nou Camp Stadium. I had got to know a few of the Forest players quite well, and they were quite friendly and outgoing; and there was a fairly good atmosphere in the squad. We held out for a 1–1 draw, which meant we won 2–1 on aggregate and became undisputed champions of Europe. I couldn't believe that I had made my debut for Nottingham Forest in a European Super Cup Final.

Fred Reacher remembers the scenes after the game: 'My most vivid recollection of Stanley was when I went into the dressing room after the second leg, and he was sitting there, deep in thought, looking at the memento that he had been given, along with the other players, for winning the competition. It was a metal figure of the Barcelona lady with an umbrella over her head. Stan looked up to me and said, "Do you know what? This is the first medal I've won in professional foot-ball." And I thought to myself, What a great waste of talent to have just picked up one memento. It seemed very sad to me.'

I gave that memento away afterwards, but the knowledge that I had won it gave me a feeling of achievement and well-being. One reporter said: 'The trophy is won. Kenny Burns puts his arm around captain John McGovern, while Stan Bowles cannot take his eyes off the first medal he has won in his richly promising career.'

I was supposed to play my first game for Forest in the league against Middlesbrough but, unfortunately, the game was called off and I even-tually made my home debut against Aston Villa at the City Ground. Although I scored, I was finding it very difficult to adapt to my new role because I was used to players giving me the ball, not the other way around. If I wanted to get into the penalty area I had to take the responsibility upon myself, which was not the kind of free role that I was used to. The fans didn't take to me immediately either, which didn't help.

Forest were an excellent passing side, and it didn't take me long to see that they were a great team. Brian Clough had been coming under pressure because of recent bad results, but there wasn't much wrong with the team at all. Trevor Francis looked a bit more skilful than he was, simply because of his speed. I thought he was a bit overrated, but he was like greased lightning over twenty yards.

After only two or three months, the Clough–Bowles relationship was on the verge of collapse. There was still an ongoing battle over the position he was playing me in, and I had suffered several barbed comments from the man himself – whose acid turn of phrase could humiliate the most experienced professional. Being me, I used to answer him back, which not many players did, and this made him even worse.

At the end of March 1980 we played at Brighton, and when Clough was asked about my performance, he said simply, 'Was Stanley out there today?' By this time I knew that I wasn't going to be at Forest for very long. Clough didn't play me in many away games – usually preferring Ian Bowyer – because he thought that I didn't put enough effort into the ninety minutes. I knew he was doing this just to aggravate me. It became very personal between us; and although I still had eighteen months of my contract to run, nobody was taking bets on how long it would last. Even I wouldn't have bet on me seeing it out, and you know my track record!

There has been a great deal of debate over the years about how talented Cloughie was as a manager, why he never became England manager, and what kind of a person he really was. I have my views.

Was Brian Clough a genius, or was he off his head? My view was that, as the old saying goes, there is a very fine line between genius and madness. It is difficult to find anyone who got close enough to Clough to make a definitive judgement, but it is certainly a subject that has been talked about in pubs, dressing rooms, and everywhere that the great mysteries of the world are debated.

One view, widely shared by my professional colleagues – and also by many in the football establishment – was that Cloughie, like some of the great but misguided Roman emperors, thought he was God – No ... he definitely knew he was God! You had to make an appointment through his secretary's secretary to see him. He would sign players without the chairman's knowledge. No one seemed to mind. The board's view was that when you are winning European Cups, you don't ask too many questions. Having that autonomy within the club gave him a feeling of invincibility. He had far greater power than any manager would have today. He would also sell players very quickly if he thought that they were not suitable; sometimes incurring a great loss for the club financially. In short, he did what he bloody well liked. Nearly everyone – board, players, media, fans – were terrified of him; and that was just the way he wanted it.

Did he know about football? I don't think he did. In Peter Taylor, he had an assistant who complemented him perfectly. Brian had an idea of the type of player that he was looking for to fill a certain role, and Peter would go out and find him. They reminded me of two policemen when interrogating a suspect. One was the hard man who would go off the deep end, and the other was the man who would put his arm around you and comfort you – the perfect foil. I wonder who played the hard man . . .

One thing was clear, however: if the signings proved successful, Cloughie took the credit and, if not, Peter took the blame. Together they had brought two unfashionable clubs – Derby County and Nottingham Forest – from Second Division obscurity to major domestic honours and then launched them on exciting European campaigns. There is no doubt that Clough and Taylor, in their prime, were very special; maybe the greatest double act in the history of English football.

Brian did things his own way, so that when you played under him you weren't able to influence him at all. He never had any great respect for the establishment, and seemed to seek out rebellious, wayward players that he thought he could mould into stars. If an assortment of mavericks and wild men could perform on the pitch, he was prepared to tolerate the more destructive side of their personalities.

Typical examples of this were myself (obviously) and Larry Lloyd, who had a reputation for being a bit uncontrollable at Liverpool, and certainly at Coventry City. Kenny Burns also fell into this 'rebel' category, as did Charlie George, and John Robertson. In fairness, Cloughie moulded Robertson – a hard-drinking, chain-smoking Scot – into probably the best left-winger in the world at the time. Brian believed that the best players had a bit of wildness about them, and that brilliance went hand and hand with a darker side.

It is my belief that his liking for misfits, rejects and bad boys, was a reflection of himself in many respects. His desire to tame them, or at least take them on board and make them part of a winning team, certainly set him apart from other managers in the game; who were usually trying to unload rebels, not sign them.

Clough's bold individuality had a kind of heroic dimension, but it proved his undoing when it came to the most prestigious job of all – manager of England. This was probably the most talked-about subject in footballing circles – or over a pint – and has been the subject of speculation ever since.

I know from talking to people who were with him at the time, that he would have loved to have been England manager, it would have been the pinnacle of a spectacular career. The vast majority of the general public thought he deserved the chance to show what he could do. He certainly had a lot of club success against the Germans, with exciting victories over Cologne, Dynamo Berlin and Hamburg. He would have relished the idea of England v West Germany at Wembley, or anywhere else, for that matter!

Sadly, Cloughie had a love–hate relationship with the establishment – at times more like a hate–hate relationship! Usually the managers who get the England job are safe bets, guys who know they mustn't rock the boat. Brian could never have been that kind of animal if he tried. He wouldn't have been able to include rebel players in his England side, and he would have had to change his management style. The football establishment wanted predictability, and Cloughie couldn't have given that. The only predictable thing about Brian Clough was his unpredictability. Since he would have come into contact with the England players only once in a blue moon, I don't think they would have understood his whims and eccentricities.

He didn't allow players to get near him. Mind you, I don't think the players wanted to be too close to him anyway – I certainly didn't. It was the same with my team-mates at the time. Although they had respect for him as a manager, if he walked into a pub where we were at the bar drinking, we felt like walking out. No one really wanted to socialise with him.

Few players got close to Brian Clough. Perhaps John McGovern, who followed Brian from Hartlepool to Derby, Leeds and Forest, was the closest. According to John:

> I played under Brian Clough for thirteen years. The biggest influence on my life has been my mother and the biggest influence on my football life has to be Cloughie.
>
> He definitely wasn't the sort of man you'd choose to go for a pint with, but as a manager he was someone you had to respect enormously. He wasn't everybody's cup of tea, but when his teams went out on to the pitch, he had everyone pulling in the same direction, which is the best thing any manager can do. Whatever else, he always got 100 per cent out of his players.
>
> People say that he was very up and down in his moods but I don't agree with that. I found him to be very constant and I always knew where I was with him. Certainly, throughout the time I played under him, he retained a passion for the game; a sort of eternal flame if you like. Other managers would have that now and again, say when they'd just won something, but with Cloughie it was always there.
>
> I had the reputation of being his blue-eyed boy, but nothing could be further from the truth. I had more rollickings off him than the rest of

them put together. He never treated anyone as special. Even in my mid-twenties, he still had me getting autographs from the lads; something that the ground staff would usually do. I suppose he made me do it to keep my feet on the ground.

I found it easy to accept his code of discipline. As far as I was concerned, it was an extension of the way I was brought up. I knew others found it a bit difficult, but I never had a problem.

Coaching wasn't his strong point. I think I was about 25-years-old before he gave me any specific coaching advice. Up until then all he'd ever say was 'If you can play, go out and play; if you can't, get out of the team.' It was Bill Shankly who used to say, 'Mums and dads make footballers, not managers or coaches.' Cloughie thought the same way. It has to be said, though, that he had an enormous knowledge of the game, and he used that knowledge very well.

As far as I'm concerned, his record in the game is second to none. Both Derby and Forest were in the doldrums when he took over, yet he managed to win two Championships and two European Cups. Other managers have collected more trophies but with the likes of Liverpool and Manchester United it's a bit easier. They had money and tradition on their side. Cloughie's teams had neither. He was definitely a one-off.

Which, I suppose, is fair enough. In my opinion, Clough was a very clever man, with a proven formula for building a winning team. He would recruit his three or four rebels, but he always made sure that the rest of the team were 'Steady Eddies'. He kept loyal players who had been with him for a long time – like McGovern, who did a reliable job – never the best player, never the worst. Others, like Viv Anderson and Tony Woodcock, who had come up through the club's youth and reserve teams, would never say anything controversial to him. They would just keep their heads down and get on with the job in hand. This strategy ensured that he couldn't really lose. He would have an effective mixture of flair, flamboyance and a stable nucleus for the team as well. For many years, Brian and Peter could visualise the players that would gel into their pattern, even if they only stayed at the club for a short time. That, in my book, was very good management.

However, it was obvious that when Clough finished nobody would be allowed to have that power again. In my short time at the club it was too late to reverse it, and the directors accepted that fact. Clough thought that because he created entertaining, winning teams, and brought millions of pounds into the club, that he was entitled to make most of the decisions.

I reckon that it was the arrival of Justin Fashanu from Norwich in August 1981 that was the catalyst for the break-up of the relationship between Peter and Brian. Now, Fashanu wasn't worth a million pence, never mind pounds! Other expensive failures, such as Ian Wallace and Peter Ward, had also been brought in around that time and the management duo were getting a bit of stick from certain quarters. Naturally, because Cloughie couldn't admit to making mistakes, poor old Peter took the blame. I think it must have got to him; because, soon after, Taylor went to Derby County and nicked John Robertson from under Cloughie's nose. They hardly ever spoke to each other again after that incident.

By the early eighties, football had become so coach-orientated that players were in danger of becoming robots. The opportunities for Brian to bring in players with real, natural skill were decreasing. The supply of Kevin Hectors, Archie Gemmills, Alan Hintons, Colin Todds, Roy McFarlands and John Robertsons had dried up. Transfer fees, on the other hand, were rocketing and no way could he find the young talent, or the maverick genius, that he had previously moulded into winning units.

The game itself was changing – and not for the better. The first question that chairmen of football clubs started to ask prospective managers was no longer, 'What have you done in the game?' It was, 'Have you got your FA coaching badge?' The old-style managers – Joe Mercer, Bill Shankly, Don Revie, Bob Paisley etc. – weren't slaves to FA coaching doctrines. But, sadly, the game was now drifting in a mundane direction. The players who had provided personality, flair and creativity, were being squeezed out of the game by athletes with outstanding fitness and pace. This made the game faster and more condensed – but a pain in the arse to watch.

No longer could Cloughie take someone like Birmingham centre forward Kenny Burns – a total nutcase who was virtually down and out, and driving a car which was falling apart – and mould him into a great central defender winner of a Championship medal and two European Cups. Kenny may even have got a decent motor out of it! Anyway, that was the kind of challenge Brian needed. It gave him a sense of fulfilment to know he had used his management skills to their fullest potential. Despite my problems with Cloughie, I think it is a great shame that those type of managers are now more or less obsolete, and will probably never re-emerge in football.

Legendary characters like Bill Shankly and Brian Clough will always be remembered with affection in the game. Directors are now almost getting to the stage where they don't trust their manager to do anything except coach and train the team. There is a widespread belief that footballers don't possess any brains, so when they emerge as managers they aren't given any say in the running of the club. Football needs maverick managers almost as much as it needs maverick players.

On the other hand, the other side of Brian's personality was very hard for the players of my era to comprehend. Larry Lloyd sums the man up in his after-dinner speeches by saying, 'Brian Clough was supposed to be with me tonight, but unfortunately he can't be here because he's doing a sponsored walk from Dover to Calais!'

Clough would insist on the team going for walks in the park. He would be in front like the Pied Piper, and we would follow behind like a bunch of dickheads. What could you do but go along with it, even if the weather was freezing? If you refused you would end up with a fine, or something. Larry and Robbo used to kick up a lot, and that, probably, cost them a few bob; but, at the end of the day you couldn't fight back – we'd all have to go. Peter Taylor would tag along with us, just to calm the troubled waters.

While Brian was marvellous at handling directors, and at creating publicity, Peter was great at finding talent, and reassuring the players. Although they made a great partnership in many ways, they didn't socialise together because I don't think that they particularly liked each other. Even so, I think Brian will always regret that they never made up after their split, and he'll probably take that regret to the grave. It was a deeply sad end to a brilliant partnership. After the two of them went their separate ways, things were never the same again at the City Ground.

My old mate, Larry Lloyd, has his own views on those times:

Certainly, after the split it was never the same. There wasn't so much laughter around the place. Everyone goes on about Cloughie, but to me Taylor was magic. He could relate to someone like Stan because there wasn't a day that went by when he didn't have a bet. They used to share a *Sporting Life* in the dressing room, and it was quite funny watching them. Stan would be sitting there with a few players, including Peter Shilton. Peter Taylor would walk in, sit in the middle of them and start picking the winners. Very often he would join the card schools on the coach when we were travelling away.

All that I could ever get out of Stan about Cloughie was when we were standing there listening to his rantings, Stan would move his mouth to one side in my direction and utter in a low voice, 'He's a fucking nutter, he is!' I think he felt differently towards Peter Taylor.

I had, of course, played against Stan when he was with QPR. I had heard from other players that he was a bit of a character, and I knew he would fit in really well with some of us. When you transfer to a new football club, it's funny, but it usually takes only one morning's training to sort out your clique – your gang. Me and Robbo were talking about going for a pint, Shilts was talking about having a bet on the horses, and Stan immediately thought, That's my mob. Not the crowd that were shouting, 'Yes boss, no boss, three bags full, boss!' You weigh up your little gang: us, like mischievous schoolchildren sitting at the back of the class, or the teacher's pets at the front who are listening intently. Stan was a back-of-the-class merchant.

Professional footballers always know when a player has ability. It comes through the grapevine, and we knew before Stan arrived at the club that he had great ability, make no mistake about it. First we thought, Shock! Horror! What's he doing coming to Forest? But the bottom line was that he could play football, and he could only improve us.

Our fans would accept two types of players. The totally committed like me, who couldn't do much with the ball but would run through a brick wall, break noses and smack people around a bit, basically doing a stopping job. The other type was Stan and Robbo, who couldn't head a ball, or tackle a fish and chip supper, but could produce a little bit of magic. Stan could sell a dummy better than Mothercare – sending 40,000 people the wrong way. That was magic and they loved it.

Prior to Stan coming to the club, I came into contact with him in the fifth round of the FA Cup in the 1977–78 season. This cup tie was a stalemate, we had drawn at QPR and also in the replay at Forest, and so there was a toss-up as to where the venue would be for the deciding game. The coin came down heads – the game would be played at the City Ground on a Thursday night. Cloughie hadn't been around for any of the previous three meetings, so we didn't expect him to be there that night. However, at twenty-five past seven, five minutes before kick-off, the door of our dressing room came off its hinges – literally. We were already shitting ourselves about the replay, but we all jumped up from our seats and there's Cloughie standing in the doorway. It either came down with one kick, or he had someone loosen the hinges beforehand. There he was, tanned and healthy, but with a face like thunder.

'You fucking bastards!' he shouted. 'You've dragged me back from Majorca to get you through this FA Cup tie against a load of shit from London!' That was Brian's team talk. We went out and beat QPR 3–1 – Stan scoring for Rangers.

The following morning Brian flew back to continue his holiday.

He had great presence, but could be very rude and ignorant. When we were out socially with the team he had waiters and waitresses shitting themselves. We used to sit there cringing as the poor little girls, trying to serve the soup, were splashing it all over the place because he'd frightened them to death.

He would also do things quite out of the ordinary. We were travelling on a coach on the M62 to play Liverpool in a cup match in the evening and there were bottles of Chablis getting passed around, and there we were getting it down us prior to a very important match.

Then, when we played in the League Cup final and arrived at the hotel about 10 o'clock the night before the game. Cloughie just said, 'Right, dump your bags in your rooms and come down to the bar.'

We were shocked because he wouldn't normally talk to us at all before a game. We congregated downstairs, and this waiter came out with half a dozen of bottles of champagne, followed by another waiter with two trays of sandwiches. John O'Hare, who was a bitter drinker through and through, said to him, 'I only like bitter, boss.'

All of a sudden, twelve pints of bitter appeared in the room. The party went on till about 1.30 in the morning, and Archie Gemmill was doing his nut because he was a 10 o'clock-to-bed man. I ended up carrying Tony Woodcock up the stairs, even though I could hardly stand up myself! As a result of this we were 1–0 down at half-time in the final, but won the game in the second half – once we'd run the booze out of our systems!

You never knew what Brian would do next. You couldn't start a conversation with him. On the odd occasion, when he would walk past you wearing his green jumper, you wouldn't dare say good morning first, or anything like that. You had to let him set the pace, depending on his mood at that particular time.

Once, I had made an appointment to see him about my contract and arrived at his office at 10 o'clock in the morning. He put two half-pint glasses down on the desk and filled them up with brandy.

'I gather you're here to talk about your contract,' he said.

'Yeah, that's right.'

'Well, let's have a drink first.'

'Oh no, I like a drink but I'm not drinking this.'

'Why not?'

'If I drink this brandy, Jimmy Gordon, the trainer, is gonna run my bollocks off when I leave here and I'm gonna spew up, and you're gonna fine me for being pissed in training aren't you?'

'Yes,' he said, 'That's right.'

'Well, fuck your drink then!'

All you ever wanted from Cloughie – all any professional footballer wants – is a pat on the back to let you know you've played well. You never got that from him. The words, 'Well played, son!' weren't part of his vocabulary.

I almost had him by the throat one day when he said that I'd bottled it against Arsenal. 'Do you know what bottled means?' I said. 'It means that I'm a coward, and I'm not taking that from anybody!' I lunged forward.

'You touch me and you're finished,' he said.

Obviously, I knew that if I'd laid hands on him I would have been finished.

Other players who had played badly would be congratulated. This was part of Cloughie's motivational technique. He knew how to press the button of each individual in the team. I've battled with Joe Jordan for ninety minutes, and Brian's never said a word to me after the game. Either he was very clever, or very lucky – I'm not quite sure. There was me with my nose across my face, and a stitch in my head having kept Joe Jordan – who was a real handful – quiet for most of the game, and Cloughie doesn't say a word. So I'm saying to myself, 'Fuck him – I'll show him next week!'

He was probably thinking, 'I know Larry'll do it next week if I ignore him.' It was a very clever way of managing the team, and it probably made him the brilliant manager that he was.'

I think Larry's views were shared by a few of us in the team. You couldn't condone or understand some of the outrageous things Clough did, but he came up with the goods when it mattered. He was arrogant and extremely temperamental, but, somehow, it worked.

He snapped one day at Wolves when a fan started to give him some verbal after a league match. Clough threw a punch, but the bloke ducked and a guy standing behind got it in the face. For once in his life

Clough panicked. He ended up escorting the victim on to our coach, trying to calm him down. He was very lucky to get away with that incident, which wasn't reported or televised. In those days there weren't so many cameras around. You have only got to fart now and a camera from Sky, or another channel, will pick it up.

While at Forest, I was able to carry on with one of my sporting loves. In my QPR days, we had often gone to race meetings at Ascot, Sandown and Kempton, all of which are fairly accessible from London. Lots of people love looking at thoroughbred racehorses, watching them in the parade ring, and so on; but I'd always stay in the bar until the off. It was the racing, and the characters, that I loved. The punters who admired the horses would be all together in one area, and the scoundrels would congregate elsewhere. I liked the atmosphere, and I still do.

Now, after joining Forest, I was able to go to Nottingham and South-well races. I used to go with Peter Shilton, and we'd make a day of it. Martin O'Neill was quite a big gambler, and Kenny Burns's father was a bookmaker.

The most I've ever won on a horse was at Southwell. I had it off and walked away with over eight grand, but the Jewish bookmaker couldn't pay me until the next meeting. In fact, he said, 'Do you want a share in the book?' meaning that he was offering me a share of the business, but I didn't fancy that – too organised for me. The most I have ever lost was when I put £4,000 on a horse at 11/4 in an ordinary meeting at Newbury, and it was beaten in a photo finish.

I got on well with Peter Taylor, and Kenny and I used to take Peter's bets. He used to have big bets on the football every Saturday, and his minimum bet would be £200 or £300 on five English matches, mainly in the First Division. But he didn't win very often, because there is always one team that lets you down.

Peter used to go to the races in disguise because he didn't want everyone to know that he was gambling. When Arsenal played Valencia in the European Cup Winners' Cup Final in May 1980, Peter wanted £4,000 on Arsenal at 6/4 to win over the ninety minutes. Even though I had no money, I said to Kenny, 'Take it!' We took £2,000 of it, and ended up a grand apiece better off. The game was a 1–1 draw, with Valencia winning on penalties. If Arsenal had won, I would have had to disappear down the M1!

All in all, the dogs took more money off me than the horses. This is mostly because I got involved in owning dogs – something I don't recommend. When I owned a dog it cost about £30 a week to keep. On top of that were the vet's fees. A greyhound might have two or three needles a week, which is another £33. With a dog, you never know whether they have had the needles or not, they can't tell you! You get a receipt, but you can't be sure that you're not being ripped-off. You're paying out on the animal; but the prize money can be as small as £40. Although it has gone up to well over £100 now, you can still really only make money out of gambling and breeding.

I was as disorganised as ever, when it came to my financial situation. In fairness to Cloughie, he did help me out once when I was being chased by the Inland Revenue. He invited the tax inspector into his office and gave him a cheque for a couple of grand to clear back taxes which I owed. I had to repay this later, but it was a kind gesture.

I also know that he helped other players out financially from time to time – all above board. He also was very benevolent when it came to charitable causes, although this was never publicised. So it just goes to show, he was a man of many faces.

People who saw Brian Clough being obnoxious on television must have wondered whether he was putting on an act for the cameras; but, let me tell you, that was the real Clough! He would insult anybody and was as arrogant as it is possible to be. I always remember one of his favourite lines: 'Rome wasn't built in a day, but I wasn't on that particular job.'

With the way the two of us were, it was only a matter of time before we had a major disagreement. Sure enough, this came as we were preparing for the 1980 European Cup Final, against SV Hamburg in Madrid.

On the Friday before we were due to leave, a testimonial had been organised for John Robertson, and I was very much looking forward to playing in the match to say thank you to John for looking after me during my early days with Forest.

Without doubt my best pal at Forest was John Robertson. As a friend he was one of the funniest, most likeable blokes anyone could hope to meet. Robbo had a great personality; often quiet, he'd choose his moment to deliver a devastating one-liner that would send us all into fits of laughter. He liked a drink too, but he was never one of those stereotypical Scots who wanted to fight everyone once he'd had one too many. He was more of a pacifist, a calming influence on and off the pitch, with a laid-back attitude on life. I'm sure his partnership with Martin O'Neill is one of the reasons why Celtic have enjoyed so much success in recent years.

How Robbo became one of the best wingers in the world is something of a mystery. His build had more in common with your average darts player than it did a professional footballer. John was an unlikely looking athlete; he had a bit of a bulge in the stomach. In all my time off the pitch I rarely saw him without a cigarette in his mouth. The wily Scottish international may have carried a bit of timber but he was certainly blessed with an uncanny ability to trick and tread his way past the very best defenders in Europe.

Robbo and I hit it off socially straight from day one despite the fact he didn't gamble. In fact thinking of it now he's probably one of a very select band of people I like that doesn't list betting as an interest.

John's style of clothing could be described as both unique and unfashionable; he was easily the worst dresser at the club despite fierce competition from Peter Shilton.

Robbo was one of those blokes that could never look smart – no matter what you did with him he'd always look like an unmade bed. You could hand him over to one of those makeover shows and a team of effeminate men and glamorous women could swarm round; decorate him from head to toe in designer gear, style his hair, remove his fag and give him a good old buff up. But no matter what they did, within minutes Robbo would manage to make the look his own – shabby, unkempt and dishevelled.

Robbo's appearance wasn't helped by a stubborn insistence on wearing his favourite pair of shocking orange/brown hush puppies. Over the years the tattered shoes had been in service, they had clocked up thousands of miles and this was visible in terms of wear and tear. Those particular hush puppies had soaked up rivers of liquid, notably rainwater, beer and piss during their loyal service. This didn't stop Robbo wearing them with dinner suits, dicky bows, or his favoured creased cotton trouser and Columbo coat combination.

Eventually, Peter Taylor got so fed up with the hush puppies that one night – in Germany – he wrenched them off Robbo and lobbed them high over the Berlin Wall somewhere deep into the dark East. As the lads watched them sail over we half expected them to be tossed straight back by a dissatisfied East German tramp. As they didn't return we can only assume that they contributed to the collapse of Communism.

Fortunately for Robbo he will be remembered at Forest for his football and not his misguided dress sense. And Robbo really was a terrific footballer. He was clever, crafty and cute all at once, often in one untidy shuffling movement. He'd lure defenders in running down the left, cut in and then go past them with a well-practised shimmy of which he had many variations. And if he didn't fancy going past a defender more often than not he'd dive over them. Robbo was an absolute master at winning penalty kicks. Forget Van Nistelrooy and Pires, I've never ever seen anyone better than Robbo at winning a spot kick. Rod Marsh was also an excellent exponent of this art, especially for a big man, but I'd have to say Robbo was even better. I remember at QPR, Don Shanks would never even attempt to tackle him in the box because he'd be too afraid of giving a penalty away.

Anyway, when the team for the testimonial was picked, I had been left out. I decided that Clough was taking the piss, so I told Peter Taylor that I was leaving the ground, and wouldn't be going to Madrid.

Peter told me that he would tell Brian Clough but, as it turned out, he didn't. Although, now I think about it, it is possible that Clough was told. He could've just been using it as an excuse to have a real go at me – a bit of psychology: poor old Brian, let down again by bad-boy Stanley Bowles. Anyway, I didn't join the Forest party which travelled to Majorca in preparation for the game, and Clough slaughtered me in the press, saying, 'I don't know why Bowles is not here. I don't know why he has not turned up. I don't know because I haven't spoken to him. But he will need to have one hell of an excuse for him to retain any hope of getting away with this action. His future at Forest must now be in very serious doubt.'

I hit back by saying that I couldn't stand Clough any more. I did an article for Kevin Moseley in the *Daily Mirror* prior to the European Cup Final. In it, I said: 'He's a virtual dictator. He bought me to help them retain the cup, yet I've never been given a chance. All I wanted to do was play but it's a standing joke at the club that I'll only be playing at home and never away.'

Things were obviously going from bad to worse, and even some of the players were giving me very little time. They tolerated Clough's behaviour because of the money and medals, but I wasn't prepared to do that – if it meant being humiliated. I could have earned a £6,000 bonus for winning the European Cup, but I told him to stick it, and young Gary Mills took my place on the subs' bench. It was ironic that the team we were due to play was Kevin Keegan's SV Hamburg, who had tried to sign me earlier. As it turned out, I would have probably been able to get on better with the Germans than I did with Clough.

Forest beat Hamburg 1–0 in the final on 28 May, with John Robertson scoring from the edge of the penalty area in the twentieth minute. But it didn't really matter to me, I knew my time at Forest was already over. Even so, Clough didn't make himself available to see me about my situation until eight days after the final. He told the press: 'We have a ten o'clock appointment this morning. It will be our first contact since Stan Bowles did his disappearing act, and as far as I'm concerned the interview will last about thirty seconds. Bowles has burned his bridges, his boats and anything else that floats.'

Actually, our meeting didn't even last that long because I had nothing to say. I haven't spoken to Clough since the day of John Robertson's testimonial.

Although I wasn't happy during my time at Forest, Jane, my girlfriend, quite enjoyed Nottingham. As far as she was concerned, one of the best things about it was that it released us from all of the hangers-on who plagued me every minute of every day in London. She thought it helped our relationship, even though during the first couple of months we were regularly going back to London by cab. We had been staying in a hotel, and so we found it quite difficult to settle, and she had put on a lot of weight in those first months.

People always thought that Jane was just out for a good time, intent on spending my money; but I can honestly say that, during our time together, she never saw a tanner of it. Although we drank champagne and went out for meals, I never gave her money for housekeeping or shopping. For her, it was a battle to get a fiver out of me to buy food. But people thought that any young actress becoming involved with a football star must be a money-grabbing social climber.

She used to love watching me play at Loftus Road, but stopped enjoying football when we moved to Nottingham because she was always a bundle of nerves, frightened that Cloughie would pull me off during a game. She knew that all Cloughie was doing was throwing down a challenge to me, and that every time I would bite.

Jane was desperately unhappy when we left Nottingham, and spent a long time saying goodbye to everyone, because our friends there were such lovely people. She knew that when we went back to London our time together would be very limited, and that I would wander back into the same old scene, with the same old hangers-on. She used to tell me that I was too good to play in a lower division, but maybe it was just because she wanted to keep me away from London.

I think I brought out the mothering instinct in Jane. No matter how bad I was, she just wanted, somehow, to protect me. Having said that, when we finally parted, years later, I think she realised within a week that her life was much better without me. She stopped feeling insecure, and felt that there really was something else to strive for. I know that, once again, I had only myself to blame.

A few weeks after the Forest–Hamburg final, Jim Gregory phoned me and said, 'There could be a good move in this for us because I could buy you back on the cheap.' So my reaction was, 'Certainly, Jim, the sooner the better.' But from what I could gather, Tommy Docherty didn't try too hard to bring me back to QPR. I didn't really fit in with his plans and we both knew it. I knew he had offered Cloughie £100,000 but when he was asked about it in the press, he said, 'Sign him back? It took me long enough to get rid of him.'

We were now in pre-season training and all the messages from the club were passed on to me by Jimmy Gordon, the Forest trainer. Clough was saying that although it hadn't worked out with me, and while the situation couldn't go on, he didn't want it to cost the club a fortune. 'We paid more than £200,000 for him, and he hasn't been with us five minutes, so there is no way we are going to let him go for peanuts,' he said.

Sheffield Wednesday came in with an offer of £110,000, and now Cloughie was admitting that he might have to lose money to wash his hands of me. The only communication between us was, as I used to say, by rumour; I knew that we would never speak again.

Fred Reacher and the Forest establishment, were also looking to make major changes. He says now: 'Stan's imminent departure coincided with a period where we, as a club, were looking at dismantling the European Cup-winning side, and reducing the age of our squad. This would not be a wholesale change, but a gradual process. We eventually achieved this objective but, unfortunately, we didn't win any more major honours after this restructuring of the team.'

In early July, Jimmy Gordon came to me on the training ground to tell me that there was a possible move back to London.

'I'll go, I don't care who it is.' My mind was made up.

It could have been an offer from the Royal Philharmonic Orchestra for all I cared.

Chapter 16

Orient – East End Stan

In July 1980 I moved to Orient, my sixth Football League club, for a club record fee of £100,000.

It was quite a bit of money for a Second Division club to lay out, but Jimmy Bloomfield, the manager, told the press that he didn't expect me to give him any headaches or sleepless nights. The reporters thought that Jimmy should go straight to the top of the league for optimism! I knew I would like Jimmy, because he had been a very good player himself. He reminded me of Ian MacFarlane, but without the violence.

I was so desperate to move from Forest that I didn't insist on a large signing-on fee. Jimmy said, 'I know one thing. Stan is certainly not greedy. His signing couldn't have been more simple. He certainly wasn't demanding.'

This was true, but the funny thing was, I was actually earning more at Orient than I had been at Forest, simply because my basic wage was bigger. At Forest, the bonuses were phenomenal – especially in European games, where we got £800 for a win, scaled all the way up to £6,000 for the final.

I liked Jimmy a good deal. I respected him as a manager, tactician and as a person. I've managed to successfully tap most of the managers I worked under for a few quid at some point during my stay, and some I found easier to milk than others. Throughout my adult existence I've tended to suffer with the week lasting longer than my pay packet, and accordingly advances, loans, subs, in fact any sort of credit, comes in double handy to plug in the gaps.

Jimmy was a nice fellow and like most nice fellows he didn't even ask for the first few subs back, expecting me to willingly return the cash in my own time. I wasn't forthcoming in handing back the cash but compromised by increasing my credit level. Sadly, this gratifying policy did not continue for as long as I would have liked. Jim began to grow tired of my frequent visits to his office asking for £60 here and

£100 there, just to tide me over. Poor Jim had completely lost track of the amount of money that was coming off my next month's wages.

One afternoon, after I finished training, I popped upstairs to see a brand-new sign sitting on Jimmy's desk boldly declaring that NO PLAYER OR MEMBER OF STAFF WILL BE ABLE RECEIVE AN ADVANCE ON THEIR WAGES UNDER ANY CIRCUMSTANCES. As I was the only player or member of staff who ever asked for an advance I deduced that this notice was directed solely at me. 'Sorry Stan,' shrugged Jimmy, 'new club policy, comes from above, nothing I can do about it.' This was undoubtedly bad news. I'd been at the club four months and been paid for seven. This meant I wouldn't be getting remunerated anytime soon.

Two months without wages did nothing for my mood. Out of desperation – two weeks later – I went up to Jimmy in a frantic state and told him he had to give me a grand in cash, there and then, or I was a dead man. Once Jimmy had stopped laughing he started laughing some more. Eventually, he asked me why I needed such a large sum and how the devil I thought he could get it. I pointed through the window to where my mate Mouse was pacing up and down next to a lamp-post.

Now Mouse is named ironically; the lamp-post was marginally taller than Mouse but nowhere near as wide. He's around six foot six, with a face like a cement mixer, a neck that looks like a pack of hot dogs. Mouse bet me once that he could kill a man with one carefully placed punch – that was one bet I was afraid to take. Mouse had a nasty scar running across his cheek. It always surprises me how men that size still seem to get attacked. I guess there are a lot of nutters around.

I told Jimmy, 'If I don't get a grand within the next hour that man I owe money to is going to come up here and break both my legs.'

As Jimmy looked out of the window again the Mouse put on his best menacing look and started to kick at a parked car, leaving it with a huge dent in the passenger door. Jimmy started spluttering, disappeared for ten minutes and came back with a sizeable wad of notes, handing it to me. 'Here's £800, all I could get, just get him away from here.'

I thanked Jim for saving my bacon and told him I was forever indebted to him; and I was, he never saw that money again!

At the time, Jimmy's ambition was to lift Orient into the First Division, and he was more concerned with the future of the club than my chequered past. But he did fire a warning shot across my bows when he said, 'If he doesn't deliver the goods, then Stan will find himself looking for manager number thirteen. And as every gambler knows, that would be unlucky.' At least I knew where I stood, which was more than could be said about my time at Forest.

Jane and I moved into rented accommodation in Lancaster Gate, about thirty yards away from the FA headquarters; which was handy if the disciplinary committee needed me. We had experienced ups and downs in our relationship, and I knew Jane definitely didn't want to leave Nottingham. Even so, she had stood by me through the turmoil of my first marriage break-up, and we were very close. I hoped she'd stick by me some more.

My Orient career didn't get off to the best of starts. In the first league game of the season, I got myself in hot water after I accused an opposing player of deliberately trying to break my leg.

We were playing against Bristol Rovers, and their defender Donnie Gillies, a Scottish Under-23 international, tried to go over the top in a tackle. As I said before, this is the worst tackle anyone can attempt, particularly when your leg is rigid and they come in below the knee. The power of the tackle could easily break a leg. Gillies got away with it and I responded by saying afterwards that all they knew about in Bristol was pig farming, and that caused quite a storm in the papers. But I knew that the tackle could quite easily have ended my career. I admit I was still a bit steamed up over the business with Gary Collier back in 1977. But even so, Gillies was well out of order.

In early October, we met QPR at Loftus Road. Jim Gregory was expecting some stick from the home fans for letting me go, particularly if I turned on the magic for Orient. Fortunately for Jim the match was a goalless non-event.

At the time, Orient were a forward-thinking club and, in December of that year, were the first London club to wear shirts with advertising on them. They finalised a deal with Everard and Ovenden, the paper manufacturers, which was worth £25,000 over eighteen months. Brian Winston, the chairman, was trying to change the image of the club, and it was a remarkable achievement that little Orient were pioneering shirt advertising in London.

Brian owned a large TV company and was well experienced in marketing initiatives. Nowadays every club in the land carries shirt advertising and it is a substantial source of income for clubs. But we were proud to be trailblazers.

One incident that stands out from that season was in February, away at Grimsby. In the game, our midfielder, Steve Parsons, had his leg broken by a terrible tackle from Clive Wigginton. I was very annoyed about this because, again, it was of the over-the-top variety. Steve, being a little bit inexperienced, didn't see it coming.

At the end of the game the crowd were giving me a bit of stick. So, as I walked towards the tunnel I went into the dugout where they keep the buckets of water, picked one up and threw it, bucket and all, over the crowd. They all scattered and the police stepped in, but no one made an official complaint. The press laughed it off by saying that it was probably my first foul throw. There's no way a player would get away with something like that nowadays, he'd probably get banned for life!

In August 1981, Jane and I were married at Marylebone Registry Office. Unfortunately, the press attempted to ruin our day by accusing me of refusing to invite my own children. They claimed that my daughter Andrea only found out about the wedding from taunting schoolmates in the school playground.

Apparently, Andrea had asked the *Sun* newspaper to send her some pictures of Jane and me because I'd let her down – as I often did. In reality she probably said things she didn't mean to say because she wasn't used to dealing with the press. It wasn't easy for us to see each other regularly, because we were separated by long distances most of the time – and neither Jane nor I were able to drive. The papers were trying to say that I was a hero to many young fans in London but neglected my own family.

Jane was twenty-four years old when we married; I was thirty-two. We'd been together for seven years. As I said, our first meeting was in a bar. She was with Robin Askwith, a mutual friend, and I pushed past them, knocking her drink and spilling it all over the place. She turned round to give me a slagging, but froze as soon as she saw me. We seemed to click straightaway, and soon became very close.

On her eighteenth birthday I took her out to dinner. While we were out, Ann, my wife at the time, came back to the flat where we were staying. Jane's sister, Linda, rang up the flat and started singing: 'Happy birthday to you, happy birthday ...' thinking Jane was on the other end of the line.

Unfortunately, Ann had picked up the phone but quickly put down the receiver, thinking it was a wrong number. Linda immediately rang again and continued with the song. She soon realised her mistake – Ann put her right on that one. Linda tried to contact us but didn't know where we had gone, so, when we arrived back at the flat, we walked right into trouble. Ann went straight for Jane, and I did the only brave thing that I'd ever done in my life and stepped in between them.

I certainly wanted to be with Jane, but I didn't want to break up with the wife and kids; so I was in a right dilemma. In our early years together, me and Jane were under a lot of pressure.

She says that she just wanted to be with me, and, as far as she was concerned, that was that. Jane was young and couldn't help herself. In hindsight, I think she's very sorry that my first marriage broke up, but she doesn't regret the time we had together. At the time the papers painted her as the 'scarlet woman', but she couldn't do it on her own – I was just as much to blame.

The first time she really became aware of the press reaction was when she was going to put a bet on for me one Saturday morning. She came down the stairs at Longfield House in Ealing, walked out of the side entrance and someone shouted, 'Jane, can we speak to you?' She reacted somewhat dramatically – covering her head while rushing up a one-way street so that they couldn't follow her in their car. She was absolutely petrified that they had seen her going into the betting shop, but she was even more scared of failing to put the bet on!

Ann soon sold her story to the press, and then I retaliated the following day by selling a photograph of me and Jane to the *Daily Express*. Jane never made any direct comments to the press but, as usual, that made no difference – they made up a few remarks and attributed them to her.

We went out to dinner one night in London, and when we came back to our flat in Lancaster Gate, the side door was open – we had been burgled. Jane ran in, with me – typically – just standing in the background. Of course, the police weren't happy when they found out that she'd left a toolbox outside the front door. Worse, our own saw had been used to force the door. Mind you, we didn't have the heart to tell the police that the key was under the mat! It had to be like that; you couldn't give me a key because I'd lose it in two minutes flat. I was always useless when it came to practical things. I suppose I still am.

In the ten years we were together me and Jane went on holiday only once – to Spain – and that was a complete disaster. We were using a friend's chalet, which had a communal shower situated about half a mile away. I'm one of those stupid people who'll lie in the sun all day, without covering up my lily-white flesh. Of course, after two days, I was in bleeding agony – moaning and groaning, tossing and turning on the bed, with my temperature shooting off the thermometer. I was as red as a lobster who'd cut himself shaving! In the chalet, there was no air-conditioning; it was like a bloody oven. Poor old Jane was stuck there, holding a wet flannel to my head, saying, 'You're not going to die Stan. I promise, you aren't going to die.'

As soon as I recovered, I went out and did exactly the same thing again – and was laid up for another two days. Talk about mad dogs and Englishmen! Jane said that it was honestly the worst holiday she'd ever had. There I was, promising her everything under the sun, just to get me back home, 'I'll never gamble again; I'll never go out again. Just get me home, please!'

When we were living in my flat in the early days, we had to keep the curtains drawn in case Ann came to the door. One night the doorbell rang when we were in the lounge with Robin; and me and him legged it into the bedroom. Jane followed to find out what we were doing, but we'd disappeared. She opened the wardrobe, and there we are – squashed together – hiding like little kids, shaking from head to foot. Another time, I had bought a greyhound and brought it back to the flat. It used to sleep at the bottom of the bed, two forlorn characters together.

Ann, obviously, deserves most of the credit for bringing up our children, and I now wish I had spent a lot more time with the kids. I was a bit wild and selfish, but, thankfully, I see them regularly now. I used to help other people's children through football, and still do so today. Perhaps that is my way of putting something back in to the game. But, unfortunately, I can't turn the clock back.

I had fully intended to see out my two-year contract with Orient, but I was being tempted towards American soccer again. There was a lot of money to be earned and many top players from Brazil and Europe were out there. Gordon Jago was heavily involved in the American League and it seemed like an exciting opportunity.

I rented a flat with the actor Robin Askwith, the cheeky chappie star of the 1970s *Confessions* film series. If you've seen one film you've seen them all. Robin would meet a lot of scantily clad women and end up having sex with them ... and there you have it. Robin, being a bit of the jack the lad, was essentially playing himself, and was very good in the role, in the same way a midget is good at being short.

Robin was a pretty easygoing guy, thoroughly pleasant company and I quickly discovered we had quite a bit in common. He had a keen interest in football and I knew very little about acting. I took the wife along to see Robin tread the boards once, or rather she dragged me.

My idea of entertainment involves watching six greyhounds chasing a hare; not looking at a bunch of screaming hams mincing about on the stage. I quickly surmised that an actor's life wasn't for me and that Robin, despite his best intentions, would have difficulty ad libbing a fart even after eating ten tins of baked beans. I didn't think it was my place to tell him that acting wasn't his strong suit.

As I didn't have a driving license I would often take the Central Line to Leyton on match days sharing the tube with travelling fans, many of whom would look at me in total disbelief. I don't suppose any of today's footballers use the tube as a medium of transport, unless they own their own line. I'm not sure if travelling by tube rather than by my previous mode of transport (the ambulance) was a progressive step. But at least I wasn't approached as much by fans when travelling in the ambulance, unless there was an accident, of course.

A bloke sat opposite me once and worryingly stared at me intently for a couple of minutes. As he got off at his stop he said out of the corner of his mouth, 'You're trying too hard to look like Stan Bowles ...' and then added, '... you ponce.' He then exited the sliding doors. I had to admire the timing and delivery of the statement. As the doors closed everyone in the carriage turned as one to look at me. I smiled uncomfortably resisting the temptation to defiantly claim that I was indeed the real Stan Bowles and not an impostor.

I'd travel with a carrier bag containing my boots and a copy of the *Sporting Life* to help pass the time on the journey. I remember having a dispute with a ticket inspector once – he thought I should have one. Ordinarily, I never bothered buying a ticket and just paid the excess fare at the other end, something you can't do now because of all the barriers. I'd tell the blokes in the peaked caps that I had boarded the tube at the stop before Leyton – at a rough hole called Stratford, if memory serves – and this saved me a small fortune.

Tragically, Jimmy Bloomfield had died of cancer, so I had lost another father figure. Around this time I was having problems with the new manager of Orient, Ken Knighton. Following a defeat in the league, I said something to him which he took exception to.

'Shut your mouth!' he said.

'Who are you talking to?' I demanded.

'If you open your mouth again, you'll be fined fifty quid,' he said.

'Well, make it a fucking hundred!' says I.

So he kept adding money on, because I wouldn't stop talking.

I was just laughing at him. 'Look,' I said, 'at the end of the day, you can make it ten grand if you want because I haven't got a fucking penny!'

So, not for the first time, I was in open conflict with a manager and I knew then that it was time to move on to pastures new. I was quite disappointed that big clubs were no longer interested in me and I generally slandered the entire Football League for turning a blind eye to my talents.

Manchester United had just paid West Bromwich Albion £1.75 million for Bryan Robson. I couldn't believe it at that time – Robson couldn't even control a ball. I remember seeing him in a League Cup match against Spurs and, while trapping a ball is a simple thing to do, he was having great difficulty. Admittedly, he came on in leaps and bounds while he was at Old Trafford, but in the early days he wasn't up to much at all. I was amazed that big clubs were laying out that kind of money on average players who couldn't play, while ignoring the likes of me – a proven ball-player.

At Orient, I was given the task of improving the game of the younger players in the squad. A prime example of this was John Chiedozie, a quick, young winger, but totally clueless when it came to the finer points of the game – like, for instance, what the ball was for! I reckon I improved Chiedozie 100 per cent. Eventually, Notts County bought him for £600,000, which was the biggest transfer fee the Orient had ever received. Before Chiedozie, the most valuable player Orient had ever produced was Glenn Roeder, who was sold to QPR for £210,000 in August 1978.

Whereas Jimmy Bloomfield had said that he was going to build a side, Orient were now selling their best prospects. I told Chiedozie that he should look after me from the transfer proceeds because of the help I had given him, and he offered me an embarrassing amount of money: £100. I declined, saying, 'Don't insult my intelligence!' Perhaps he thought that was all I was worth. I just hope he wasn't right!

A lot of people have said that Jimmy Bloomfield made a big mistake by paying out big money for players who were at the end of their careers. He brought in Peter Taylor, Tommy Taylor, and the chocolate teapot, Ralph Coates; and yours truly, of course. Although he did sell some youngsters to balance the books, I disagree with Bloomfield's critics; he needed to bring in experience to help the kids along. Anyway, I think the Chiedozie story demonstrates that. Before I worked with him, Orient were going to let him go for £100,000. So, we has-beens must have made some impact.

One night I was out with Mouse Morris, Chrissy Morris's father. We were on our way to the Crown & Sceptre, after an evening in a gambling club. Just as we were driving down Bloemfontain Road – by the QPR stadium – we were stopped by the Special Patrol Group. The official reason they pulled us up was that we had no rear light, but they had the entire road blocked off.

As it happened, unknown to me, Mouse had stashed twelve stolen chequebooks in the dashboard. The SPG duly searched the car, found the chequebooks, and we were both arrested and carted off to Notting Hill nick. When we got there, they split us up – to interrogate us separately, as they do.

When you come into a police station, and see the sergeant at the reception desk, they have a cell close by which is a bit better than the main holding cells. At Notting Hill, the desk sergeant knew me, and he said, 'Do you want to go in there then?', pointing to the reception cell. I says, 'Yes please.' So they put Mouse in the holding cell with some other detainees, and put me in the nice one, all on my own. Then three detectives came in and started pushing me about. If you get beaten up in a police station they don't do you any serious, visible damage. They just do you in the balls, the stomach and the side – no bruises. So they dished out a bit of that.

For some reason, they thought I was connected to an international chequebook fraud, which operated across Continental Europe. They reckoned I was passing on information, but I knew nothing about it. If I had, I'd admit it now, since it doesn't matter any more; but I was completely innocent. It turned out that Mouse was involved in the fraud. He was carrying chemicals to wipe the signatures off credit cards. Now, Mouse was very good at forging signatures – it didn't matter how you signed your name, he could copy it very well and very quickly. After a couple of attempts, he would copy any signature – perfectly. This didn't really help him much, though as he ended up getting three years for his part in the scam.

All that happened to me was that I got kept in the cells overnight – once again. The next day Orient played up at Preston, and I got sent off. Great weekend, that was!

Chapter 17 •

Brentford –
One Last Sting for the Bees

With my time at Orient over, I was waiting for someone to come in for me. As the only club that did was Brentford, I signed for them in a deal worth around £25,000.

The Bees were a middle-of-the-table Third Division side with a few up-and-coming youngsters.

I was quite happy with the wages that Martin Lange, the chairman, and Fred Callaghan, the manager, had offered me. As it happens, there were arrears left on my contract with Orient, and Fred told me that I was entitled to four grand. I rang them from Fred's office and spoke to Peter Barnes, the secretary. I told Peter to tell Brian Winston that if I didn't receive the money I wouldn't sign for Brentford. They would have to put up with me for the rest of my contract; I think this is called blackmail. Anyway, whatever it was it worked because, after a few telephone calls, they eventually agreed. When the deal went through, I was at St Bart's Hospital with Bill Songhurst – the Orient physio – having a check-up. While we were there, Peter Barnes, who is now the secretary at Tottenham, brought me the £4,000 in readies. I went straight off to the dogs at White City, and didn't come home with much change.

The next day I had lunch with Fred Callaghan at the Kensington Hilton and signed on the dotted line. I had known Fred for a long time, and I was quite happy to work for him because he was an easygoing character, like myself. As long as you did the business for him, he was all right.

I was now back in the middle of my old patch in West London, just ten minutes away from Shepherd's Bush. On the first day, I went into the dressing room to change for training and met my new team-mates. We enjoyed a bit of banter – which was always the same and probably still is to this day – and everything seemed to be going well. All of a sudden this bleeding great yeti appeared out of the bathroom: hair halfway down his back, great big beard and two earrings hanging out.

Underneath all the hair was Terry Hurlock, who became my best friend at Brentford – and he still is today. Terry's appearance alone got him into trouble with referees, but he was a very good player. I believe that he could have played for one of the big English clubs quite easily. Eventually, Glasgow Rangers recognised his worth and took him north of the border.

I was pleased to be living in Brentford, as the geography of the place suited me well. Terry used to take me to see his friends in Walthamstow, and I reciprocated with my friends in Notting Hill. All in all, we went out a great deal together. One night his friends came over to Brentford and we all got quite drunk at the local pubs. Griffin Park, Brentford's ground, is probably unique in that it's got a pub on every corner of the stadium. There's The Royal Oak, The New Inn, The Griffin, and The Princess Royal. At two in the morning all ten of my mates decided to have a race, stark bollock naked, round the ground for a £50 prize. Sensibly, I declined to take part because I was too well-known in the area.

So, the guys all stripped off, and started to race round the block. As they came into the home straight, which was approaching Brentford's main gates, a Panda car pulled up, saw me, and looked at the naked bodies running up the road towards us. The policeman, recognising me, wound down his window, and said, like this was an everyday occurrence, 'Stan, get them to put their clothes on now. Otherwise, they're nicked.' And off he drove.

Terry Hurlock remembers our playing days:

I was in my early twenties when Stan joined Brentford. He played out wide and was absolutely brilliant. I had a bit of go in me, and I used to give him the ball. His control and passing skills were superb. At thirty-three, he was a class player, so God only knows what he was like when he was younger. He got on well with everyone, and had bundles of manners. He was never flash, and fitted in straightaway.

One of my most vivid recollections of Stan goes back to the night of 1 February 1983, when Brentford Football Club caught fire. At the time, I lived right opposite the gates, and I looked out of the window to see the old groundsman come running out – breathing out of his arse – smoke billowing round his body. It must have been about two in the morning, and the night air was filled with the noise of ambulances and fire engines. The TV reporters decided to use my house as a base. By this time the fire was getting a hold on the ground. They were interviewing people and using the phone in my house – it was pan-demonium! All of a sudden, I saw this figure in the distance walking up the road, wearing a Crombie overcoat, hands tucked firmly in the pockets. It was about three o'clock by then; he must have been on his way home from the pub, or the spieler.

'All right, Stan?' I shouted.

There was mayhem all around Stan as he stood in the middle of the road. He moved his head to one side, and looked at the smoke billowing into the night sky. 'Just my fucking luck, isn't it?' he said.

'What?' I said. 'What are you talking about?'

'A big fire right near my house, and the wind's blowing in the wrong direction. Just my fucking luck!'

'What do you mean?'

'If my house was to burn down, I could claim on the insurance.'

And he carried on walking, muttering to himself, totally oblivious to the situation around him. I was always learning from Stan, and he was a pleasure to be with.

Thank you, Terry, but I can't teach you how to change the direction of the wind, that's a secret!

After settling in at Brentford, I decided to take another step into the business world. A long-standing friend of mine, David Carroll – who later worked with Frank Warren and Don King – decided to open up a wine bar in Ladbroke Grove, in a former gambling club called The Hole in the Wall. Back in the seventies, I had stood bail for David – about £10,000 – when he was up on a big charge. He'd never forgotten that, so he asked me to be a partner in his new venture.

The wine bar was called Tropics, and he spent a fortune doing it up. On reflection, I was probably not the ideal man for such a business venture, but David asked me, and I agreed. I was really only there to add a bit of glamour, and to use my name to promote the place.

Tropics started off promisingly. Sting sent us a telegram to wish us well, and Phil Lynott was involved in the official opening. Dave asked me how much Phil would want to open the club, and I said, 'It's got to be at least a monkey.'

In the meantime, I asked Phil what he wanted, and he said, 'I'll be happy with a bottle of Jack Daniels.' So I copped the monkey, and Phil got the Jack Daniels – I always knew that I had business acumen! Dave never knew about that, so I hope he doesn't get too upset.

It became quite a venue for the pop world and other celebrities, and we had a nice clientele from around Holland Park. Dave would occasionally give me a few quid and, for a while, the prospects looked good. Unfortunately, the owner of the freehold said that too many undesirables were frequenting the establishment. That wasn't the case, except perhaps for a few of my friends from Notting Hill. The owner refused to renew the lease, so Dave decided to cut his losses and do other things.

At that time I had the courts chasing me for outstanding personal debts. They were piling up and I was having trouble paying them – as always! They said that I would go bankrupt but, luckily, a solution presented itself just at the right time. Two national newspapers, when reporting this story, wrote that I was *already* bankrupt.

So Martin Lange, the Brentford chairman, said, 'You've never been bankrupt, have you, Stanley?'

'No, I haven't,' I said, indignantly.

'Well,' he said, smiling, 'there are a couple of newspapers who are saying that you have been. That's defamation of character, that is.'

So we went ahead with this claim for damages, and the money we received in settlement paid off my debts. So the papers bailed me out, and Lady Luck shone on me again.

In the meantime, I was almost back to my best on the football field, as Fred Callaghan remembers:

Stan was the best signing I ever made. We took £12,500 extra on the gate the first time he played for us, which made the £25,000 signing-on fee look ridiculous. He also brought a lot of colourful stories to the dressing room, and he was an incredible player.

I went to a football forum with Stan early on in his days with us and a woman in the audience asked a question. 'Mr Bowles, can you tell us the highlight of your career?' she asked politely.

I thought Stan would say playing for England was the pinnacle of his career, but he said, 'Yes, I can. It was when a football manager gave me £10,000 in a brown envelope.' I don't know whether that answered her question, but he was full of outlandish remarks like that.

When he first joined us he was a little unfit, and we used to have cross-country running. The first time he joined in, he finished last, a long way behind all the other players. But he said, 'Next time we do this, I will finish in the first six.' And he did. Stan was a committed trainer who never liked to be beaten, a genuine man when it came to football. The younger lads in the club looked up to him, and he was a model professional. I used to try and help him with his finances by paying half of his wages on a Friday, and the rest on a Monday, so that he could survive until the next pay cheque.

I remember taking a team to the *Daily Express* five-a-side tournament at Wembley Arena. There was a young kid who was in a wheelchair by the side of the pitch, and Stan said, 'If I win anything tonight, son, you can have it.'

During the matches he was absolutely superb and he won the Player of the Tournament award: a big statue of a footballer, and a plaque. As he received it, he walked straight over to the young lad in the wheelchair, gave it to him, and walked out of the arena. That was Stanley.

At the end of the 1982–83 season, after playing about eighty games for Brentford, I finished playing full-time professional football altogether. Frank McLintock and John Docherty arrived at the club. Frank became the manager, and John, who used to play in the reserves at QPR, when I was there, was his assistant. Johnny and I never really saw eye to eye. After a training session one day I realised that it was all wrong. I went to see Frank and said, 'That's it, mate, I'm finished.' There was no animosity between Frank and myself, and we parted on the best of terms.

I had played for eight league clubs from 1967 till 1983. Sixteen years – a long time when you consider the average career-span of a footballer. I had scored two goals on my debut for Manchester City, got carried away with the high life, had two punch-ups with assistant manager Malcolm Allison, and been thrown on the scrap heap at Bury. I had clawed my way back at Crewe and Carlisle, found true happiness at QPR, won my only medal at Nottingham Forest, and had some laughs at Orient and Brentford.

My seven years at QPR mean more to me than my time at all the other clubs put together, and I loved playing in the 1976 team with Gerry Francis, Frank McLintock, David Webb and everybody else. That team must have been one of the finest English club sides never to win a trophy. I regard the night I broke the British goalscoring record in Europe – previously held by my hero Denis Law – as the highlight of my career. Of course, football never stands still, and four years later another Scot, John Wark, beat my eleven goals when he scored fourteen as Ipswich won the UEFA Cup in 1981.

It was strange to reflect that I had played five times for England under three managers, and that my first game was Sir Alf Ramsey's last match in charge.

It had been a long and sometimes strange career, never dull and littered with highs and lows. But, now it was over.

Chapter 18 •

Another Fine Mess?

So, after gambling my way through about half a million quid, I ended up on the dole. Jane was standing by me, and telling the press that she still loved me. We both knew that my career had to come to an end sometime, and now I had plenty of time on my hands. How would I use it?

Badly, that's how!

One very hot summer's day, I went out – as was my custom at the time – with a friend of mine, Chrissy Morris, to an illegal gambling club, owned by David Carroll. I said to Chrissy, 'You put my bet on, and I'll go over the road and order the beers.' The club was facing an Irish pub called the Kensington Park Hotel – known locally as the KPH – and so I strolled over and ordered two pints. As I came back to the door of the pub, I heard someone shout, 'Go! Go!' Suddenly, about forty coppers appeared from nowhere and swarmed on the gambling club, smashing down the door with axes – It was like an episode of *The Sweeney*!

The police arrested everyone in the club, including Chrissy, and they were all led away in handcuffs to spend a night behind bars. I was standing at the pub doorway, looking totally innocent, as they were frogmarched into Black Marias.

I had a little chuckle to myself, and went back into the pub. If the police had done their homework, they would have known that the door they had just smashed down was unlocked all the time anyway, so they could have just walked in. They wrecked the whole place: searching the ceiling voids, under the carpets, everywhere. After that, I kept my head down, and didn't see Chrissy for three days. The police let him go, but they got two convictions out of it – one bloke went down for three years.

That narrow escape was probably the only piece of good luck I have ever had – at least since 1970, when Paul Hince gave me that three bob for a train ticket to Crewe. I made a statement in the press saying, 'It was almost enough to turn me to Christianity, because I knew that somebody up there was looking after me.'

Although I'd retired from professional football, a friend, Nipper Houston – who had been jailed during the Notting Hill riots years previously – had bought a big pub in Epping called The Cock and Magpie. He said, 'I've just taken over a football team, Stan. Come over to the pub – I'll pay your expenses – because I've got something to discuss with you.'

So I went over to the pub and they offered me a few quid to play some games for Epping Town in the Isthmian League Division Two in 1983–84. Johnny Donner, one of Terry Hurlock's mates from Walthamstow, was the chairman, and he wanted the place livening up a bit. So I played a few games for Epping. This was good fun until it all ended abruptly in glorious farce. One day, we were short of players, and the chairman had to play. Now, Johnny didn't mind a fight – any time of the day or night – and he had a bit of a row with a couple of the opposing players. He knocked one of them spark out, and started chasing the other player through the woods at the back of the pitch.

After that fracas, Epping were thrown out of the league and the ground was closed down. I had to laugh because Johnny never caught up with the other player, who ran through the woods like a hare; and we've never seen him to this day. He didn't even come back to the dressing room to get changed, so he's probably still in his kit sitting in Epping Forest!

About this time, I remember Joey Leach expressing concern about Phil Lynott. Phil was very down because his career was at a standstill. He'd done a tour of America, which he'd financed himself, and, unfortunately for Phil, it wasn't very successful. He was also in conflict with his management. The last straw for him was the fact that he wasn't included on the bill for Live Aid in July 1985. That snub affected him a great deal, and I can understand why.

Phil had given many people a helping hand, and some of them became stars in their own right. He had people in his band like Snowy White, Jimmy Bain, and Gary Moore – who all made their name through Thin Lizzy – and Phil had also used Midge Ure on keyboards. Since Bob Geldof and Midge Ure were the main organisers behind the Band Aid single, and the Live Aid concert at Wembley, Phil was devastated to be left out of proceedings. Both Joey and I could not understand how or why this had happened, particularly as Geldof, and his management, controlled the event. In the early days in Cricklewood, Bob Geldof used to come and visit Phil regularly, and they were very close, which made it even more of a mystery. Phil was very depressed about being left out of the biggest gig of the eighties.

In late 1985, I went to a party at Phil's house in Kew, and he was obviously completely gone by then. There were lots of people from the pop world there, but Phil was just sitting in an armchair watching old videos of Thin Lizzy – totally oblivious to what was going on around him. That night was the last time I ever saw him alive. I had been told that he was doing the heavy stuff – heroin – and he died from a drug overdose soon after.

To see Phil in that state was tragic. He had always enjoyed life to the full, so for it to end like that was an horrific waste of a talented musician, and, most of all, a genuinely kind and caring person.

That Christmas and New Year was the worst Joey and I ever had. Joey's wife, Pam, died on 4 December 1985, and Phil died on 4 January 1986. For a long time, Joey didn't know whether he was coming or going; and it almost destroyed me as well, because Phil and I were like brothers.

Up in Manchester, Joey was also having serious problems. One of our friends, Kevin Taylor, a professional card player, was successfully involved in a property deal which netted him a few million pounds. All of a sudden, right out of the blue, Kevin was in the running as a Conservative candidate for our local area. He started to rub shoulders with the nobs, and didn't want to know his mates any more.

He became friendly with John Stalker, who was the Deputy Chief Constable for Manchester. They were near neighbours and their children went to school together. When the IRA 'Shoot to Kill' situation was going on there were a lot of important people trying to control John Stalker, and keep him quiet. Stalker was telling the truth, but they tried to discredit him through his connections with Kevin Taylor. Obviously, Joey had been one of Kevin's associates, and the Establishment reckoned that, although they couldn't discredit John Stalker or Kevin Taylor, they would have a go at them through Joey Leach.

They'd spoken to Joey and indicated that they would squash a potential five-year sentence if he helped them discredit Stalker. Joey told them to stuff it: Stalker was telling the truth as far as he was concerned, and had done nothing wrong; so why were they trying to sling him out of office? What kind of people were they? Needless to say, Joey didn't get any answers.

Joey Leach was used as a pawn in a very big game of chess. Because

Kevin had become a big-shot, they were trying to drag Joey into it by association. Joey was on bail for two years, and his court case eventually fell through, but they were trying to manipulate him. Joey would have been a back-up option for them if they couldn't get to Stalker some other way. It was a very political situation that Joey found himself in, and I was worried about his chances. It was a close-run thing. There are some people out there, in high places, that you just don't mess with.

Everywhere I went, things seemed to end in chaos; but, fortunately, my old mate Jim Gregory came to the rescue. He'd promised me a testimonial match because of the seven good seasons I'd given QPR, and I knew he'd keep his word. It was just a question of where and who the opponents should be. Gordon Jago had talked about bringing the Tampa Bay Rowdies over from America but when that didn't happen, Jim decided that we should play the match at Brentford.

So I organised the game with Brentford, to take place on 15 May 1987. The kick-off had to be put back half an hour because of the size of the crowd – which was about 8,000; a big gate for the club. The Brentford team included Andy Sinton and Ian Holloway, both of whom later played under Gerry Francis after he became manager of QPR in May 1991.

The QPR team was Tony Roberts, Warren Neill, Wayne Fereday, Sammy Lee, Gary Chivers, Gavin Maguire, Ian Dawes, myself, John Byrne, Rodney Marsh and Mike Fillery. Rodney came over from America to play, and all we paid him was his air fare, which was a lovely gesture on his part. I played the second half for Brentford, scored from a penalty, and QPR won 3–2. Gerry Francis played as a substitute. George Best was supposed to come, but he didn't turn up – he was drunk somewhere in Chelsea. Bestie later apologised, saying, 'I got the days mixed up, Stan.' I replied, 'Don't worry, I get a bit like that myself from time to time!'

The day went really well. The managing director of the Hoover company, who had been a long time admirer of my footballing skills, gave me £1,000 – which was very generous and totally unexpected.

I got about £30,000 out of it altogether. I heard that Harper and Cox, a local bookmaker, put £500 into the kitty and said, 'We consider it as a temporary loan.' And they were quite correct. On top of that money, I had about £27,000 from the sale of my house. So, I had a total of fifty-seven grand in my pocket; I was set up for life.

Unfortunately, I think that windfall lasted me about four or five months tops. After that I was back on skid row. Certainly, the White City bookmakers were glad that I'd been given a testimonial. I went down the pan at a fast rate of knots. Jane had left me, and I can't say that I blame her because I'd started on the vodka non-stop, and was smoking eighty fags a day.

The drink was getting the better of me on a daily basis, and this had a predictably bad effect on our marriage. I'd wake up in the morning and worry that that was the best I was going to feel all day. I just couldn't wait to get in the pub and start drinking again to shut out my troubles – if only for a few hours. I don't think I would call myself an alcoholic, I suppose I was more of a drunk; the difference being I didn't attend any meetings. It would take only one drink to get me drunk, usually the thirteenth or fourteenth, by which time everything was a blur. And as a blur things looked considerably better.

Around this time, I had a fling with a woman called Sue, whom I eventually moved in with after a brief bar-room courtship. It wasn't a serious affair and in all honesty I can't remember too much about it; for me it was just somewhere to stumble back to and kip down of a night. Sue liked a drink herself, she'd wake up with a hangover and trot off to work in a bad mood, with me still out for the count in her bed. The trouble is nobody can keep up that lifestyle of drinking all day – well not for long. I think after a while my mere presence began to grate on Sue's nerves. She'd mope around the house with a towel wrapped round her head, spluttering out subtle comments like, 'Are you still here?' Obviously the conditions of my tenancy were under review.

One morning before she left for work she handed me a shopping list the size of an unravelled toilet roll, a £10 note (which would probably have bought the first three items), and asked me to go to the super-market and stock the cupboards in preparation for the month ahead. I mumbled that 'two can live as cheaply as one' to which she replied, 'yeah, for half as long'. I awoke mid-morning, stuck the tenner on a dog in the first race at Catford and when it failed to oblige I took it as a sign from above, that fate had decreed the relationship to be over. I packed my belongings into two carrier bags and went on my merry way. The funny thing was that I saw Sue a couple of weeks later in the pub and she didn't even raise the subject of my disappearance, or the missing shopping. She probably considered the ten quid as money well spent.

*

So, within six months of getting the best part of sixty grand, I was penniless again. I'd blown the lot on vodka and tonic, gambling and fags. Looking back, I think I overdid it on the tonic!

Eventually, I wound up in the West Middlesex hospital. The bloke in the next bed had suffered a stroke, and kept talking to me in French; he died while I was in there. On the other side of me was a chap who kept calling me Eric. He was always waking me up in the middle of the night, saying, 'C'mon, Eric, we've got to catch a train in ten minutes.'

The geezer kept asking me for cigarettes, and he used to hide them in different places so the sister wouldn't find them. I didn't know how dangerous it was until she caught me one day giving him a fag. 'What do you think you're doing? Don't you know that he is on oxygen! If he lit up a cigarette near his bed, the whole place would go up in flames!' The sister nearly exploded herself.

I wanted to leave, but they wouldn't let me discharge myself.

I called a nurse over and said, 'Nurse, this place is full of bleeding nutters!' The nurse looked at me with a funny smile, as if to say, Don't you know why you're here ... Then it struck me – I was one of the bleeding nutters!

I tell you, it frightened the life out of me. I was out of there within five days. The episode really shook me up, but, later on, I saw the funny side of it. After that I was basically living on the streets, or sleeping on people's sofas. It was a very rough time for me.

Things began to improve for me dramatically after that bad patch. I met another girl called Sue – a cleaner for Ronnie Wood of the Rolling Stones, and some other rock people, including a Scottish guy who was a mate of Billy Connolly's. We lived together for four years, and Ronnie Wood and his missus bought Sue a car.

Also I started doing a bit of charity work. George Best was travelling around the country playing football with his team 'The George Best Newhaven Select XI' and he asked me if I'd like to join them for a few games. We played on Sundays, and that went on through most of the summer, attracting pretty good crowds.

I remember one match against a celebrity side which included Terry Marsh – the former lightweight boxing champion – who is quite small but has legs like tree trunks. I pushed the ball through his legs and, after scoring, I was walking back up the field when he said, 'If you do that again, I'm gonna punch your fucking head in!' Terry Marsh had these mad eyes. I could see the fury in them, and, as he gave me a dirty look, I thought, That's my lot! I believed that if I went past him again, he was going to really hurt me; so I went over to the other side of the pitch. I can assure you I didn't nutmeg him again.

On TV at the time there was a series called *Big Deal*, which was quite near the mark about gambling – portraying it more or less as it is. Ray Brooks played Robbie Box, the main character, and the papers compared me with him. They said that people like us drift from day to day, and the days of the week are all the same to us. We go to sleep, we wake up if we are lucky, and we waste our lives ducking and diving. There you go, then.

It was well known by fans, reporters, TV people and friends that my base in Brentford was The Bricklayer's Arms. It became more of an office than a boozer, where I conducted my business on the telephone. Out of every hundred calls they received, probably eighty were for me. Recently, a man came up to me in there and told me that he was at Loftus Road in 1976, after QPR had won the last match of the season against Leeds, when some of the players had thrown their shirts into the crowd. He had grabbed my number 10 shirt and still had it all those years later. He told me: 'I'll never, ever let that go.'

It makes you think, that kind of thing.

At Loftus Road in 1993, I was invited to take five penalties against one of the Rangers goalkeepers for a charity event organised by QPR. We both got changed in the same dressing room, and I actually told him that I was going to hit them all to his right-hand side. The first four went into the net as I had promised him, and every time he went the wrong way. So, I decided to place the last penalty to his left for a change, just to see what happened. Of course, for the first time he dived to his right. Unfortunately, I shot wide!

Throughout all my ups and downs, some things have stayed the same. My mum, for instance, is exactly the same as she's always been. She always takes things in her stride. She was never overly impressed with my being a footballer; I was, in her eyes, no different to the rest of her family. The only time she really took an interest was when I made my England debut. She told me that listening to the national anthem being sung before the game, brought a lump to her throat. I think that was one time she was especially proud of me.

Her two great loves are bingo and cooking. She is a very good cook my mum, and she still cooks a Sunday roast every week and my kids usually go round to her. She used to write all the names on the plates, and then go off to the bingo. When the kids arrived, they'd find out which plate of food was theirs and would put it in the microwave. If one of them couldn't make it on the Sunday, she would put it in the fridge and they'd have it the next day.

I still see her quite regularly and I try to phone once a week, but, I have to admit, it can be a couple of months between calls sometimes. The rest of the family pop round to see her all the time. I see quite a lot of one of my brothers – Steve. As a family, I don't suppose we're great ones for talking. When I see Steve, we might just sit there reading the papers for most of the time. But at least we all know that we're there for each other – well I think we do!

Steve's not really into football, although he did once have a trial for Manchester City. He was a pretty good player, but wasn't all that interested. On top of that, I think he got pissed off with people at Maine Road saying that they hoped he didn't turn out like me.

My other brother, Mark, likes a bet, almost as much as I do. So much so, that he's even been a bookmaker. He took over from a bloke he used to work for and was in his element. He travelled around the racecourses all the time, so I didn't really see that much of him.

My boy, Carl, played a bit of football and even had a trial at Brentford with Webby. Ann sent him down to the club without even telling me, but he's quite a shy lad, and I don't think he came across as what they wanted.

I see them all a lot more than I used to. My dark secret is that I'm a grandfather. Some people say that I get on better now with my ex-wives than I ever did when we were married. I hope that's not entirely right.

Diane, my third ex-wife, used to say that I was trying to catch up with Mickey Rooney, who had seven!

I just have a few small bets these days; ten, twenty quid. I used to write little betting slips out for three or four pounds, and leave them in my pockets. If my wife found them, she would think, Well, that's not too bad.

Diane had a habit of getting my trousers mixed up with her own, so I sometimes hid money. One time I hid £100 in the bathroom, under the carpet by the toilet. But, as luck had it, she spilled a bucket of water, and the carpet round the bowl became soaking wet. She pulled it up, and there was my stash, so she kept it; well, not all of it – she gave me a score. Thanks very much. I have learned that you have to keep changing your hiding places, or, at least, make sure they're waterproof.

My marriage to Diane started promisingly but declined steeply, pretty much straight after the honeymoon in fact. Diane had a very lively spur-of-the-moment personality and we had started off having some good times together. However, towards the end of our relationship the laughs were few and far between.

I remember once when we were walking together in Brentford and about thirty Hell's Angels raced past us on motorbikes and parked up in a greasy spoon café a few hundred yards ahead of us. Once the Angels had dismounted, they duly began to do what Hell's Angels do best, that is look dangerous and admiringly eye up each other's motorcycles.

Instinctively, I veered away from the mob pretending something of interest had caught my eye on the other side of the road. All of a sudden I realise Diane is no longer by my side but dashing towards the posse of Hell's Angels. Without a word she jumps on one of the Harley Davidsons, pretends to rev it up and starts making convincing engine sounds. Well, these bikes are sacrosanct to these fellows and I'm thinking she's going to get a whack from one of these very big greasy blokes, unless, that is, their scruples wouldn't allow them to hit a lady, in which case I would get thumped instead. Fortunately, they saw the funny side of it and one of them even took her for a spin round the block on the bike. Unfortunately, he brought her back.

I've never been under the illusion that I'm an easy person to live with and I guess our marriage was put under added pressure by me not having a regular income. This was a constant source of rows as well as me spending what meagre income I did receive, on things I shouldn't have – you can guess what was top of the list. In due course we decided to call time on our relationship, and both of us were delirious about it.

Don Shanks always maintains that our biggest undoing was that we never dated any women who were richer than us. It's probably the most incisive reflection on our lives that he has, or ever will articulate.

I have definitely settled in Brentford, now. I did some coaching for Dave Webb when he was manager of Brentford FC. He set me back on my feet, and gave me some opportunities to do little jobs with the media as a result. According to Dave Webb at the time:

I've given him the chance at Brentford Football Club to put something back into the game as a part-time coach, and hope that things might open up for him. He is like a flower that has blossomed and died too soon in the game. I want him to bounce back, and if he can pass on any of his magical skills to young players, then football will be the better for it. Many clubs don't open up their doors to older ex-players, and I think that club managers should be more respectful of tradition and allow these guys to be involved in some small capacity; to make them feel that football hasn't turned its back on them.

During the season I was doing the coaching a few times a week and I was there for a couple of years. The players were a great bunch of lads, and I loved it. I was working with the first-team squad, mostly on their 'touch'. They were not Premiership standard, of course, but with some of them you never knew what the future might hold. They were very raw and inexperienced and did far too much running sometimes; they needed to learn to make the ball do the work now and again. When the main training session finished, Webby would send a small group over to me for a bit of fine-tuning. We'd work for an hour or so on shooting, passing and crossing. It was nice to be back in a tracksuit, a great feeling, but entirely unexpected.

For one season I worked with their star player, Nicky Forster – on his touch. He had tremendous pace but sometimes lacked the touch to make him a very good player. I can tell you it's a great joy to see things we'd practised on the training pitch pay off on a Saturday afternoon. It's funny, but, when I was playing, I never really thought I would be involved in the coaching side of the game – it had never interested me before. I suppose that when you're playing, you don't think about the future, unless, of course, you're Terry Venables, Gerry Francis or Dave Webb!

I also did a bit of scouting for Brentford, which, with my well-known dislike of watching football, might surprise some people. But I'd been away from the game for a few years and I started to look at things differently. So, if Webby wanted a second opinion, I was his man.

As I said, I was doing a few bits and bobs in the media. I got a fair bit of work through John Hollins at QPR; celebrity games and the like. I also started doing a fair bit of radio work: commentating, commenting, that sort of thing. I've done some telly work for Sky and LWT and made a few videos, such as *The Onion Bag*, with Paul Ross. So things were looking positive in that direction as well.

One of those little jobs was for *Loaded*, the magazine which celebrates laddish behaviour. They asked Tina Partridge, the wife of publicist Rob Partridge, if I would like to go out for the day to a big pop festival at Stratford-upon-Avon. She said there would be a five-a-side tournament in which a team from *Loaded* would play various celeb-rities. The event would carry on while the music was happening. She said, 'I have specifically rung you up because I know you like Van Morrison, and he's one of the headliners. Bob Dylan is also headlining. Van Morrison will be on at four o'clock in the afternoon.' So I said, 'Certainly!'

I went with Diane, and Alan Hudson and his wife. We were picked up in a white stretch limousine, provided by *Loaded*, and zoomed off down the M40 with Adam Black and Phil Robinson, two guys from the magazine.

We were chatting away, and the subject of Dave Sexton came up. Alan, throughout his career, never got on with Dave at all, and calls him Old Stiff-neck. When Alan was at Chelsea and came in drunk to training, Dave would have him thrown in the shower to sober him up. Alan and I had had this conversation before, and previously I had just said, 'It's a waste of time talking to me, I like the guy.'

So, in the car, Alan says, 'You like Old Stiff-neck, don't you?' And I said, 'As it happens, I do,' hoping this would shut him up. But Alan kept rambling on and on about Sexton, and then he started saying, 'I don't like smoking in the car.' It wasn't even his car! I said, 'Leave it out, I ain't travelling two hours down the fucking motorway without a fag!' So we just keep on smoking and he just keeps on whingeing like an old woman. Who'd have thought you could be really pissed off in a stretch limo?

Anyway we arrive, and the *Loaded* team has a lot of games to play in the Phoenix 95 Red Bull five-a-side tournament. We kept winning, and got through to the final – against the Royal Shakespeare Company! There was quite a long break between the semi-finals and the final, so time was getting on. In the final I scored a couple of goals, and we were 3–1 up at half-time. I knew that Van Morrison was only going to do a forty-minute set, and just as the second half was about to start, I heard Van's band strike up on stage, about fifty yards away from the football arena. So I told Adam I was off to see Van Morrison. Still in my football kit, I got a bottle of champagne out of the limo and went over with my wife, and stood there thoroughly enjoying the music.

When I came back we'd won the final 7–3, and all the pictures had been taken. Later in the evening, after I had got changed, they took another photo of me. That was why I was the only person in the magazine wearing a tie. On the way home from Stratford, Alan kept opening the electric windows in the limo because of the cigarette smoke. Then, fortunately, he fell asleep, and that's when his wife had a fag: he doesn't like her smoking! Next time I get to go in a stretch limo, remind me never to go with Alan.

In February 1996, Barry Hearn, the Orient chairman, invited me over to a match. For special guest appearances they put a red carpet out to the centre of the pitch, and you walk along it, wave to the crowd, walk back, and get paid. So I did this, and then watched them beat Cardiff 4–1. George Best had been guest-of-honour the week before. Apparently, Bestie arrived in a big limousine; walked out to the middle, waved to the punters, walked back, got his money, climbed back into the motor and left!

I am still playing life a day at a time, but there's a future for me – in some capacity – connected with football. I do a lot of coaching with kids around the Brentford area, and go in to schools. There must be something wrong somewhere with the system in this country because so few great players are being produced these days. But, I do keep thinking that there must be loads of kids out there who are just as good as I was in the late fifties.

Looking back, the seventies were very enjoyable times for a lot of people, especially footballers, fans and even referees. I am very glad that I played when I did. The referees in the seventies were like ringmasters, watching and influencing the show as it was going on. The referee would come on to the pitch, and let the spectacle unfold, without feeling the need to turn in an Oscar-winning performance himself. Nowadays, referees are so in control of the game that they sometimes destroy the flow. The rules in those days were interpreted within the spirit of the game, as opposed to now, where they are interpreted too strictly to the letter of the law; little or no leeway is given.

I regarded the crowd as an audience, who wanted me to go out and perform for them. I could talk to them, and get close to them, almost saying, Look, I'm the same as you, really.'

That created a certain rapport between the crowd and players like me. People could perform as individuals within the framework of the team, and that was accepted as part of the profession in those days. If you could do your trapeze act, that's fine. If you can do your trapeze act and juggle a few balls at the same time, that's even better – that's showbiz, and the crowd loved it.

Players are not allowed to do that today; I think that it's more of a war to win. Results, which were always important, have become the be-all-and-end-all. Winning is everything now, and the pressures on players are incredible. I think that the mid-to-late eighties was the time when attitudes began to change.

Back then, we all played as part of a team, but there was always scope to demonstrate your own individual flair or party-trick, and there was no one there to say, 'Don't do that.' It was accepted, allowed and almost encouraged.

The referees then, knew that people had paid money to see those few moments of magical entertainment, and it didn't matter so much if your team lost. This was absent in the condensed game of the eighties and early nineties. Chants of 'one-nil, one-nil' are, to me, a sad indictment of football. Mind you, it was a bit of a pleasant shock to hear the fans singing 'four–nil to the Enger-land' during the Euro 96 game against the Dutch!

Saying that, there are managers now, particularly in the Premiership, who have set out their stall to try and introduce skilful, attacking football. Many of these managers played in the seventies and would love to re-create those heady days. The likes of Keegan, for example, believe in the concept of entertainment, and natural talent being nurtured and developed.

Fifteen years back, it was all a bit faceless – a lot of not very good players getting far more money than they deserved. All that big boot, hustle and bustle stuff was a bloody disgrace. As far as I'm concerned it could have killed off the game in this country. Thankfully, though, since the formation of the Premier League it has improved beyond recognition. I think we've woken up to the fact that the rest of the world was leaving us behind. Players are still getting more money than they deserve, but fair play to them – I'd have done the same given half the chance!

People talk about us trying to play the 'Ajax way', and things like that, but we can't really do it. It's all well and good managers having what they call 'progressive ideas', but if you haven't got the players to do the job, it's never going to work out. We've got some, but nowhere near enough. I think we need to change the way we bring up the kids – there's too much emphasis on winning at all costs and not enough emphasis on skills. There are some very good youngsters coming through – Wayne Rooney for example – but I do wonder where the next Best, Hudson, Marsh and the like will come from. They must be out there somewhere. Once upon a time, flair players could be found in every team in the land, but now they're the exception rather than the rule.

The main flair players in this county at the moment are, for the most part, the foreign imports; I'm not too sure if all the overseas stars coming in is a good idea. It's true that our youngsters can only learn from them, but it does have a downside as well. I think it hampers our youngsters from coming through. Managers are buying names from abroad for now, and not thinking about the future. It's true that teams like Man U and Liverpool have excellent youth policies; but for many, if you can pick up a star Moldovian for a couple of bob, why bother to go out looking for the new George Best?

The foreign players tend to be more skilful, and those that can adjust to the pace of the game like Thierry Henry, Robert Pires, and van Nistelrooy are great talents and a joy to watch. I have to say that Thierry Henry is one of the best players I've ever seen. Charlie George, who still works at Highbury, has nothing but admiration for the man. His attitude is spot on; his work-rate, pace and unselfishness in front of goal, make him a special player. Defenders aren't as clever or talented as strikers. I used to run at them and they just didn't know what to do. The crowds just love players who can dribble and beat defenders and I'm just the same, which is why I've always been a great admirer of the sublimely talented Ryan Giggs.

Today's game has changed markedly from when I played, mainly for the better. I think the changes in the law would have suited my style, with defenders not being allowed to tackle you from behind, and today they tend to get treated more severely. This would have helped the flair players in my day. The game is quicker today but the playing surfaces are like carpets, whereas we used to play in mud baths. The ball is a lot lighter too.

Yes, the game has progressed in many ways: you can't run down the clock any more by passing the ball back to the keeper, or kicking it into row Z. Off the pitch clubs and players have become a great deal more professional as wages have rocketed, and players' diets have improved. Instead of getting £1,000 a week today's players are getting upwards of £50,000 and such an incentive focuses the mind: getting into shape, and staying fit and healthy.

I think some of the rule changes that have come about in the last few years have helped the game. However, others, such as bookings for shirt-pulling are ridiculous – those types of incidents should be part and parcel of the game. Football's a man's game; it's not bleeding synchronised swimming! There are far too many bookings, and it's only going to get worse. Soon we'll be having one-a-side games.

Some of the other ideas being bandied around – kick-ins instead of throw-ins and making the goals bigger – are just plain daft. The use of a 'third official' is a good idea – in theory, but it would totally interrupt the flow of the game. Also, human error is an integral part of the sport and mistakes do tend to balance out over a season. I'm intrigued by the rule of 'sudden death' extra-time, where the winners are the side who scores first after the regulation ninety minutes. The only trouble is that some teams couldn't score if they played until midnight. Still, at least the fans get their money's-worth, even if they'd have to invest in sleeping bags and cocoa.

That said, I think the game is heading in the right direction. England's performances in Euro 96 gave the game a lift. We may not be able to play 'total football', but we can demonstrate a bit of skill again, as well as strength and running. We're not quite the laughing-stock we were a few years ago. Terry Venables – take a bow!

Like most football fans across the country I also enjoyed watching the 2002 World Cup, despite the competition being played out in South Korea and Japan, and relayed back here at unsavoury early morning hours.

I thought Sven's men did well to qualify from the so-called 'group of death', but like most other observers I was extremely disappointed with the tame manner of our exit to eventual winners, Brazil.

I watched most of England's matches from my Brentford base, the Bricklayer's Arms. Mine host was kind enough to provide me early morning coffee and sausage sandwiches, in return for some 'expert' analysis. Even armed with the best intentions, the flow of coffee soon gave way to drinks of a more potent nature.

I tend to be a bit picky when it comes to pundits, presenters and commentators. I find the painfully articulate Garth Crooks particularly irritating, and Barry Davies over-opinionated. I've noticed when the Olympics are on that Davies commentates on about fifty different sports including tennis, ice-skating, rowing, gymnastics, badminton and hockey. He even does the Lord Mayor's Show! Unsurprisingly, he considers himself an expert on every single one of those sports. I've also noticed too, that the BBC seem to be intent on turning the statistically obsessed sheepskin that is John Motson, into a 'character'. Somehow I don't think they'll succeed.

I've never really been keen on Gabby Logan, who co-hosted most of the live games with housewives' favourite Des Lynam. Women are the first to complain about sexism, and rightly so, but quite a few lady presenters in the sports world get by on looks and a skimpy knowledge of the subject. Gary Lineker, Alan Hansen assisted by fence squatter Trevor Brooking, are altogether more unattractive, but are undoubtedly the best of the bunch – in my opinion anyway.

England got off to an all too predictable start drawing against Sweden in their opening match making the encounter against Argentina all the more important. The match was far from entertaining but the result was always going to be more important and the luck, for a change, went our way. We produced another scrappy display against Nigeria, but did enough to qualify and secure a tie against Denmark in the knockout stages.

Elsewhere there were shocks aplenty with the holders France – the team I had backed at the start of the competition – incredibly knocked out without winning, or scoring a goal: the old Stan Bowles betting curse. Portugal lost to South Korea with two of their players sent off. The bookies must have had a good World Cup.

I watched the Denmark match with my old mucker Charlie George, whom I first formed a friendship with at Forest. We've kept in touch since, mainly through a shared interest in gambling. Charlie's as bad with the bookies as me – he once wanted to bet me that he could give up gambling. Charlie failed to see the irony in taking the bet. That's one he's never paid me out on.

At least Charlie gets a regular income from Arsenal with whom he does some hospitality work. All credit to Arsenal for looking after their former players. Unfortunately when QPR went into administration my hospitality work evaporated. I was getting only £100 a time for it but that did come in handy. I guess Charlie was a bit luckier to play for a team that stayed in the top flight, whereas my lot have struggled in recent years. Oh, well, if you can't make it good, at least try and make it look good.

The best thing about England's 3–0 win over Denmark was Rio Ferdinand scoring the first goal. I'd backed him for £20 at 50/1 on a pal's phone-betting account. I didn't really expect him to score but liked the idea of pocketing a grand. When Rio scored I was delighted and bought the whole pub a drink and that cost £112. The next day my pal, whose account I had used, rang me to say that the bookies weren't going to pay out on Ferdinand because they thought it was an own goal.

My hangover was made ten times worse on receiving that bombshell. I rang William Hill up myself and pleaded the case on how Rio had smashed the ball into the back of the net. FIFA's policy had been more than generous in accrediting strikers with dubious looking own goals, and they had awarded the goal to Ferdinand. Eventually, after a bit of arguing, Hills decided to allow the Ferdinand goal as a 'goodwill gesture' – I was much relieved, and a grand better off.

Of course everyone knows England lost their next game to Brazil. The lack of passion was noticeable but you have to remember the humidity out there was draining and I don't think Beckham and Owen, our key players, were anywhere near match-fit. That said, it was still a hugely disappointing way to go out of the competition.

Domestically, things are bright for the Premiership but I worry about the others outside the elite. I do believe that we're going to see more and more clubs go into administration or change to semi-pro.

One thing hasn't changed: the players with real and exceptional talent, are still the first to be crucified. Apparently the 'establishment' expect all professional footballers to be clean-living diplomats, who set an example to the rest of society.

Unfortunately, that is impossible. It is only recently that the Football Association decided to do something to help players with potentially disastrous problems, claw their way back to the top. Players, especially young ones in very successful teams like Manchester United, Arsenal and Liverpool, can't always live up to the high expectations that surround them. I am pleased that finally there is a coming together of the powers that be and the players. A more sympathetic understanding of the many demands and pressures placed on young men like Wayne Rooney, is welcome, both inside and outside of the game. In my day, that support was never forthcoming. We were slated for any indiscretion. So, some things have improved there, too.

In many ways, my life today is the same as it was all those years ago – a mixture of the glamorous and the ordinary. For example, during Euro 96 I played in a seven-a-side ex-internationals match before the big England v Scotland clash. In the England team alongside me were Glenn Hoddle, Ray Wilkins, Kenny Sansom and Graham Rix. Gordon Strachan and Asa Hartford turned out for Scotland. They beat us 3–1, but it was a delight to see old friends again. The commentator on the radio said that Stan Bowles was up to his old tricks again – now what did he mean by that?

The big England v Scotland main attraction was a great occasion. The atmosphere was a bit special; I've never known anything like it for an international at Wembley. The crowd lifted the players like you can't imagine. I don't think the game itself was up to all that much, but Gascoigne's goal was something else. Gazza looked a bit tired at times, but I can't think of another English player who could pull such a piece of magic out of his bag of tricks, and that's why I would have picked him every time in his heyday.

After the game we went to the banqueting room and had a drink with the current England players of the time. I had a nice little chat with Gazza, who seemed a really nice, genuine bloke. He told me that Terry Venables had said to him that I was even more crackers than he was. Now, I don't know if that's a compliment or an insult, but we'll let it rest.

That night, as a complete contrast, I was in Ealing, doing a presentation for John Stokes's pub team. They'd done the treble in their Sunday League and were having a big do in the Caernarvon Hotel. I'd managed to get an England shirt from the team that afternoon, and all the players had signed it, so I put it up as a raffle prize. Everyone there wanted to win it because everyone dreams of pulling on the shirt of their national team. Whether you play in the Premier League or turn out for your local pub side, that's what it's all about – dreaming. It's where we all start from, but only a handful achieve it, but that doesn't mean that the dreams have to end.

Chapter 19 •

Eskimo Stanley

I went to Bavaria once to play a match, Old England v Old Germany to re-create the 1966 World Cup team. Geoff Hurst and Martin Peters were in the team as were other guest players like Jimmy Johnstone, Mike Summerbee, Brian Kidd and Tommy Gemmell. We got hammered 7–2. The Germans might have been getting on in years but they had all stayed in shape and were a darn site fitter than our lads, who in the main, had come armed with the motto 'win or lose we'll be on the booze'. There was a bit of a fight on the pitch when Mike Summerbee head-butted one of the Germans. After the match we retired to the bar for a few beers and it wasn't long before another brawl threatened to break out again.

Jimmy Johnstone – the diminutive fiery red-headed Scotsman – had taken full advantage of the free bar on offer. In fact, I don't think he was offside all night, and that was evident when he streaked naked on the long table during the after-match dinner both sides attended. I thought it was hilarious but Martin Peters and Geoff Hurst, who were always a little strait-laced for my liking, were disgusted with Jimmy's behaviour and walked out. Geoff Hurst said to me, 'I don't know how you can hang about with people like that.'

'They'll do for me,' I replied, making sure they got the point.

As the wine flowed some of the Germans grew increasingly agitated with Jimmy's behaviour and a couple of them threatened to give him a whack. I remember Tommy Gemmell getting one of them by the throat and telling him that if anyone wanted to take a pop at Jimmy then they would have to go through him. Tommy was a huge beast of a man – you wouldn't want to mess with him in an alleyway, no matter how well it was lit. After that, the two teams peeled off to separate sections of the bar. Jimmy, Tommy and I were the last to leave, and Tommy had Jimmy slung over his shoulder when we eventually staggered home.

We had another party in 1996, at Terry Venables's club Scribes to launch the publication of the original edition of my autobiography. The place was packed and included some of my scallywag friends from Manchester. A few of the guys I'd played with, and against, also turned up; the likes of Alan Hudson, Dave Webb, Steve Parsons and Terry Hurlock. Even comedian Jim Davidson, who was a good pal of Brian Wright, a mutual friend, attended to add some colour to the occasion.

Terry Venables put on a lovely spread and the grub there was some of the best I've ever tasted. Jim Davidson told Terry that he hadn't seen food like it since he last flew with British Airways. The press were there in force and so were the cameras from LWT, and after a few drinks everyone was in good spirits. Someone had gone to the trouble of constructing a life-size cardboard cut-out of me and propped it up inside the club. There it stood with me in my footballing pomp complete with sideburns and shoulder-length hair. Tommy Carr, a good friend of mine, had brought his young teenage son along and late on in the afternoon, little Tommy suddenly and unexpectedly, dashed towards the cut-out grabbed it and sprinted off down Kensington High Street with it tucked under his arm. A couple of lady guests, sipping their wine, couldn't believe what had happened and wanted to call the police. Jim Davidson said that the police were already aware that a cardboard cut-out thief was operating in the area.

When I met up with Tommy some months later, he told me he had travelled home on the tube with my cardboard likeness sitting next to him and nobody batted an eye lid. Tommy said he even slipped his tube ticket into the cardboard hand just in case an inspector boarded the train.

Every so often, a journalist will manage to track me down to whichever watering hole or backstreet bookie I'm frequenting. They will ask me for my opinions on this or that, usually on the footballing stories that are making the headlines at the time. Obviously, I get the call every time a betting-related story breaks. One week *Kilroy* and *Esther* both wanted me to appear on their shows, in the same week, discussing gambling addictions in general and its effects on society. What it had to do with me I wasn't quite sure. The people from *Kilroy* sent a car round to pick me up but I wasn't in – I'd already left for Cheltenham races.

I am more than happy to swap my stories in exchange for a small financial inducement. I always tend to insist on cash transactions for the sake of simplicity and to cut back on form-filling. These payments are invariably absorbed in whatever establishment I'm residing in at the time – usually within hours. Easy come, easy go, that's the way I see things. Up till now I've lived my life on a day-to-day basis and the onset of middle age has not made me adapt nor adjust my philosophy in that respect. The only discernible differences are that my hair is now grey and the gap between pay days is wider. Still, I'm not one to complain.

Following our divorce, Diane has moved from Brentford to South Shields. Her son Tommy, whom I have become very close to over recent years, has stayed in Brentford and moved in with his father Dave Ratcliffe, who is a good friend of mine. I normally meet Dave in the Royal Oak most days along with the rest of the 'rat pack' – Roger Cunningham, Colin Sherbourne, John Marriot, John Kemp (The Bear), and QPR terrace legend Tommy Collins. We study the day's racing and play cards.

My new partner, Hannah, works for the mental health unit at West Middlesex Hospital. This means that she does a lot of unpaid overtime in the evenings – trying to look after me. Hannah recollects how we met:

It was just over three years ago when Stan was staying with friends of mine. I am mad about rugby, having been born and bred in Bath and love the national game. I was in the local pub and left my rugby hat on the table, while I went to the toilet. When I returned it had disappeared. Stan had taken it, and I told him to give it back or I would take him outside and sort him. At that time I didn't know that Stan was this massive footballing star. My friends by this time were laughing but also slightly horrified – I had just invited the great Stan Bowles outside to give him a good hiding. My only excuse was that I'd never heard of him before. So that's how we met.

Eventually, we decided that we would give it a go together and see what happened, so Stan moved into my flat in Brentford. That was over three years ago and he's still there. Even now it is difficult to try and imagine him as this footballing icon. However, two seasons ago, I had an introduction to 'Stan mania'.

QPR were playing at home and, after the match, the fans decided to congregate outside Loftus Road in a demonstration against Chris Wright, the chairman of the club. Stan and I waited in the bar for half an hour or so to let things calm down before attempting to leave.

Eventually, we decided it was time to make a move. As soon as Stan opened the doors and the fans saw him, the chanting stopped. Their full attention was redirected towards Stan.

The cheering, passion and admiration they showered on their idol will never leave me. I had to hold on to the back of Stan's coat as fans streamed over for him to sign anything: season ticket vouchers, programmes, shirts, arms, faces. One woman even offered her boobs; needless to say he got a dig in the back for that one!

Then he was hoisted on to the shoulders of three or four fans and everyone starting singing his name. It was quite an experience and the first time that I came face to face with 'Stan Bowles, the footballer'.

Hannah usually comes face to face with Stan, the neurotic man!

One of the more unusual requests to land on my lap came, sometime in 1999, from a company named Borkowski PR. A chap called me and, after the usual polite, but insincere enquiries as to health were exchanged, he tentatively suggested I might want to take a trip to Greenland for five days, to play football in the 'prestigious' Smirnoff Ice Challenge Cup. These marketing boys are something else, I thought. It was however an undoubtedly interesting development because the furthest I had planned to travel that week was to the Bricklayer's Arms in Brentford. As you know this is my office, or so I tell the many journalists who have traced my tracks through circuitous routes to this friendly little boozer.

The PR company, headed up by a chap called Borkowski, were of the opinion that if myself, Mark Hateley (who once scored against Brazil), Gary Gillespie (the ex-Liverpool defender), and Brian Hornsby (apparently an ex-Arsenal player whom I later discovered didn't write *Fever Pitch*, nor did he ever have an accompanying band called The Range), should form the basis of an English five-a-side team to play local teams from Greenland. It was never made clear to me how a group of retired footballers, playing football somewhere in the Arctic Circle, would result in the sale of more bottles of Smirnoff Ice in this, or any other country. But then that wasn't really my problem, so I didn't think to raise the matter for debate.

It made sense on several fronts to make the trip. Firstly, to ease a severe shortage of funds that was again threatening to hamper the enjoyment of even the most modest of my daily plans – like eating. Secondly, my marriage to wife number three was in its death throes. I was getting a frostier reception at home than I could ever get in Greenland.

My fears of flying and entering into the unknown were assuaged, somewhat, by a few loose assurances that the inappropriately named Greenland – a place I'd only ever seen on a RISK board – was a beautiful, tranquil and relaxing place and that the flight there would be direct.

It all sounded ever so straightforward. I would spend one day playing football, and another five in a hotel relaxing in a bar. The alternative was being broke in Brentford and having barneys with the missus. Not for the first time the thought entered my head – what did I have to lose?

Greenland had just applied for membership of the game's international governing body, FIFA. There was a campaign to get Greenland instated into the World Cup qualifiers and apparently this might help. The likes of St Vincent/Grenadines, Dutch Antilles, Aruba, and São Tomé and Principe were in the hat for Japan, but not Greenland.

On landing, after a long three-stop flight, I decided immediately that Greenland was a desperate place – colder than Carlisle with even less to do. Every town in Greenland is small and almost exclusively engaged in fishing; and every town is on the coast. The central area of the country is uninhabitable and the population is scattered around the edges. A mere 55,000 people – mostly fishermen and hunters – live in a country that is nine times the size of the UK; it is the biggest island in the world. To put that in context: Greenland's population is about a quarter that of a typical London borough. If Greenland ever get to play at Wembley's new stadium every single Greenlander would fit into the stadium, and there'd still be room for 30,000 opposition fans.

A delegation was sent to meet and greet us; they were a sturdy group of around thirty burly Eskimos, looking less than hospitable. They started shouting things at us and generally began to get agitated. Now, after being around a bit, I know instinctively when someone is hurling an insult at me, even if it is in a different language, and so sensibly I took a discreet step behind Mark Hateley. The crowd became more raucous and threatening. Then, suddenly, someone threw a fish at Hateley. Needless to say Mark failed to bring it under control.

One of our interpreters started speaking to the group in an attempt to calm them down, and discovered that the locals thought we were from Greenpeace, and that we were there to stop them fishing; dehorn antelope; club seals; or whatever it was they did to make a living. I told our interpreter to make it known to them, that we had no beef with any of the above activities and that we were there simply to play football. Once reassured we were of no threat to them, the crowd's attitude softened and someone at the back shouted, 'Bobby Charlton'. I pointed to Hateley whose hair had thinned in a similar manner to the Manchester United legend. This gesture raised a laugh from the crowd and helped lighten, but not warm, the atmosphere.

The temperature was twenty below, the entire country was covered in snow and the sky was as black as I'd ever seen it. It was probably the first time I'd ever felt that homesick for Collyhurst.

The route to the Arctic hotel, where we would be staying, was located miles away across snowy mountainous terrain, and the transport provided us were thirteen huskies tied to a sledge. There are more dogs in Greenland than people. The driver of the sledge obviously wasn't a dog lover, as he whipped the poor animals every thirty seconds. I felt sorry for those little creatures, running about in the freezing cold pulling a load of people and getting whipped for their trouble. No way to treat man's best friend, I thought to myself. Two of the dogs were toiling badly through exhaustion, but the driver simply untied them, slid them along the ice while they were still alive, and laughingly pointed to a big black bird that was circling above. The bird had its sights set on dinner. There's no sentimentality in Greenland. I only hoped I wouldn't be getting the same treatment if I took ill.

When we eventually arrived at the hotel we were all suffering from a mild form of frostbite, as well as very sore backsides. We took lunch at the Hong Kong Café – these Chinese restaurants get everywhere. It was the first time I'd eaten a Chinese meal since my childhood days in Collyhurst. They had ice cream on the menu just in case anyone was feeling the need to cool down.

We were advised – for our own safety – not to go out in the evenings. There was nothing to do in the country but drink and the Inuits, as they preferred to be called weren't too keen on foreigners. One of the visiting reporters called a local an Eskimo, and got a swift kick in the bollocks for his mistake.

As soon as I got into the hotel I went up to my room, climbed into bed, shut my eyes and stayed there. After a couple of days the woman in charge of the party came up to see if I wanted to come sightseeing. 'No thanks,' I replied, 'I've seen the icebergs.' By night, and you only get around three hours daylight, you can see the Northern Lights. They looked quite nice as lights go, but then so do the Blackpool illuminations – I've never been big on lights as a form of entertainment.

The Inuits hang all their fish outside at night-time, which also made for a strange sight – no need for freezers in Greenland.

I'm told that Greenland is a beautiful place in their summer, but I shan't be reserving a spot for a holiday. I took to drinking heavily to help pass the time. We spent an evening in the community hall in Disko Bay, listening to a band called Sumi, whom we were assured were the second-best rock band in Greenland. Their finale was a cover of 'The Vengabus' by the Vengaboys. I think that speaks for itself.

The Smirnoff Ice Challenge Cup itself was played over one day in a gymnasium; the rules were never fully explained. What was clear was that the tournament consisted of a number of seven-minute games, with no end-changing – the traditional 'head high' rule did not apply. The referee, dressed in jeans and a durable anorak, kept play flowing from a standing position. Our training for the event had involved a lot of late-night drinking and it showed.

We lost the first game 2–1, with me scoring our goal. We also lost our second game by the same margin, and our third by five goals to nil. We salvaged some pride with a 7–1 victory in our last game, with Hateley and myself scoring hat-tricks and Gillespie chipping in with the other. One thing we all agreed on: we wouldn't be renewing our challenge for the Smirnoff Ice Challenge any time soon.

At present I do a bit of writing for various football magazines, and some hospitality work at QPR. There is even talk of turning my life story into a film. Several TV companies have been looking at buying the film rights to the Stan Bowles Story. I'd like to play myself, but don't think I'm good looking enough.

From time to time I get some television work. Some guy rang me up recently from London Weekend and said they were quite keen to do something with me. He started buttering me up by saying what a terrific player I had been, one of the most skilful of my generation. I'm thinking to myself, Yeah, tell me something I don't already know. Then he skips the bit about what show he wants me to appear in, and says it's £350 for a morning's shoot.

Well, this bloke carries on praising me up and I start to think £350 will come in quite handy, so I don't even mind if I have to appear on the worst show on television – *Blankety Blank* or *Tomorrow's World*. Then he drops the bombshell. He wants me to appear in a show entitled *After They Were Famous*. The fucking cheek, I thought I still *was* bloody famous. Then it dawns on me. I remembered watching the show once when I was drunk – you have to be very drunk to watch this show. In fact, you have to be drunk to the point that the remote control isn't within arm's reach, and you can't be bothered to get up and kick the telly over.

The thing that struck me was that the people who were on the show weren't even very famous in the first place. Bob Carolgees (with Spit the Dog) appeared on the episode I had seen. Even he was baffled how he'd managed to be on telly for so long, before the public realised that a dog that spits isn't very funny in the first place – the joke starts to wear pretty thin after ten years. He now runs an antiques shop – that's Spit the Dog not Carolgees. Apparently the puppet used to operate him!

Patti Boulay, the singer, was also on that show. If I recall correctly she's now turned into a Tory activist. God only knows what crimes she was responsible for in her last life to cause that much grief on to the public on two counts.

Then this chap who wants me to do the show starts suggesting locations for the various scenes: a pub; an illegal gambling den one of my mates operates (changed to the bookies because my mate gets raided a good deal); and another pal's tile shop. Obviously LWT were trying to paint a picture of me as an unqualified success. I told 'em straight that I wasn't interested – I still had my integrity, my pride; and you can't put a price on that. Then the fellow said, 'How about £400 – in cash?' We shot the scenes the following morning.

In a similar vein, Virgin got in touch recently and said they were interested in 'working with me'. They wanted me to appear in an advert for them, which in itself was a surprise because I know their goofy governor – Richard Branson – rarely misses an opportunity to project his own personality on television. That is when he's not messing about in balloons.

The guy from Virgin asked me if I would be interested in 'starring' in an advertisement. You can guess my immediate response, to which he replied, 'Oh, don't worry Mister Bowles, you shall have a very attractive remuneration package.' I replied, 'Never mind that, how much?' He then mentioned a tidy little sum for one day of filming. They wanted to pay me £5,000, well in excess of what I had been expecting. I told him I had a window in my business diary for the entire year, so I would be available at any given time.

Unfortunately, I never heard back from the guy, which I found pretty annoying. I had thought up a few ways to spend the money, most of which involved a day out at the races. Then, a few months later I saw a Virgin advert with that bloke Geoffrey from the children's TV show *Rainbow* looking all washed-up and weather-beaten. The voice-over said, 'Don't you wish you had invested your money more wisely?'

Those cheeky sods at Virgin only wanted to use me as an example of a failure. They had the whole country to choose from and it comes down to a straight shoot-out between me and Geoffrey from *Rainbow* as to who is the biggest loser in the country.

And to add insult to injury, Geoffrey just edges me out and bins £5,000. I suppose it's nice to know there is always someone worse off than you, although I'd rather have been the top loser and bagged the money. Typical of Stanley Bowles's luck. If I entered a competition to find the biggest loser in the world I'd probably be the winner.

Over the years there has been a great deal of paper talk about my private life – away from the football arena – so I have welcomed this opportunity to tell you the real facts behind my various adventures.

So that's more or less it. But, before I go, I particularly want to thank five people who helped me further my career, and for whom I have lasting respect.

Jim Gregory, chairman of Queens Park Rangers, did more for me than anyone else. I used to get the impression that we played a game between ourselves: the multimillionaire versus the wayward footballer. I didn't have a business brain, but I stood up to him. He liked that, and our relationship developed as we played by our own privately evolved rules.

I will always remember one Sunday morning, when I was sitting in a room at the Royal Lancaster Hotel in Bayswater waiting for Jim, being questioned and propositioned by a party of Germans from SV Hamburg. They wanted to sign me, and offered me over £400 per week plus bonuses, but all I could think about was, 'Where is he?' So I interrupted the meeting, rushed to the phone, and rang Jim at his home.

'What's the matter?' said Jim in a sleepy voice.

'What's the matter ... You are supposed to be here with me for the meeting with the Hamburg officials.'

'Do you want to go?' he said.

'Well, no ... not really.'

'Listen, I'll give you £2,000 in cash on Monday morning, and we'll negotiate a new contract, how about that?'

I agreed, replaced the receiver and, without stopping to look back, walked out of the hotel. I took a cab and went straight to Jim's house, staying for Sunday lunch, and sipping pink champagne all afternoon. That's how close we were. It's funny to think that if I had gone to SV Hamburg, they wouldn't have signed Kevin Keegan, and he probably wouldn't have gone on to become European Footballer of the Year. But I've always known that I was their first choice.

Not many people know this, but QPR are known as St Jude's, a fact I found out myself only recently. St Jude is apparently the patron saint of lost causes so it's no surprise that I've got an affinity with him. I couldn't say for certain if St Jude was a gambler but it is highly probable that he was.

Ernie Tagg, the manager of Crewe, was a funny man and a good friend who looked after me very well during my time at Gresty Road – after I had been sacked by Manchester City.

Ian MacFarlane, the straight-talking Scot who managed Carlisle, was a larger-than-life character whom I liked and respected. He played a major role in my rehabilitation as a professional footballer.

Joe Mercer, a generous father figure to me at Manchester City, was a true gentleman. Unfortunately, I let him down when I walked out on the England squad during the Home Internationals, and I suppose I regret that. It was, basically, due to a certain stubbornness in me. In those days, the slightest thing would spark me off and, although I have learned over the years to control this part of my personality, it is still there. My father and brother are exactly the same.

I also owe a debt to Malcolm Allison, Joe's assistant manager. This might seem strange, but I would have been lost to football, long before I reached my full potential, if Malcolm hadn't kicked me out in 1970. I know that sounds cock-eyed, but Malcolm did me a big favour. At the time it came as a blow, because it was my father's dream that I play for City, being born and bred in Collyhurst. I knew I'd let my father down, and felt guilty about that for a long time.

The rest of the football establishment wouldn't give me the time of day. Some people in authority looked down on me, and talked to me as if I was a lesser being. When I moved from Crewe to Carlisle, they said that it wouldn't last; that it would only be a matter of months. But I knew in my own mind that I could ride all of their criticism, and build a career for myself. I felt that it was Stan Bowles versus the football establishment – and that was just the challenge I needed.

I also want to say a special thank you to all of my fans – past and present. I was always very close to them, and generally used the pubs nearest to the ground after the game, and enjoyed socialising with supporters. This was frowned upon by the clubs, mainly because they received letters from certain people complaining that they had seen me frequenting local pubs and greyhound stadiums. I used to smile because they must have been there also to have seen me! It was a natural way for me to unwind and enjoy some of my free time, and I did this throughout my career at Crewe, Carlisle and QPR.

I have never planned anything in my life, and, needless to say, I have never voted because it doesn't matter to me whether Labour or the Tories are in government. I think Gerry Francis was right when he said I am a happy-go-lucky type who lives from day to day, and can't be changed. I don't think I could have lived my life any other way. That ninety minutes on a Saturday was an outlet for me; as it was for Don Shanks. Frank McLintock and Webby couldn't believe that I could go through so many traumas and still perform on the field – but I loved it. I had no worries while I was out there, except trying to win the game.

Talking of Don Shanks ... I expect you're wondering why he hasn't had a mention for quite a while. You shouldn't be surprised; Don flits in and out of my life, as he has done for a good few years now. He's still up to his old tricks: ducking and diving. Mind you, he must be doing pretty well for himself because dear old Mr Donald is part-owner of a racehorse! Through his racing connections, he also does a bit of chauffeuring for rich Arabs who own racehorses in this country. So he'll definitely be making a few bob off them!

I still see my old mate from time to time. He turns up like a bad penny usually when he's skint, then we spend some time together being skint. Don left Rangers when Terry Venables became manager. The two of them came to an agreement that if Don left, QPR wouldn't ask a fee for him. Around about three months later Don joined Brighton when Mark Lawrenson left to go to Liverpool.

Don spent two years at Brighton until Bobby Moore asked him to be his assistant player-manager for a team in Hong Kong called Eastern FC. They were fairly successful, finished second in the league and got to the Cup final. Unluckily for Don, Brighton also got to the Cup final that year – against Manchester United. He had played every single game for them that year up until Christmas, so typically, Don missed out on some big bonuses! United ultimately beat Brighton in a replay.

After his time in the Far East, Don returned to Britain, played one game for Wimbledon, didn't like their style of football and went off to live in Tampa, Florida where he got involved with the semi-pro soccer scene. Rodney Marsh was the manager of the Tampa Bay Rowdies at the time. Don was instrumental in helping out when Roy Wegerle transferred to Chelsea from Tampa.

When the soccer league was temporarily disbanded in the US, Don came back to England and put a soccer school together with Alan Hudson and Frank Worthington. Being Don, he then decided to go and do a coaching job in Lagos, Nigeria coaching a team called Concorde FC. They finished third in the league and won the Cup but it was a little too volatile for Don who realised he'd most likely live a lot longer by living somewhere else. They offered him sackfuls of money – Don never needed encouragement when it came to an earner. There was a civil war going on out there at the time; but I can't remember if Don started it.

He spotted a couple of players out there that he thought Brentford might be interested in, but nothing ever came of it – one of them was seven foot tall.

At that time Don owed me a lot of money, so he said, 'Come out here and I'll get it for you, no problem.'

Now Collyhurst may have been quite a rough place to grow up in, but it doesn't prepare you for a civil war, so I declined Don's offer. As it turned out, Shanksy never got his money. The bloke who was supposed to pay him just disappeared – as tends to happen in civil wars – so I'm bloody glad I didn't risk Shanks's safari!

Don has always got four or five projects on the go at any one time. A while back he phoned me up and asked if I wanted to go to Thailand with him to coach a team there, for £200 a week. Don reckons that sort of dough is equivalent to getting a grand in this country. I didn't think I could leave my home comforts behind me, and besides, the hot, humid climate has never really suited my pasty complexion. So I had to decline, much to Don's annoyance. I told him that if he was so keen then he should go to Thailand on his own, to which he solemnly replied, 'I would, but nobody has bloody well heard of *me* out there!'

I met up with Don recently for a session down the local. We found a spot in the corner of the pub, settled down together, ordered up the drinks and before long we began reminiscing about the 'good ol' days'. After several pints and a few belly laughs Don said, 'You know something, Stan? I think if the two of us had never hooked up we might both have had a bit more money; but never would we have had as much fun.' Then he looks me squarely in the eyes and says, 'You know something else, Stan? I wouldn't swap those memories for all the tea in China.' I smiled slowly, and replied nostalgically, 'You're right mate, we might not have much in monetary terms, but you can't measure happiness. Yes, we sure had some great times.' We both took another sip of beer and sat in a contented silence for a minute, reflecting quietly. After a pause Don looked thoughtfully into the muddy remnants of his glass and says, 'Who am I trying to kid? Give me money any day of the week and you can keep the soddin' memories.'

He's keeping well and I expect he'll turn up again soon. No doubt he'll appear at my shoulder – like the Devil with a decent tan – going through my pockets and telling another tall tale. With Don Shanks, you always know he'll land on his feet. Now, I can reveal that the Stan Bowles and Don Shanks roadshow is set to take-off in late 2004, doing the after-dinner speech circuit. This is not to be missed as we have been nominated as the best double act since Morecambe and Wise!

If I could have my time again, I would try to save a few quid because it's a fact of life that you can't live without money. I had a house in Ealing but had to sell it before it got repossessed. I also had one in Brentford, but had to sell that too – although I actually made a few quid on that one because the eighties boom was on. The mortgage company were quite good about it because I was well over a year behind with the payments. I wouldn't get away with that nowadays.

If I was playing in the Premiership today, I would probably be earning £80,000 a week, so it would be nice to think that I could gamble £70,000, and still have ten grand left at the end of the week. But, of course, gambling addicts never save money. People may think of me as a footballer who gambled far too much, but really I'm a gambling addict who happened to be a good footballer.

I think that Frank Worthington summed up my life quite well when he said, 'Stan has spent all of his money on gambling, booze and birds.' I respond to that by saying, 'Well, at least I didn't waste it!'

As it happens, you can't say fairer than that.

People still come up to me and say how well they remember me and how they'd like to chat with me for a while and not all of them are debt collectors. One question I am asked virtually on a daily basis is: Do I regret playing in an era when there was next to no money in the game? I can honestly answer, No, never. I enjoyed a great career as a professional footballer spanning eighteen years and eight clubs. I'm not saying today's money wouldn't have been nice, and I'm pretty sure I'd have found ways to spend it fairly quickly. But, at the end of the day (footballers are required to use this phrase wherever they can), my working life consisted of running round a park and getting paid for it. For that I'll always be grateful. They say that the meek will inherit the earth – who wants earth?

I've some great memories as a player, and I wouldn't swap them for anything in the world except hard cash. I only needed money to finance the necessities in life, like gambling. And besides, I have enough money to last me the rest of my life – provided I drop dead at 4.30 this afternoon. I also have a big mortgage to pay off – my bookie's.

Oh well, I started out with nothing and I pretty well still have most of it left.

Accreditations

CATHY IONA
LINDSAY COLLINS
CAROL ALLEN
ROHIT PATEL
J. P. SHAW (for being involved in editing this book)
A big thank you to Don Shanks for his invaluable contribution

Index